THE TRANSLATIONS OF
EZRA POUND

The
TRANSLATIONS OF
EZRA POUND

With an Introduction by
HUGH KENNER

faber and faber
LONDON · BOSTON

First published in 1953
by Faber and Faber Limited
3 Queen Square London WC1N 3AU
An enlarged edition published in 1970
Reissued in 1984

Printed in Great Britain by
Redwood Burn Limited
Trowbridge Wiltshire
All rights reserved

Acknowledgement
Poems included here from *The Spirit of Romance* are
reprinted by permission of Peter Owen Limited

British Library Cataloguing in Publication Data

Pound, Ezra
The translations of Ezra Pound
1. Literature—Collections
I. Title
808.8   PN6014
ISBN 0-571-13307-X

CONTENTS

(dates of original publication in brackets)

8

INTRODUCTION
by Hugh Kenner

Pope translated the *Iliad* into heroic couplets, Chapman into fourteeners. Numerous foreign poems have been shoved into an idiom invented by Milton, which goes flat the moment the atmosphere is cleared of sulphur. Ezra Pound never translates 'into' something already existing in English. The Chinese or Greek or Provençal poem being by hypothesis something new, if it justifies the translator's or the reader's time—

> *Dagas sind gewitene,*
> *ealle onmedlan eorþan rices;*
> *nearon nu cyningas ne caseras*
> *ne goldgiefan, swylce iu waeron ...*

—something correspondingly new must be made to happen in English verse:

> Days little durable
> And all arrogance of earthen riches,
> There come now no kings nor Caesars
> Nor goldgiving lords like those gone.
> Howe'er in mirth most magnified,
> Whoe'er lived in life most lordliest,
> Drear all this excellence, delights undurable!
> —*The Seafarer*

Other translators of Anglo-Saxon verse have been content to take the English language as they found it, or to teutonize from word to word without quite knowing what was happening; only Pound has had both the boldness and resource to make a new form, similar in effect to that of the original, which permanently extends the bounds of English verse. Other poets after him have used these schemes of assonance and alliteration; it was Pound who built them their speech.

INTRODUCTION

Underlying conspicuous success of the *Seafarer* order is Pound's conception of what the poet's job is: the rendering, without deformation, of something, within him or without, which he has clearly apprehended and seized in his mind:

> as the sculptor sees the form in the air
> before he sets hand to mallet,
> and as he sees the in, and the through,
>   the four sides . . .

Translating does not, for him, differ in essence from any other poetic job; as the poet begins by seeing, so the translator by reading; but his reading must be a kind of seeing.

Hence the miraculous accomplishment of Pound's translations; sitting down before a text, he doesn't chafe at restrictions unusual to his lyric practice. A good translation seems like a miracle because one who can read the original can, so to speak, see the poem before the poet writes it, and marvel at the success of his wrestle to subdue his own language to the vision; but Pound has always written as if to meet a test of this kind, in a spirit of utter fidelity to his material, whether a document or an intuition. He has told of working six months to fix a complex instantaneous emotion in fourteen words. Translation is indeed for Pound somewhat easier than what is called 'original composition'; those six months were spent less on finding the words than in bringing the emotion into focus, and a text to be translated, once grasped, doesn't wobble. The technical difficulty is comparable, but the emotional discipline, if no less exacting, less exhausting. Pound has for this reason recommended translation as an exercise to young poets plagued by the tendency of what they are trying to express to undergo expedient transformations.

It is because so many Poundian principles meet in the translator's act that the best of his translations exist in three ways, as windows into new worlds, as acts of homage, and as personae of Pound's. The Personae of his first published volume do not differ in principle from the translations of a few years later. In his earliest work, *Cino, Marvoil, Altaforte, Piere Vidal Old,* Pound builds in English an imitation of the accent and speech and rhythm of certain dead men: usually dead poets, since it is the poet who of all men is most alive to his ambience, and the ambience is what Pound is trying to seize.

> Bah; I have sung women in three cities,
> But it is all the same;
> And I will sing of the sun.
>
> Lips, words, and you snare them,
> Dreams, words, and they are as jewels,
> Strange spells of old deity,
> Ravens, nights, allurement:
> And they are not;
> Having become the souls of song.
> —*Cino*

This isn't the English soul of 1908; the rubric, 'Italian Campagna 1309, the open road' implies that it is an emotion Pound has generated in himself in contemplating a time 600 years gone. A persona crystallizes a modus of sensibility in its context. It derives from an attempt to enter an unfamiliar world, develop in oneself the thoughts and feelings indigenous to that world, and articulate them in English. A translation, by extension, is a rendering of a modus of thought or feeling in its context after it has already been crystallized, by a Cavalcanti or a Rihaku. The same clairvoyant absorption of another world is presupposed; the English poet must absorb the ambience of the text into his blood before he can render it with authority; and when he has done that, what he writes is a poem of his own following the contours of the poem before him. He does not translate words. The words have led him into the thing he expresses: desolate seafaring, or the cult of the plum-blossoms, or the structure of sensibility that attended the Tuscan anatomy of love.

Since he doesn't translate the words, he may deviate from the words, if the words blur or slide, or if his own language fails him. 'Eorþan rices' doesn't mean 'earthen riches' but 'kingdoms of the earth'; 'kings' in the next line enforces however an alteration, and the available synonyms for 'kingdoms', such as 'realms', have the wrong connotations: 'royaume' for instance implies something too settled, too sumptuous. Hence the recourse to 'riches', a sort of pun on the word in the text, which has a slightly wrong meaning but a completely right feeling.

If he doesn't translate the words, the translator remains faithful to the original poet's sequence of images, to his rhythms or the effect produced by his rhythms[1], and to his tone. Insofar as he is faithful, he does homage to his predecessor's knowledge of his job, his success in securing from point to point the precise images and gestures to embody a vision which is neither his property nor that of the translator. Pedantry consists in supposing that the importance of a moment of thought or feeling lies in the notation somebody else found for it. The Poundian homage consists in taking an earlier poet as guide to secret places of the imagination.

The labour that precedes translation is therefore first critical in the Poundian sense of critical, an intense penetration of the author's sense; then technical in the Poundian sense of technical, an exact projection of one's psychic contents, and so of the things on which one's mind has fed. The reorientation of the terms 'critical' and 'technical' sums up Pound's service to letters, so far as that service can be abstracted from the work he has actually done. His best translations exist between pedagogy on the one side and personal expression on the other, and in touch with both. At the left, however, is a body of work produced with the strictly pedagogic aim of guiding the reader to certain qualities of past literature: the numerous versions in *The Spirit of Romance,* and the translations of Arnaut Daniel which have the avowed aim of showing us what the rhyme-patterns look and sound like. At the right are the adaptations from Heine and Propertius, which while borrowing and turning phrases with endless virtuosity, are rather *personae* than translations. The original author's attitude of mind passes through the words, but the primary intentions are those of Pound. Pound calls the Propertius sequence a *Homage,* largely in

[1] English hexameter, for instance, sounds pedantic, especially in the specimens Arnold produced as triumphs. Pound's version of the Homeric *Nekuia* (Canto I) went into adapted *Seafarer* rhythms, not synthetic hexameters, with startling success; and the *Seafarer* itself rather reproduces the feel of alliterative Anglo-Saxon verse than obeys its rules.

a futile attempt to keep it from being mistaken for an attempt at translation. Thomas Hardy, seeing that Pound vs. Imperial Britain was the 'subject,' and Sextus Propertius a factor in the 'treatment,' advised him to focus attention on subject rather than treatment by leaving Propertius' name out of the title; thereby revealing himself a shrewder reader than the sequence has usually met with.[1]

In the *Cathay* poems, made from Ernest Fenollosa's notes and cribs to the ideograms of Rihaku (Li Po), Pound is at his best both as poet and as translator; he is amazingly convincing at making the Chinese poet's world his own. If the series of *Noh* dramas is somehow less successful, it is because there is less of Pound in them, though we are teased from time to time by traces of Yeats, whose conversation in a cottage in Sussex provided the milieu in which the work was done.

> And looking upon the waves at Ise and Owari,
> He longed for his brief year of glory:
> The waves, the breakers return,
> But my glory comes not again,
> Narihira, Narihira,
> My glory comes not again.
> He stood at the foot of Asama of Shinano,
> and saw the smoke curling upwards.
> —*Kikitsubata*

We have only to put this beside something from *Cathay*—

> March has come to the bridge head,
> Peach boughs and apricot boughs bend
> over a thousand gates,
> At morning there are flowers to cut the heart,
> And evening drives them on the eastward-flowing waters . . .
> —*Poem by the Bridge at Ten-Shin*

—to sense a remoteness, a sense on Pound's part that he is doing

[1] Hardy made an impractical suggestion *re* title, but in such a way as to indicate that he, Hardy, would have had his mind on the subject rather than the treatment of it. E. P.

something exotic, thin, appreciated rather than lived, that just prevents the *Noh* sequence from standing, as *Cathay* does, with his finest original work. Though the tone of the best work varies continually through Provençal, Chinese, Greek, Latin, and Tuscan modalities, the voice is always the voice of Pound, submitting to the discipline of translation in order to realize persona after persona with unfaltering conviction.

Behind certain ideograms in the Confucian Analects Mr. Arthur Waley sensed a sage embroidered on tapestry expounding the Way:

'The Master said, Who expects to be able to go out of a house except by the door? How is it then that no one follows this Way of ours?'

and Pound a live man speaking pregnant sense:

'He said: The way out is via the door, how is it that no one will use this method.'

To say that one can hear Pound speaking these words is to say that he has lent Confucius his own voice; but to say that he was able to make what he found in the ideograms so much his own is to say that his translation gives us, as can no other, a realization of how the Confucian books have survived dynasty after dynasty in defiance of the shifting conventions of preciosity and of 'effects.' Confucius after twenty-four centuries stirs Pound into speech; Pound after twenty-four centuries lends Confucius his voice. The translations of Confucius are not represented in the present collection, as they require a volume to themselves. But it is equally true of them and of the translations in this book, that they are interchanges of voice and personality with the dead, the handful of enduring dead, across centuries and millenia of snow-drifting events.

H. K.

CAVALCANTI POEMS

PUBLISHERS' NOTE

Although these translations were originally published at different times, and some of them were revised for later publication, they are reprinted here in the same order as that of the Italian text.

INTRODUCTION

'Cimabue thought that in portraiture
He held the field; now Giotto hath the cry
And all the former fame is turned obscure;
Thus hath one Guido from the other reft
The glory of our tongue, and there's perchance
One born who shall un-nest both him and him.'

Even the qualification in the last line of this speech which
Oderisi, honour of Agobbio, illuminator of fair pages, makes to
Dante in the terrace for the purgation of Pride, must be balanced
by Dante's reply to Guido's father among the burning tombs
(Inf. X), sic.

Cavalcante di Cavalcanti:
  'If by the height of genius thou dost go
  Through this blind prison house; where is my son?
  Why is he not with thee?'
Dante:
  'I come not of myself,
  But he, who awaiteth there (i.e. Virgil), doth lead me
    through.'

After these passages from 'The Commedia' there should be
small need of my writing introductions to the poems of Guido
Calvacanti, for if he is not among the major prophets, he has at
least his place in the canon, in the second book of The Arts, with
Sappho and Theocritus; with all those who have sung, not all
the modes of life, but some of them, unsurpassedly; those who in
their chosen or fated field have bowed to no one.

It is conceivable the poetry of a far-off time or place requires a
translation not only of word and of spirit, but of 'accompaniment',
that is, that the modern audience must in some measure be made
aware of the mental content of the older audience, and of what
these others drew from certain fashions of thought and speech.

Six centuries of derivative convention and loose usage have obscured the exact significances of such phrases as: 'The death of the heart,' and 'The departure of the soul.'

Than Guido Cavalcanti no psychologist of the emotions is more keen in his understanding, more precise in his expression; we have in him no rhetoric, but always a true description, whether it be of pain itself, or of the apathy that comes when the emotions and possibilities of emotion are exhausted, or of that stranger state when the feeling by its intensity surpasses our powers of bearing and we seem to stand aside and watch it surging across some thing or being with whom we are no longer identified.

The relation of certain words in the original to the practice of my translation may require gloze. *L'anima* and *la Morte* are feminine, but it is not always expeditious to retain this gender in English. *Gentile* is 'noble'; 'gentleness' in our current sense would be *soavitate*. *Mente* is 'mind,' 'consciousness,' 'appercep-tion.' The *spiriti* are the 'senses,' or the 'intelligences of the senses,' perhaps even the 'moods,' when they are considered as 'spirits of the mind.' *Valore* is 'power.' *Virtute*, 'virtue,' 'potency,' requires a separate treatise. Pater has explained its meaning in the preface to his 'The Renaissance,' but in reading a line like

'Vedrai la sua virtù nel ciel salita'

one must have in mind the connotations alchemical, astrological, metaphysical, which Swedenborg would have called the corres-pondences.

The equations of alchemy were apt to be written as women's names and the women so named endowed with the magical powers of the compounds. *La virtù* is the potency, the efficient property of a substance or person. Thus modern science shows us radium with a noble virtue of energy. Each thing or person was held to send forth magnetisms of certain effect; in Sonnet XXXV, the image of his lady has these powers.

It is a spiritual chemistry, and modern science and modern mysticism are both set to confirm it.

'Vedrai la sua virtù nel ciel salita.'

The heavens were, according to the Ptolemaic system, clear

concentric spheres with the earth as their pivot; they moved more swiftly as they were far removed from it, each one endowed with its *virtue*, its property for affecting man and destiny; in each its star, the sign visible to the wise and guiding them. A logical astrology, the star a sort of label of the spiritual force, an indicator of the position and movement of that spiritual current. Thus 'her' presence, his Lady's, corresponds with the ascendancy of the star of that heaven which corresponds to her particular emanation or potency. Likewise,

> '*Vedrai la sua virtù nel ciel salita.*'

Thou shalt see the rays of this emanation going up to heaven as a slender pillar of light, or, more strictly in accordance with the stanza preceding: thou shalt see depart from her lips her subtler body, and from that a still subtler form ascends and from that a star, the body of pure flame surrounding the source of the *virtù*, which will declare its nature.

I would go so far as to say that 'Il Paradiso' and the form of 'The Commedia' might date from this line; very much as I think I find in Guido's 'Place where I found people whereof each one grieved overly of Love,' some impulse that has ultimate fruition in Inferno V.

These are lines in the sonnets; is it any wonder that 'F. Z.' is able to write:

'His (Guido's) canzone solely on the nature of Love was so celebrated that the rarest intellects, among them 'il beato Egidio Colonna,' set themselves to illustrating it with commentaries, of which the most cited is that of Mazzuchelli.'

Another line, of which Rossetti completely loses the significance is

> '*E la beltate per sua Dea la mostra.*' (Sonnet VII, 11.)

'Beauty displays her for her goddess.' That is to say, as the spirit of God became incarnate in the Christ, so is the spirit of the eternal beauty made flesh dwelling amongst us in her. And in the line preceding,

> '*Ch' a lei s'inchina ogni gentil virtute*'

means, that 'she' acts as a magnet for every 'gentil virtue,' that is, the noble spiritual powers, the invigorating forces of life and beauty bend toward her; not

> 'To whom are subject all things virtuous.'

The *inchina* implies not the homage of an object but the direction of a force.

In the matter of these translations and of my knowledge of Tuscan poetry, Rossetti is my father and my mother, but no one man can see everything at once.

The twelfth ballata, being psychological and not metaphysical, needs hardly be explained. Exhausted by a love born of fate and of the emotions, Guido turns to an intellectual sympathy,

> 'Love that is born of loving like delight,'

and in this new force he is remade,

> *'formando di disio nova persona'*

yet with some inexplicable lack. His sophistication prevents the complete enthusiasm. This 'new person' which is formed about his soul

> *'amar già non osa'*

knowing 'The end of every man's desire.'

The facts of Guido's life, as we know them from other evidence than that of his own and his friends' poems, are about as follows: Born 1250 (circa), his mother probably of the Conti Guidi. In 1266 or 1267 'Cavalcante dei Cavalcanti gave for wife to his son Guido one of the Uberti,' i.e., the daughter of Farinata. Thus Villani. Some speak of it as a 'betrothal.' In 1280 he acted as one of the sureties of the peace arranged by Cardinal Latino. We may set 1283 as the date of his reply to Dante's first sonnet. In 1284 he was a member of the grand council with Dino Compagni and Brunetto Latino. In party feuds of Florence Guelf, then a 'White' with the Cherci, and most violent against Corso Donati. 1292-96 is the latitude given us for the pilgrimage to the holy house of Galicia. Corso, it is said, tried to assassinate him on this pilgrimage. It is more plausible to accept 1292 as the date of the feud between the Cavalcanti and the Buondelmonti, dating so the sonnet to Nerone. For upon his return from the pilgrimage which had extended only to Toulouse, Guido attacks Corso in the streets of Florence, and for the general turmoil ensuing, the leaders of both factions were exiled. Guido was sent with the 'Whites' to Sarzana, where he caught his death fever. Dante at this time (1300) being a prior of Florence, was party to decree of exile, and perhaps aided in procuring Cavalcanti's speedy recall. 'Il nostro Guido' was buried on August 29, whence writes Villani, 'and his death is a great loss, for as he was philosopher, so was he man of parts in more things, although somewhat puncti- lious and fiery.' Boccaccio considers him 'probably' the 'other just man,' in Dante's statement that there were two in Florence.

Benevenuto says so positively, *alter oculus Florentiae.*' In the Decameron we hear that, 'He was of the best logicians in the world, a very fine natural philosopher. Thus was he *leggiadrisimo,*' and there is much in this word with which to confute those who find no irony in his sonnets; 'and habile and a great talker.' On the 'sixth day' (novel nine) the queen herself tells how he leapt over an exceeding great tomb to escape from that bore Betto Brunelleschi. Other lines we have of him as: 'noble and pertinent and better than another at whatever he set his hand to'; among the critics, Crescimbene notes, *robustezza e splendore*'; Cristoforo Landiano, *sobrio e dotto,* and surpassed by a greater light he be- came not as the moon to the sun. Of Dante and Petrarcha, I speak elsewhere.'

Filippo Villani, with his translator Mazzuchelli, set him above Petrarch, speaking of him as 'Guido of the noble line of the Cavalcanti, most skilled in the liberal arts, Dante's contemporary and very intimate friend, a man surely diligent and given to specu- lation, 'physicus' (? natural philosopher) of authority . . . worthy of laud and honor for his joy in the study of 'rhetoric,'[1] he brought over the fineness of this art into the rhyming compositions of the common tongue (*eleganter traduxit*). For canzoni in vulgar tongue and in the advancement of this art he held second place to Dante nor hath Petrarch taken it from him.'

[1] 'Rhetoric' must not here be understood in the current sense of our own day. 'Exact and adequate speech' might be a closer rendering.

Dino Compagni, who knew him, has perhaps left us the most apt description, saying that Guido was *'cortes e ardito, ma sdegnoso e solitario,'* at least I would so think of him, 'courteous, bold, haughty and given to being alone.' It is so we find him in the poems themselves.'

Dante's delays in answering the elder Cavalcante's question (Inf. X) 'What said you? "He (Guido) *had*?" Lives he not still, with the sweet light beating upon his eyes?' This delay is, I think, a device for reminding the reader of the events of the year 1300. One who had signed a decree of exile against his friend, however much civic virtue was thereby displayed, might well delay his answer.

And if that matchless and poignant ballad,

> *'Perch' io non spero di tornar già mai'*

had not reached Florence before Dante saw the vision, it was at least written years before he wrote the tenth canto of the Inferno.

Guido left two children, Andrea and Tancia. Mandetta of Toulouse is an incident. As to the identity of 'our own Lady,' that Giovanna 'presumably' of whom Dante writes in the Vita Nuova, sonnet fourteen, and the prose preceding, weaving his fancy about Primavera, the first coming Spring, St. John the Forerunner, with Beatrice following Monna Vanna, as the incarnate love: Again in the sonnet of the enchanted ship, *'Guido vorrei . . .'* we find her mentioned in the chosen company. One modern writer would have us follow out the parallels between the Commedia and 'Book of His Youth,' and identify her with the 'Matilda' of the Earthly Paradise. By virtue of her position and certain similarities of phrasing in Purgatory XXVIII and one of the lives of the saint, we know that Matilda in some way corresponds to or balances John the Baptist. Dante is undoubtedly reminded of his similar equation in the Vita Nuova and shows it in his

> *'Tu mi fai remembrar, dove e qual era*
> *Proserpina, nel tempo che perdette*
> *La madre lei, ed ella primavera.'*

Dante's commentators in their endless search for exact corres-pondences, seem never to suspect him of poetical innuendo, of calling into the spectrum of the reader's mind associated things which form no exact allegory. So far as the personal Matilda is concerned, the great Countess of Tuscany has some claims, and we have nothing to show that Giovanna was dead at the time of the vision.

As to the actual identity of Guido's lady—granting her to have been one and not several—no one has been rash enough to suggest that *il nostro Guido* was in love with his own wife, to whom he had been wedded or betrothed at sixteen. True it would have been contrary to the laws of chivalric love, but Guido was not one to be bound by a convention if the whim had taken him otherwise. The discussion of such details and theories is futile except in so far as it may serve to bring us more intimately in touch with the commune of Florence and the year of grace one thousand three hundred.

As for the verse itself: I believe in an ultimate and absolute rhythm as I believe in an absolute symbol or metaphor. The perception of the intellect is given in the word, that of the emotions in the cadence. It is only, then, in perfect rhythm joined to the perfect word that the two-fold vision can be recorded. I would liken Guido's cadence to nothing less powerful than line in Blake's drawing.

In painting, the colour is always finite. It may match the colour of the infinite spheres, but it is in a way confined within the frame and its appearance is modified by the colours about it. The line is unbounded, it marks the passage of a force, it continues beyond the frame.

Rodin's belief that energy is beauty holds thus far, namely, that all our ideas of beauty of line are in some way connected with our ideas of swiftness or easy power of motion, and we consider ugly those lines which connote unwieldy slowness in moving.

Rhythm is perhaps the most primal of all things known to us. It is basic in poetry and music mutually, their melodies depending on a variation of tone quality and of pitch respectively, as is commonly said, but if we look more closely we will see that music is, by further analysis, pure rhythm; rhythm and nothing else, for the variation of pitch is the variation in rhythms of the individual notes, and harmony the blending of these varied rhythms. When we know more of overtones we will see that the tempo of every masterpiece is absolute, and is exactly set by some further law of rhythmic accord. Whence it should be possible to show that any given rhythm implies about it a complete musical form—fugue, sonata, I cannot say what form, but a form, perfect, complete. Ergo, the rhythm set in a line of poetry connotes its symphony, which, had we a little more skill, we could score for orchestra. *Sequitur*, or rather *inest*: the rhythm of any poetic line corresponds to emotion.

It is the poet's business that this correspondence be exact, i.e., that it be the emotion which surrounds the thought expressed. For which cause I have set here Guido's own words, that those few of you who care, may read in them the signs of his genius. By the same token, I consider Carducci and Arnone blasphemous in accepting the reading

E fa di claritate tremar l' are

instead of following those *mss.* which read

E fa di clarità l'aer tremare.

I have in my translations tried to bring over the qualities of Guido's rhythm, not line for line, but to embody in the whole of my English some trace of that power which implies the man. The science of the music of words and the knowledge of their magical powers has fallen away since men invoked Mithra by a sequence of pure vowel sounds. That there might be less interposed between the reader and Guido, it was my first intention to print only his poems and an unrhymed gloze. This has not been practicable. I can not trust the reader to read the Italian for the music after he has read the English for the sense.

These are no sonnets for an idle hour. It is only when the emotions illumine the perceptive powers that we see the reality. It is in the light born of this double current that we look upon the face of the mystery unveiled. I have lived with these sonnets and ballate daily month in and month out, and have been daily drawn deeper into them and daily into contemplation of things that are not of an hour. And I deem, for this, that *voi altri pochi* who understand, will love me better for my labor in proportion as you read more carefully.

For the rest, I can but quote an envoi, that of Guido's Canzone 'Donna mi prega':

> Thou mayest go assurèd, my Canzone,
> Whither thou wilt, for I have so adorned thee
> That praise shall rise to greet thy reasoning
> Mid all such folk as have intelligence;
> To stand with any else, thou'st no desire.

Ezra Pound

November 15, 1910

SONETTO I

Voi, che per gli occhi miei passaste al core,
E svegliaste la mente che dormia,
Guardate a l' angosciosa vita mia,
Che sospirando la distrugge Amore,

E' va tagliando di sì gran valore,
Che i deboluzzi spiriti van via:
Campa figura nova in signoria,
E boce e quando mostra lo dolore:

Questa vertù d' Amor, che m'ha disfatto,
Da' vostri occhi gentil presta si mosse,
Lanciato m' ha d' un dardo entro lo fianco;

Sì giunse il colpo dritto al primo tratto,
Che l'anima tremando si riscosse,
Veggendo morto il cor nel lato manco.

SONNET I

You, who do breech mine eyes and touch the heart,
And start the mind from her brief reveries,
Might pluck my life and agony apart,
Saw you how love assaileth her with sighs,

And lays about him with so brute a might
That all my wounded senses turn to flight.
There's a new face upon the seigniory,
And new is the voice that maketh loud my grief.

Love, who hath drawn me down through devious ways,
Hath from your noble eyes so swiftly come!
'Tis he hath hurled the dart, wherefrom my pain,

First shot's resultant! and in flanked amaze
See how my affrighted soul recoileth from
That sinister side wherein the heart lies slain.

SONETTO II

Io vidi gl ochi dove amore si mise
Quando mi fece di se pauroso
Che mi sguardaro chome fosse noioso
Allora dicho che l cor si divise

E se non fosse che lla donna rise
Io parlerei di tal ghuisa doglioso
Ch amor medesimo ne farei anghoscioso
Chon quello inmaginar che mi conquise.

Di ciel si mosse uno spirto in quel punto
Che quella donna non ghuardo ghuardare
E vennesi a posar nel mio pensero

E poi mj conta sj d amore il vero
Che ogni sua virtu ver di me pare
Sj com jo fossj nel suo chor gia giunto.

SONNET II

I saw the eyes, where Amor took his place
When love's might bound me with the fear thereof,
Look out at me as they were weary of love.
I say: The heart rent him as he looked on this,

And were't not that my Lady lit her grace,
Smiling upon me with her eyes grown glad,
Then were my speech so dolorously clad
That love should mourn amid his victories.

The instant that she deigned to bend her eyes
Toward me, a spirit from high heaven rode
And chose my thought the place of his abode

With such deep parlance of love's verities
That all Love's powers did my sight accost
As though I'd won unto his heart's mid-most.

SONETTO III

O donna mia, non vedestu colui,
Che 'n su lo core mi tenea la mano,
Quand' io ti rispondea fiochetto e piano
Per' la temenza de gli colpi sui?

El fú Amore, che trovando nui
Meco ristette, che venìa lontano
A guisa d' uno arcier presto soriano,
Acconcio sol per ancidere altrui,

E trasse poi degli occhi miei sospiri
I quai mi seattò nel cor sì forte,
Ch'io mi partii sbigottito fuggendo.

Allor mi parse di seguir la morte,
Accompagnata di quelli martìri,
Che soglion consumar altrui piangendo.

SONNET III

O Lady mine, doth not thy sight allege
Him who hath set his hand upon my heart,
When dry words rattle in my throat and start
And shudder for the terror of his edge?

He was Amor, who since he found you, dwells
Ever with me, and he was come from far;
An archer is he as the Scythians are
Whose only joy is killing someone else.

My sobbing eyes are drawn upon his wrack,
And such harsh sighs upon my heart he casteth
That I depart from that sad me he wasteth.

With Death drawn close upon my wavering track,
Leading such tortures in his sombre train
As, by all custom, wear out other men.

SONETTO IV

S' io priego questa donna, che pietate
Non sia nemica del suo cor gentile,
Tu di ch' io sono sconoscente e vile,
E disperato e pien di vanitate.

Onde ti vien sí nova crudeltate?
Gia rassomigli a chi ti vede umile,
Seggia, adorna, ed accorta, e sottile,
E facta a modo di soavitate.

L'anima mia dolente e paurosa
Piange nel sospirar che nel cor trova,
Sì che bagnati di pianto escon fore.

Allhor mi par che ne la mente piova
Una figura di donna pensosa,
Che vegna per veder morir lo core.

SONNET IV

If I should pray this lady pitiless
That Mercy to her heart be no more foeman,
You'd call me clownish, vile, and say that no man
Was so past hope and filled with vanities.

Where find you now these novel cruelties?
For still you seem humility's true leaven,
Wise and adorned, alert and subtle even,
And fashioned out in ways of gentleness.

My soul weeps through her sighs for grievous fear
And all those sighs, which in the heart were found,
Deep drenched with tears do sobbing thence depart,

Then seems that on my mind there rains a clear
Image of a lady, thoughtful, bound
Hither to keep death-watch upon that heart.

SONETTO V

Gli miei folli occhi, che 'n prima guardaro
Vostra figura piena di valore,
Fur quei, che di voi, donna, m' accusaro
Nel fiero loco, ove tien corte Amore.

Immantenente avanti a lui mostraro,
Ch' io era fatto vostro servitore,
Perchè sospiri e dolor mi pigliaro
Vedendo, che temenza avea lo core.

Menarmi tosto senza riposanza
In una parte la 've trovai gente
Che ciaschedun si dolea d' Amor forte.

Quando mi vider, tutti con pietanza
Dissermi: Fatto sei di tal servente,
Che mai non dei sperare altro che morte.

SONNET V

Lady, my most rash eyes, the first who used
To look upon thy face, the power-fraught,
Were, Lady, those by whom I was accused
In that harsh place where Amor holdeth court.

And there before him was their proof adduced,
And judgment wrote me down: 'Bondslave' to thee,
Though still I stay Grief's prisoner, unloosed,
And Fear hath lien upon the heart of me.

For the which charges, and without respite,
They dragged me to a place where a sad horde
Of such as love and whom Love tortureth

Cried out, all pitying as I met their sight,
'Now art thou servant unto such a Lord
Thou'lt have none other one save only Death.'

SONETTO VI

Tu m'hai si piena di dolor la mente
Che l'anima sen briga di partire:
E li sospir, che manda il cor dolente,
Dicono a gli occhi, che non puon soffrire.

Amore, che lo tuo gran valor sente,
Dice: El mi duol, che ti convien morire
Per questa fera donna che neente
Par, che pietate di te voglia udire.

Io fo come colui, ch'è fuor di vita,
Che mostra a chi lo guarda ched el sia
Fatto di pietra, o di rame, o di legno:

Che si conduca sol per maestria,
E porti nello core una ferita,
Che sia, com' egli è morto, aperto segno.

SONNET VI

Thou fill'st my mind with griefs so populous
That my soul irks him to be on the road.
Mine eyes cry out, 'We cannot bear the load
Of sighs the grievous heart sends upon us.'

Love, sensitive to thy nobility,
Saith, 'Sorrow is mine that thou must take thy death
From this fair lady who will hear no breath
In argument for aught save pitying thee.'

And I, as one beyond life's compass thrown,
Seem but a thing that's fashioned to design,
Melted of bronze or carven in tree or stone.[1]

A wound I bear within this heart of mine
Which by its mastering quality is grown
To be of that heart's death an open sign.

[1] Moved only by mechanical device. E.P.

SONETTO VII

Chi è questa che vien, ch' ogni uom la mira,
Che fa di clarità l' aer tremare,[1]
E mena seco Amor, sì che parlare
Null' uom ne puote, ma ciascun sospira?

Ahi, Dio, che sembra quando gli occhi gira?
Dicalo Amor, ch' io nol saprei contare:
Cotanto d'umiltà donna mi pare,
Che ciascun' altra in vêr di lei chiam' ira.

Non si potria contar la sua piacenza,
Ch' a lei s' inchina ogni gentil virtute,
E la beltate per sua Dea la mostra.

Non fu sì alta già la mente nostra,
E non si è posta in noi tanta salute,
Che propriamente n' abbiam conoscenza.

[1] This is by far the better reading if the sonnet is spoken, but the other reading: *tremare l'are*, can be sung, and that perhaps explains the persistent divergence between the best manuscripts at this point.

SONNET VII

Who is she that comes, makyng turn every man's eye
And makyng the air to tremble with a bright clearenesse
That leadeth with her Love, in such nearness
No man may proffer of speech more than a sigh?

Ah God, what she is like when her owne eye turneth, is
Fit for Amor to speake, for I can not at all;
Such is her modesty, I would call
Every woman else but an useless uneasiness.

No one could ever tell all of her pleasauntness
In that every high noble vertu leaneth to herward,
So Beauty sheweth her forth as her Godhede;

Never before was our mind so high led,
Nor have we so much of heal as will afford
That our thought may take her immediate in its embrace.

SONETTO VIII

Perchè non furo a me gli occhi miei spenti,
O tolti sì, che de la lor veduta
Non fusse ne la mente mia venuta
A dire: Ascolta se nel cor mi senti?

Una paura di nuovi tormenti
M' apparve allor sì crudele ed acuta,
Che l' anima chiamò: Donna, or ci aiuta,
Che gli occhi, ed io non rimagniam dolenti.

Tu gli hai lasciati sì, che venne Amore
A pianger sovra lor pietosamente
Tanto che s' ode una profonda voce,

La qual dà suon: Chi grave pena sente,
Guardi costui, e vederà 'l suo core
Che Morte 'l porta in man tagliato in croce.

SONNET VIII

Ah why! why were mine eyes not quenched for me,
Or stricken so that from their vision none
Had ever come within my mind to say
'Listen, dost thou not hear me in thine heart?'

Fear of new torments was then so displayed
To me, so cruel and so sharp of edge
That my soul cried, 'Ah mistress, bring us aid,
Lest the eyes and I remain in grief always.'

But thou hast left them so that Love's self cometh
And weepeth over them so piteously
That there's a deep voice heard whose sound in part

Turned unto words, is this: 'Whoever knoweth
Pain's depth, let him look on this man whose heart
Death beareth in his hand cut cruciform.'

SONETTO IX

A me stesso di me gran pietà viene
Per la dolente angoscia, ch'io mi veggio
Di molta debolezza: quand' io seggio,
L'anima sento ricoprir di pene.

Tanto mi struggo, perch'io sento bene
Che la mia vita d'ogni angoscia ha l' peggio.
La nova donna, a cui mercede io chieggio,
Questa battaglia di dolor mantiene.

Però che quand'io guardo verso lei,
Drizzami gli occhi de lo suo disdegno
Sì fieramente che distrugge il core.

Allor si parte ogni vertù da' miei;
Il cor si ferma per veduto segno,
Dove si lancia crudeltà d'Amore.

SONNET IX

I am reduced at last to self compassion,
For the sore anguish that I see me in;
At my great weakness; that my soul hath been
Concealed beneath her wounds in such a fashion:

Such mine oppression that I know, in brief,
That to my life ill's worst starred ills befall;
And this strange lady on whose grace I call
Maintains continuous my stour of grief,

For when I look in her direction,
She turns upon me her disdeigning eyen
So harshly that my waiting heart is rent

And all my powers and properties are spent,
Till that heart lieth for a sign ill-seen,
Where Amor's cruelty hath hurled him down.

SONETTO X

Deh spirti miei, quando voi me vedite
Con tanta pena, come non mandate
Fuor de la mente parole adornate
Di pianto, doloros e sbigottite?

Deh, voi vedete che 'l core ha ferite
Di sguardo, e di piacere e d' umiltate.
Deh, io vi priego, che voi 'l consoliate,
Che son da lui le sue vertù partite.

Io veggio a lui spirito apparire
Alto e gentile, e di tanto valore,
Che fa le sue vertù tutte fuggire.

Deh, io vi priego, che deggiate dire
A l' alma trista, che parla in dolore,
Com' ella fu, e fia sempre d' Amore.

SONNET X

Alas, my spirits, that ye come to find me
So painful, poor, waylaid in wretchedness,
Yet send no words adorned with deep distress
Forth from my mind to say what sorrows bind me.

Alas, ye see how sore my heart is wounded
By glance, by fair delight and by her meekness;
'Las! Must I pray ye that ye aid his weakness,
Seeing him power-stripped, naked, confounded.

And now a spirit that is noble and haut
Appeareth to that heart with so great might
That all th' heart's virtues turn in sudden flight.

Woe! and I pray you greet my soul as friend,
Who tells through all her grief what things were wrought
On her by Love, and will be to the end.

SONETTO XI

Se merce fosse amica a' miei desiri,
E 'l movimento suo fosse dal core,
Di questa bella donna il suo valore
Mostrasse-la vertute a' miei martìri,

D' angosciosi diletti i miei sospiri,
Che nascon de la mente, ov'è Amore,
E vanno sol ragionando dolore,
E non trovan persona, che gli mìri,

Girieno agli occhi con tanta vertute,
Che 'l forte, e duro lagrimar, che fanno,
Ritornerebbe in allegrezza e 'n gioia.

Ma si è al cor dolente tanta noia,
Ed a l' anima trista tanto danno,
Che per disdegno uom non dà lor salute.

SONNET XI

If Mercy were the friend of my desires,
Or Mercy's source of movement were the heart,
Then, by this fair, would Mercy show such art
And power of healing as my pain requires.

From torturing delight my sighs commence,
Born of the mind where Love is situate,
Go errant forth and naught save grief relate
And find no one to give them audience.

They would return to the eyes in galliard mode,
With all harsh tears and their deep bitterness
Transmuted into revelry and joy;

Were 't not unto the sad heart such annoy,
And to the mournful soul such rathe distress
That none doth deign salute them on the road.

SONETTO XII

Una giovane donna di Tolosa
Bella e gentil, d' onesta leggiadria,
Tant' è diritta, e simigliante cosa
Ne' suoi dolci occhi de la donna mia;

Che fatto ha dentro al cor desiderosa
L'anima in guisa, che da lui si svia,
E vanne a lei; ma tanto è paurosa,
Che non le dice di qual donna sia.

Quella la mira nel suo dolce sguardo,
Ne lo qual fece rallegrare Amore,
Perchè v' è dentro la sua donna dritta:

Poi torna piena di sospir nel core,
Ferita a morte d' un tagliente dardo,
Che questa donna nel partir le gitta.

SONNET XII

The grace of youth in Toulouse ventureth;
She's noble and fair, with quaint sincerities,
Direct she is and is about her eyes
Most like to our Lady of sweet memories.

So that within my heart desirous
She hath clad the soul in fashions peregrine.[1]
Pilgrim to her he hath too great chagrin
To say what Lady is lord over us.

This soul looks deep into that look of hers,
Wherein he rouseth Love to festival,
For deep therein his rightful lady resteth.

Then with sad sighing in the heart he stirs,
Feeling his death-wound as that dart doth fall
Which this Tolosan by departure casteth.

[1] Vita Nuova XLI, 46, and sonnet 24 and sonnet V, l. 4: '*In guisa che da lui si svia e vanne a lei.*'

SONETTO XIII

Per gli occhi fiere un spirito sottile,
Che fa in la mente spirito destare,
Dal qual si muove spirito d' amare,
Ch' ogn' altro spiritello fa gentile.

Sentir non può di lui spirito vile,
Di cotanta vertù spirito appare.
Questo è lo spiritel, che fa tremare
Lo spiritel, che fa la donna umile.

E poi da questo spirito si muove
Un altro dolce spirito soave,
Che segue un spiritello di mercede.

Lo quale spiritel spiriti piove,
Ch' ha di ciascuno spirito la chiave,
Per forza d' uno spirito, che 'l vede.

SONNET XIII

Concerning the source, the affects and the progeny of the little spirit of pure love:
  Born of the perception of beauty, he arouseth that power of the mind whence is born that quality of love which ennobleth every sense and every desire; misunderstood of base minds who comprehend not his power, he is the cause of that love in woman which teacheth modesty. Thus from him is born that love in woman whence is born Mercy, and from Mercy 'as a gentle rain from heaven' descend those spirits which are the keys of every spirit, perforce of the one spirit which seeth.

A breath of thy beauty passes through my eyes
And rouses up an air within my mind
That moves a spirit so to love inclined
It breedeth, in all air, nobilities.

No vile spirit to discern his vertu is able
So great is the might of it,
He is the spryte that putteth a trembling fyt
On spirit that maketh a woman mercyable.

And then from this spirit there moveth about
Another yet so gentle and soft that he
Causeth to follow after him a spirit of pity

From the which a very rain of spirits poureth out,
And he doth carry upon him the key
To every spirit, so keen is his breath to see.

SONETTO XIV

Certo non è da l' intelletto accolto
Quel che stamen ti fece disonesto.
Or come ti mostrò mendico presto
Il rosso spiritel, che apparve al volto.

Sarebbe forse, che t' avesse sciolto
Amor da quella, ch' è nel tondo di Sesto,
O che vil raggio t' avesse richiesto
A far te lieto, ov' io son tristo molto?

Di te mi duole in me puoi veder quanto:
Che me ne fiede mia donna a traverso,
Tagliando ciò, che Amor porta soave.

Ancor dinanzi mi è rotta la chiave,
Che del disdegno suo nel mio cor verso;
Sì che amo l' ira, ed allegrezza e 'l pianto.

SONNET XIV

Surely thy wit giveth not welcome place
To that which this morn madeth thine honour to want,
Fye, how swiftly art thou shown mendicaunt
By that red air that is suffusing thy face.

Perhaps thou art let on rampage
By love of what is caught in Sesto's ring
Or some vile beam is come here to engage
Thee to make merry, whereof I am sorrowing,

Aye, sorrowing, so much as thou mayst see
In that before my Lady I dare not to flaunt,
Whereby I lose all of love's agrement;

The key brok'n off before me, her disdeign
Stuck in my heart to turn, making me
To love confusion, or to be gaye, or playne.

Tondo di Sesto, printed *tondo sesto* and unexplained or atrociously explained in previous editions.
'Taken in an empty hoop of sophistries.'
I find in Fr. Fiorentino's 'Manuale di Storia della Filosofia':
Sesto Empirico . . . Ogni sillogismo è per lui un circolo vizioso, perchè la premessa maggiore dovrebbe essere assicurata da una induzione completa: ora, affinchè possa dirsi completa, è evidente che vi si debbia trovar compressa anche la conclusione del sillogismo che ancora si ha da dimostrare, etc.
The application here must be considered in relation to the whole philosophic and scholastic background, the attribution of 'Da più a uno fece sillogismo', etc.

SONETTO XV

Avete in voi li fiori, e la verdura,
E ciò che luce, o è bello a vedere,
Risplende più che' l sol vostra figura,
Chi voi non vede, mai non può valere.

In questo mondo non ha creatura
Sì piena di beltà, nè di piacere,
E chi d'Amor temesse, l'assicura
Vostro bel viso, e non può più temere.

Le donne, che vi fanno compagnia
Assai mi piacen per lo vostro amore;
Ed io le prego per lor cortesia,

Che qual più puote, più vi faccia onore,
Ed aggia cara vostra signoria,
Perchè di tutte siete la migliore.

SONNET XV

Thou hast in thee the flower and the green
And that which gleameth and is fair of sight,
Thy form is more resplendent than sun's sheen;
Who sees thee not, can ne'er know worth aright.

Nay, in this world there is no creature seen
So fashioned fair and full of all delight;
Fearers of Love who fearing meet thy mien,
Thereby assured, do solve them of their fright.

The ladies of whom thy cortège consisteth
Please me in this, that they've thy favour won;
I bid them now, as courtesy existeth,

To prize more high Thy lordship of their state,
To honour thee with powers commensurate,
Since Thou dost shine out far above them all.

SONETTO XVI
A GUIDO ORLANDO

La bella donna, dove Amor si mostra,
Che tanto è di valor pieno ed adorno,
Tragge lo cor de la persona vostra,
Che prende vita in far con lei soggiorno.

Perchè ha sì dolce guardia la sua chiostra,
Che 'l sente in India ciascun Unicorno:
E la vertù de l' armi a farvi giostra
Verso di noi fa crudel ritorno.

Ch' ella è per certo di sì gran valenza,
Che gia non manca a lei cosa da bene,
Ma che natura la creo mortale.

Poi mostra, che in ciò mise provvidenza;
Che al vostro intendimento si conviene
Far pur conoscer quel, che a lei sia tale.

SONNET XVI

This fayre Mistress, whereby Love maketh plain
How full he is of prowesse, adornèd to a marvel,
Tuggeth the heart out of thy masking-shell,
The which enhaunceth his life in her domain.

For her quadrangle is guarded with such a sweet smell
Every unicorn of India smelleth it out,
But her vertue against thee in jousting-bout
Turneth against us for to be cruel.

She is, certes, of such great avail
Nothing of all perfectness in her lacketh
That can be in creature subject to death,

Neither in this mortality did foresight fail.
'Tis fitting thy wit make known
Only that which it can take, or mistake, for its own.

SONETTO XVII
A BERNADO DA BOLOGNA

Ciascuna fresca, e dolce fontanella
Prende in Liscian sua chiarezza, e vertute,
Bernardo amico mio; e sol da quella,
Che ti rispose a le tue rime acute.

Perocchè in quella parte ove favella
Amor de le bellezze, che ha vedute,
Dice che questa gentilesca e bella
Tutte nuove adornezze ha in sè compiute.

Avvegnachè la doglia io porti grave
Per lo sospiro, che di me fa lume,
Lo core ardendo in la disfatta nave,

Mando io a la Pinella un g. ande fiume
Pieno di lamie, servito da schiave,
Belle, ed adorne di gentil costume.

SONNET XVII

Concerning Pinella, he replies to a sonnet by Bernardo da Bologna and explains why they have sweet waters in Galicia (Liscian).

Every fresh and sweet-flavoured water-spring
Hath in Galicia its taste and its clearness,
Bernardo, my friend, from but the one enchanteresse;
It was she that answered thy sharp rhyming.

And in that Court where Love himself fableth
Telling of beauties he hath seen, he saith:
This pagan and lovely woman hath in her
All strange adornments that ever were.

Though I be heavy with the pain of that sigh
That maketh my heart burn but as a light
In shipwracke, I send Pinella a river in full flood

Stockèd with Lamia-nymphs, that are foreby
Served each with her slave hand-maids, fair to sight
And yet more fair by manner of gentlehood.

SONETTO XVIII

Beltà di donna di piagente core,
E cavalieri armati che sian genti,
Cantar d' augelli e ragionar d' amore,
Adorni legni in mar forti e correnti,

Aire sereno quand' appar l' albore,
E bianca nieve scender sensa venti,
Rivera d' aigua e prato d' ogni fiore,
Oro, argento, azzurro in ornamenti

Passa la gran beltate e la piagensa
De la mia donna el suo gentil coraggio,
Siche rassenbra vile à chi cio sguarda,

E tanto apiò d' ogn altra canoscenza
Quanto lo celo dela terra è maggio:
Assimil di natura ben non tarda.

SONNET XVIII

Beauty of woman, of the knowing heart,
And courtly knights in bright accoutrement
And loving speeches and the small birds' art,
Adorned swift ships which on high seas are sent,

And airs grown calm when white the dawn appeareth
And white snow falling where no wind is bent,
Brook-marge and mead where every flower flareth,
And gold and silver and azure and ornament:

Effective 'gainst all these think ye the fairness
And valour of my Lady's lordly daring?
Yea, she makes all seem base vain gathering,
And she were known above whome'er you'd bring
As much as heaven is past earth's comparing;
Good seeketh out its like with some address.

SONETTO XIX

Novella ti so dire, odi Nerone,
Che i Buondelmonti trieman di paura,
E tutti i Fiorentin non gli assicura
Udendo che tu hai cor de lione.

E più treman di te, che d' un dragone,
Veggendo la tua faccia, che è sì dura
Che non la riterrian ponti, ne mura,
Ma sì la tomba del Re Faraone.

O come fai grandissimo peccato,
Sì alto sangue voler discacciare,
Che tutti vanno via senza ritegno!

Ma ben è vêr che rallargar lo pegno,
Di che potresti l' anima salvare,
Se fussi paziente del mercato.

SONNET XIX

He suggests to his kinsman Nerone that there may be one among all the Buondelmonti of whom they might in time make a man.

News have I now for thee, so hear, Nerone,
How that the Buondelmonti shake with fear,
And all the Florentines can not assure them,
Seeing thou hast in thee the lion-heart.

They fear thee more than they would fear a dragon,
Seeing that face of thine, how set it is
That neither bridge nor walls could hold against it
Lest they were strong as is King Pharo's tomb.

Oh how thou dost of smoky sins the greatest
In that thou wouldst drive forth such haughty blood
Till all be gone, gone forth without retention.
But sooth it is, thou might'st extend the pawn
Of one whose soul thou *mightest* give salvation
Wert thou more patient in thine huckstering.

SONETTO XX

L'anima mia vilmente è sbigottita
De la battaglia, ch' ella sente al core;
Che se pur si avvicina un poco Amore
Più presto a lei che non soglia, ella muore.

Sta come quella che non ha valore,
Ch' è per temenza dal mio cor partita:
E chi vedesse com' ella n' è gita,
Diria per certo: questa non ha vita.

Per gli occhi venne la battaglia in pria,
Che ruppe ogni valor immantenente,
Sì che dal colpo fier strutta è la mente.

Qualunque è quel, che più allegrezza sente,
S' ei vedesse il mio spirito gir via,
Sì grande è la pietà che piangeria.

SONNET XX

So vilely is this soul of mine confounded
By strife grown audible within the heart
That if toward her some frail Love but start
With unaccustomed speed, she swoons astounded.

She is as one in whom no power aboundeth;
Lo, she forsakes my heart through fearfulness,
And any seeing her, how prone she is,
Would deem her one whom death's sure cloak surroundeth

Through th' eyes, as through the breach in wall, her foes
Came first to attack and shattered all defense,
Then spoiled the mind with their down-rained blows.

Whoe'er he be who holdeth joy most close
Would, should he see my spirit going hence,
Weep for the pity and make no pretense.

Cf. Sonnet I.

SONETTO XXI

Veder poteste, quando vi scontrai,
Quello pauroso spirito d' Amore,
Lo qual suol apparer quand' uom si more,
Che in altra guisa non si vede mai.

Egli mi fu sì presso, che pensai,
Ch' egli ancidesse il mio dolente core.
Allor si mise nel morto colore
L'anima trista in voler tragger guai.

Ma poi si tenne quando vide uscire
Da gli occhi vostri un lume di mercede,
Che porse dentro al cor una dolcezza.

E quel sottile spirito che vede,
Soccorse gli altri, che credean morire
Gravati d'angosciosa debolezza.

SONNET XXI

THE DRED SPIRIT

Thou mayest see, who seest me face to face,
That most dred spirit whom Love summoneth
To meet with man when a man meets with Death;
One never seen in any other case.

So close upon me did this presence show
That I thought he would slay my heart his dolour
And my sad soul clad her in the dead colour
That most accords the will and ways of woe.

Then he restrained him, seeing in true faith
The piteous lights forth-issue from your eyes
The which bore to my heart their foreign sweetness,

While the perceptive sense with subtle fleetness
Rescued those others[1] who had considered death
The one sure ending for their miseries.

[1] The senses or the spirits of the senses.

SONETTO XXII

Vedesti al mio parere ogni valore
E tutto gioco, e quanto bene uom sente,
Se fusti in pruova del signor valente,
Che signoreggia il mondo de l' onore;

Poi vive in parte, dove noia muore,
E tien ragion ne la pietosa mente;
Si va soave ne' sonni a la gente,
Che i cor ne porta senza far dolore.

Di te lo core ne portò, veggendo,
Che la tua donna la morte chiedea:
Nudrilla d' esto cor, di cio temendo.

Quando t' apparve, che sen gia dogliendo,
Fu 'l dolce sonno, ch' allor si compiea,
Che 'l suo contrario lo venìa vincendo.

SONNET XXII

To Dante, in answer to the first sonnet of the Vita Nuova.

Thou sawest, it seems to me, all things availing,
And every joy that ever good man feeleth.
Thou wast in proof of that lord valorous
Who through sheer honour lords it o'er the world.

He liveth in a place where baseness dieth,
And holdeth reason in the piteous mind,
Moving so gently to mankind in sleep
That the heart bears it 'thout the feel of pain.

Love bore away thy heart, because in his sight
Was Death grown clamorous for one thou lovest,
Love fed her with thy heart in dread of this,

Then, when it seemed to thee he left in sadness,
A dear dream was it which was there completed
Seeing it contrary came conquering.

Note: Dante, V. N. III. 'The true significance of the dream was not then seen by anyone.'

SONETTO XXIII

Io vengo il giorno a te infinite volte,
E trovoti pensar troppo vilmente;
Molto mi duol de la gentil tua mente,
E d' assai tue virtù, che ti son tolte.

Solevan ti spiacer persone molte,
Tuttor fuggivi la noiosa gente;
Di me parlavi sì coralemente,
Che tutte le tue rime avei accolte.

Or non mi ardisco, per la vil tua vita,
Far dimostranza, che 'l tuo dir mi piaccia;
Nè 'n guisa vegno a te che tu mi veggi.

Se 'l presente sonetto spesso leggi
Lo spirito noioso, che ti caccia,
Si partirà da l' anima invilita.

SONNET XXIII

To Dante, rebuking him for his way of life after the death of Beatrice.

I daily come to thee uncounting times
And find thee ever thinking over vilely;
Much doth it grieve me that thy noble mind
And virtue's plenitude are stripped from thee;

Thou wast so careless in thy fine offending,
Who from the rabble alway held apart,
And spoke of me so straightly from the heart
That I gave welcome to thine every rime.

And now I care not, sith thy life is baseness
To give the sign that thy speech pleaseth me,
Nor come I to thee in guise visible,

Yet if thou 'lt read this sonnet many a time,
That malign spirit which so hunteth thee
Will sound forloyn[1] and spare thy affrighted soul.

[1] The recall of the hounds.

SONETTO XXIV

Se vedi Amore, assai ti prego, Dante,
In parte, la've Lapo sia presente,
Che non ti gravi di por sì la mente,
Che mi riscrivi, s'egli il chiama amante:

E se la donna gli sembra aitante,
E se fa vista di parer servente.
Che molte fiate così fatta gente
Suol per gravezza d'Amor far sembiante:

Tu sai che ne la corte, là ove regna
Non può servire uomo, che sia vile,
A donna che là dentro sia renduta.

Se la soffrenza lo servente aiuta,
Puoi di leggier conoscer nostro stile,
Lo quale porta di mercede insegna.

SONNET XXIV

Dante, I pray thee, if thou Love discover
In any place where Lappo Gianni is,—
If 't irk thee not to move thy mind in this,
Write me these answered: Doth he style him 'Lover?'

And, 'Doth the lady seem as one approving?';
And, 'Makes he show of service with fair skill?';
For many a time folk made as he is, will
To assume importance, make a show of loving.

Thou know'st that in that court where Love puts on
His royal robes, no vile man can be servant
To any lady who were lost therein;

If servant's suff'ring doth assistance win,
Our style could show unto the least observant,
It beareth mercy for a gonfalon.

SONETTO XXV

Guarda, Manetto, quella sgrignutuzza,
E pon ben mente com' è sfigurata,
E come bruttamente è divisata,
E quel che par, quand' ella si raggruzza.

E s' ella fosse vestita d' un' uzza
Con cappellina e di vel soggolata,
E apparisse di dì accompagnata
D' alcuna bella donna gentiluzza,

Tu non avresti iniquità sì forte,
Nè tanta angoscia, o tormento d' amore,
Nè sì rinvolto di malinconia,

Che tu non fossi a rischio de la morte
Di tanto rider, che aprirebbe il core;
O tu morresti, o fuggiresti via.

SONNET XXV

'Hoot Zah!!!'

Come, come Manetto, look upon this scarecrow
And set your mind upon its deformations,
Compute th' extent of its sad aberrations,
Say what it looks like where she scarcely dare go!

Nay, were she in a cloak most well concealèd
And snugly hooded and most tightly veiled
If, by her, daylight should once be assailed
Though by some noble woman partly healèd,

Still you could not be so sin-laden or quite
So bound by anguish or by love's abstractions
Nor so enwrapped in naked melancholy

But you were brought to deathly danger, solely
By laughter, till your sturdy sides grew fractions,
'Struth you were dead, or sought your life in flight.

SONETTO XXVI

Certe mie rime a te mandar vogliendo
Del grave stato quale il mio cor porta,
Amor m'apparve in un' imagin morta,
E disse: Non mandar, ch' io ti riprendo

Però che se l' amico è quel ch' io intendo,
E' non avrà già sì la mente accorta,
Ch' udendo la 'ngiuriosa cosa e torta,
Ch' io ti fo sofferir tuttora ardendo,

Temo non prenda tale smarrimento,
Che avante che udito abbia tua pesanza,
Non si diparta da la vita il core.

E tu conosci ben ch' io sono Amore,
E ch' io ti lascio questa mia sembianza,
E portone ciascun tuo pensamento.

SONNET XXVI

Nay, when I would have sent my verses to thee
To say how harshly my heart is oppressed,
Love in an ashen vision manifest
Appeared and spake: 'Say not that I foredo thee,

For though thy friend be he I understand
He is, he will not have his Spirit so inured
But that to hear of all thou hast endured,
Of that blare flame that hath thee 'neath its hand,

Would blear his mind out. Verily before!
Yea, he were dead, heart, life, ere he should hear
To the last meaning of the portent wrought.

And thou; thou knowest well I am Amor
Who leave with thee mine ashen likeness here
And bear away from thee thine every thought.'

SONETTO XXVII

S'io fossi quello che d' Amor fu degno,
Del qual non trovo sol che rimembranza,
E la donna tenesse altra sembianza,
Assai mi piaceria sì fatto segno.

E tu, che se' de l' amoroso regno
Là onde di mercè nasce speranza,
Riguarda, se 'l mio spirito ha pesanza,
Ch' un presto arcier di lui ha fatto segno;

E tragge l' arco, che li tese Amore,
Sì lietamente che la sua persona
Par che di giuoco porti signoria.

Or odi maraviglia, ch' ella fia,
Lo spirito fedito li perdona,
Vedendo che li strugge il suo valore.

SONNET XXVII

Were I that I that once was worthy of Love
(Of whom I find naught now save the remembrance)
And if the lady had another semblance,
Then would this sort of sign please me enough.

Do thou, who art from Love's clear realm returned,
Where Mercy giveth birth to hopefulness,
Judge as thou canst from my dim mood's distress
What bowman and what target are concerned.

Straining his arc, behold Amor the bowman
Draweth so gaily that to see his face
You'd say he held his rule for merriment,

Yet hear what's marvelous in all intent:
The smitten spirit pardoneth his foeman
Which pardon doth that foeman's power debase.

Anyone who can, from the text as it stands, discern what happens to whom in
the final lines of this sonnet, is at liberty to emend my translation.

SONETTO XXVIII

Un amoroso sguardo spiritale
M' ha rinovato Amor tanto placente,
Che assai più che non suole ora m' assale,
Ed a pensar mi stringe coralmente

Ver la mia donna, verso cui non vale
Mercè nè pietà, nè star soffrente,
Che sovent' ore mi dà pena tale,
Che' n poca parte il cor la vita sente.

Ma quando sento che sì dolce sguardo
Per mezzo gli occhi passò dentro al core,
E posevi uno spirito di gioia,

Di farne a lei mercè giammai non tardo;
Così pregata fosse ella d' Amore
Che un po' di pietà no i fusse noia.

SONNET XXVIII

A love-lit glance with living powers fraught
Renewed within me love's extreme delight,
So love assails me with unwonted might,
And cordially he driveth me in thought

Towards my lady with whom 'vaileth not
Mercy nor pity nor the suffering wrought,
So oft and great, her torments on me fall
That my heart scarce can feel his life at all.

But when I feel that her so sweet regard
Passeth mine eyes and to the heart attaineth
Setting to rest therein spirits of joy,

Then do I give her thanks and without retard;
Love asked her to do this, and that explaineth
Why this first pity doth no annoy.

SONETTO XXIX

Dante, un sospiro messagger del core
Subitamente m' assalì dormendo;
Ed io mi disvegliai allor temendo,
Ched egli fosse in compagnia d' Amore:

Poi mi girai, e vidi il servitore
Di Mona Lagia, che venia dicendo,
Aiutimi pietà, sì che piangendo
Io presi di pietà tanto valore,

Ch' io giunsi Amore, che affilava i dardi;
Allor lo domandai del suo tormento,
Ed elli mi rispose in questa guisa:

Dì al servente, che la donna è presa,
E tengola per far suo piacimento,
E se no 'l crede, dì che agli occhi guardi.

SONNET XXIX

Dante, a sigh, that's the heart's messenger
Assailed me suddenly as I lay sleeping,
Aroused, I fell straightway into fear's keeping,
For Love came with that sigh as curator.

And I turned straight and saw the servitor
Of Monna Lagia, who came there a-crying,
'Ah pity! Aid me!' and at this his sighing
I took from Pity this much power and more.

That I found Love a-filing javelins
And asked him of both torment and solution,
And in this fashion came that Lord's replies:

'Say to the servant that his service wins.
He holds the Lady to his pleasure won.
If he'd believe it, let him watch her eyes.'

SONETTO XXX

Io temo che la mia disavventura
Non faccia sì, ch' io dica: Io mi dispero;
Però ch' io sento nel cor un pensiero,
Che fa tremar la mente di paura.

E par ch' ei dica: Amor non t'assicura
In guisa che tu possa di leggiero
A la tua donna sì contare il vero,
Che morte non ti ponga in sua figura.

De la gran doglia, che l' anima sente,
Si parte da lo core un tal sospiro,
Che va dicendo: Spiritei fuggite.

Allor null' uom, che sia pietoso, miro,
Che consolasse mia vita dolente,
Dicendo: Spiritei, non vi partite.

SONNET XXX

I fear me lest unfortune's counter thrust
Pierce through my throat and rip out my despair.
I feel my heart and that thought shaking there
Which shakes the aspen mind with his distrust,

Seeming to say, 'Love doth not give thee ease
So that thou canst, as of a little thing,
Speak to thy Lady with full verities,
For fear Death set thee in his reckoning.

By the chagrin that here assails my soul
My heart's parturèd of a sigh so great
It cryeth to the spirits: 'Get ye gone!'

And of all piteous folk I come on none
Who seeing me so in my grief's control
Will aid by saying e'en: 'Nay, Spirits, wait!'

SONETTO XXXI

O tu che porti negli occhi sovente
Amor tenendo tre saette in mano,
Questo mio spirto, che vien di lontano,
Ti raccomanda l' anima dolente;

La quale ha già feruta ne la mente
Di due saette l' arcier soriano,
E a la terza apre l' arco, ma sì piano,
Che non m' aggiunge, essendoti presente;

Perchè saria de l' alma la salute,
Che quasi giace infra le membra morta
Di due saette, che fan tre ferute.

La prima dà piacere e disconforta,
E la seconda desìa la virtute
De la gran gioia, che la terza porta.

SONNET XXXI

You, who within your eyes so often carry
That Love who holdeth in his hand three arrows,
Behold my spirit, by his far-brought sorrows,
Commends to you a soul whom hot griefs harry.

A mind thrice wounded she[1] already hath,
By this keen archer's Syrian shafts twice shot.
The third, less tautly drawn, hath reached me not,
Seeing your presence is my shield 'gainst wrath.

Yet this third shot had made more safe my soul,
Who almost dead beneath her members lies;
For these two arrows give three wounds in all:

The first: delight, which payeth pain his toll;
The second brings desire for the prize
Of that great joy which with the third doth fall.

[1] I.e. The Soul. I have kept the Italian gender in those few sonnets where there is no danger of confusing 'her', the soul, with the subjects of other feminine pronouns.

SONETTO XXXII

Se non ti caggia la tua Santalena
Giù per lo colto tra le dure zolle,
E venga a man di qualche villan folle,
Che la stropicci e rendalati appena;

Dimmi, se 'l fructo che la terra mena,
Nasce di secco, di caldo o di molle;
E qual è 'l vento, che l' ammorta, e tolle;
E di che nebbia la tempesta è piena;

E si ti piace, quando la mattina
Odi la voce del lavoratore,
E 'l tramazzar dell' altra sua famiglia.

Io ho per ceto, che se la Bettina
Porta soave spirito nel core,
Del nuovo acquisto spesso ti ripiglia.

SONNET XXXII

TO CECCO

If Santalena does not come unto you
Down in the plow-lands where the clods are hard,
But falls into the hands of some hot clod-pole
Who'll wear her out and hardly then return her;

Then tell me if the fruit which this land beareth
Is born of drought or heat or from the dampness,
And say what wind it is doth blight and wither
And which doth bring the tempest and the mist.

Say if it please you when at break of morning
You hear the farmer's workman bawling out
And all his family meddling in the noise?

Bigod! I think that if your sweet Bettina
Beareth a mellow spirit in her heart
She'll rescue you once more from your last choice.

SONETTO XXXIII

Morte gentil, rimedio d' cattivi,
Merzè, merzè, a man giunte ti chieggio,
Viemmi a vedere, o prendimi, che peggio
Mi face Amor chè miei spiriti vivi

Son consumati e spenti sì che quivi,
Dov' io stava gioioso, ora m' avveggio
In parte lasso là, dov' io posseggio
Pene e dolor, e 'n pianto vuol ch' arrivi,

E molto maggior mal, s'esser più puote.
Morte, or è il tempo, che valer mi puoi
Di tormi da le man di tal nimico.

Aimè lasso, quante volte dico:
Amor, perchè fai mal sol pure a' tuoi,
Com' fa quel de l' inferno, che percuote?

SONNET XXXIII

Death who art haught, the wretched's remedy,
Grace! Grace! hands joined I do beseech it thee,
Come, see and conquer for worse things on me
Are launched by love. My senses that did live,

Consumèd are and quenched, and e'en in this place
Where I was galliard, now I see that I am
Fallen away, and where my steps I misplace,
Fall pain and grief; to open tears I nigh am.

And greater ills He'd send if greater may be.
Sweet Death, now is the time thou may'st avail me
And snatch me from His hand's hostility.

Ah woe! how oft I cry 'Love tell me now:
Why dost thou ill only unto thine own,
Like him of hell who maketh the damned groan?'

SONETTO XXXIV

Amore, e Mona Lagia, e Guido, ed io
Possiam ben ringraziare un Ser costui,
Che n' ha partiti, sapete da cui?
Nol vo' contar per averlo in oblio.

Poi questi tre più non v' hanno disio;
Ch' eran serventi di tal guisa in lui,
Che veramente più di lor non fui,
Ymaginando ch' elli fosse Iddio.

Sia ringraziato Amor, che se ne accorse
Primieramente, poi la donna saggia,
Che in quel punto li ritolse il core.

E Guido ancor, che n' è del tutto fore,
Ed io ancor, che' n sua virtute caggia;
Se poi mi piacque, non si crede forse.

SONNET XXXIV

Amore and Mona Lagia and Guido and I
Can give true thanks unto Ser Such-a-one
Who hath now rid our lot of Know-you-who?
I'll name no name for I'd have it forgotten.

And these three people have no wish for it
Though they were servants to him in such wise
That they, in sooth, could not have served him more
Had they mistaken him for God himself.

Let Love be thanked who was first made aware,
And then give thanks unto the prudent lady
Who at Love's instance hath called back her heart;

Then thanks to Guido[1] who's not here concerned
And to me too who drove him back to virtue,
If then he please me, think it not perchance.

[1] I.e. Guido Orlando.

SONETTO XXXV

Una figura de la donna mia
S' adora, Guido, a San Michele in Orto,
Che di bella sembianza, onesta e pia,
De' peccatori è refugio e conforto:

E quale a lei divoto s' umilia
Chi più languisce più n' ha di conforto:
Gl' infermi sana, i demon caccia via,
E gli occhi orbati fa vedere scorto.

Sana in pubblico loco gran languori:
Con reverenza la gente l' inchina;
Due luminara l' adornan di fuori.

La voce va per lontane cammina;
Ma dicon, ch' è idolatra, i Fra' Minori,
Per invidia, che non è lor vicina.

SONNET XXXV

He explains the miracles of the madonna of Or San Michele, by telling whose
image it is.

My Lady's face is it they worship there.
At San Michele in Orto, Guido mine,
Near her fair semblance that is clear and holy
Sinners take refuge and get consolation.

Whoso before her kneeleth reverently
No longer wasteth but is comforted;
The sick are healed and devils driven forth,
And those with crooked eyes see straightway straight.

Great ills she cureth in an open place,
With reverence the folk all kneel unto her,
And two lamps shed the glow about her form.

Her voice is borne out through far-lying ways
'Till brothers minor cry: 'Idolatry',
For envy of her precious neighborhood.

MADRIGALE

O cieco mondo, di lusinghe pieno,
Mortal veleno è ciascun tuo diletto,
Fallace, è pien d' inganni, e con sospetto.

Folle è colui che ti addrizza il freno,
Quando per men che nulla quel ben perde,
Che sovra ogn' altro Amor luce e sta verde.
Però già mai di te colui non curi,
Che 'l frutto vuol gustar di dolci fiori.

MADRIGAL

O world gone blind and full of false deceits,
Deadly's the poison with thy joys connected,
O treacherous thou, and guileful and suspected:
Sure he is mad who for thy checks retreats
And for scant nothing loseth that green prize
Which over-gleans all other loveliness;

Wherefore the wise man scorns thee at all hours
When he would taste the fruit of pleasant flowers.

BALLATA I

Poichè di doglia il cor convien ch' io porti,
E senta di piacere ardente foco,
Che di virtù mi tragge a sì vil loco:
Dirò come ho perduto ogni valore.

Io dico, che miei spiriti son morti,
E 'l cor, ch' ha tanta guerra e vita poco.
E se non fosse che 'l morir m' è gioco,
Fare' ne di pietà piangere Amore.

Ma per lo folle tempo, che m' ha giunto,
Mi cangio di mia ferma opinione
In altrui condizione;
Sì ch' io non mostro quant' i' sento affanno,
Là ond' io ricevo inganno:
Che dentro da lo cor mi passa amanza,
Che se ne porta tutta mia speranza.

BALLATA I

Sith need hath bound my heart in bands of grief,
Sith I turn flame in pleasure's lapping fire,
I sing how I lost a treasure by desire
And left all virtue and am low descended.

I tell, with senses dead, what scant relief
My heart from war hath in his life's small might.
Nay! were not death turned pleasure in my sight
Then Love would weep to see me so offended.

Yet, for I'm come upon a madder season,
The firm opinion which I held of late
Stands in a changèd state,
And I show not how much my soul is grieved
There where I am deceived
Since through my heart midway a mistress went
And in her passage all mine hopes were spent.

Note: This is not really a ballata but is the first stanza of a lost canzone, one
mentioned by Dante in the D.V.E.

BALLATA II

Io vidi donne con la donna mia:
Non che niuna mi sembrasse donna;
Ma simigliavan sol la sua ombria.

Già non la lodo, se non perch' è 'l vero,
E non biasimo altrui, se m'intendete:
Ma ragionando muovesi un pensiero
A dir: Tosto, miei spiriti, morrete.
Crudei, se me veggendo non piagete;
Che stando nel pensier gli occhi fan via
A lagrime del cor, che non la oblia.

BALLATA II

Fair women I saw passing where she passed;
And none among them women, to my vision;
But were like nothing save her shadow cast.

I praise her in no cause save verity's
None other dispraise, if ye comprehend me.
A spirit moveth speaking prophecies
Foretelling: Spirits mine, swift death shall end ye,
Cruel! if seeing me no tears forelend ye,
Sith but the being in thought sets wide mine eyes
For sobbing out my heart's full memories.

BALLATA III

Se m' hai del tutto obliato mercede,
Già peró fede
   Il cor non abbandona;
Anzi ragiona
   Di servire a grato
Al dispietato
   Core.
E qual ciò sente, simil me non crede,
Ma chi tal vede?
   Certo non persona;
Ch' Amor mi dona
   Un spirito in suo stato,
Che figurato
   More:
Che quando quel piacer mi stringe tanto,
Che lo sospir si mova,
Par che nel cor mi piova
Un dolce amor sì buono,
Ch' io dico: Donna, tutto vostro sono.

BALLATA III

Tho' all thy piteous mercy fall away
Not for thy failing shall my faith so fall,
That Faith speaks on of services unpaid
To the unpitied heart.

What that heart feeleth? Ye believe me not.
Who sees such things? Surely no one at all,
For Love me gives a spirit on his part
Who dieth if portrayed.

Thence when that pleasure so assaileth me,
And the sighing faileth me,
Within my heart a rain of love descendeth
With such benignity
That I am forced to cry: 'Thou hast me utterly.'

BALLATA IV

Vedette, ch'io son un, che vo piangendo,
E dimostrando
        il giudizio d'Amore;
E già non trovo si pietoso core,
Che me guardando
        una volta sospiri.

    Novella doglia m' è nel cor venuta,
La qual mi fa dolere e pianger forte;
E spesse volte avvien, che mi saluta
Tanto d' appresso l' angosciosa morte,
Che fa in quel punto le persone accorte,
Che dicono in fra lor: Questi ha dolore;
E già secondo che ne par di fore,
Dovrebbe dentro aver nuovi martiri.

    Questa pesanza ch' è nel cor discesa,
Ha certi spiritei già consumati,
I quali eran venuti per difesa
Del cor dolente, che gli avea chiamati;
Questi lasciaro gli occhi abbandonati;
Quando passo nella mente un rumore,
Il qual dicea: Dentro biltà che more;
Ma guarda che biltà non vi si miri.

BALLATA IV

Weeping ye see me, in Grief's company,
One showing forth Love's jurisdiction.
Of pity-shrouded hearts I find not one
Who sigheth, seeing me disconsolate.

   New is the grief that's come upon my heart,
And mournful is the press of my deep sighs,
And oft Death greeteth me, by tricksome art
Drawn close upon me with his agonies,
Yea close, drawn close till every dullard sees;
I hear their murmuring, 'How grief hath bent
'This man! And we from the apparent testament,
         Deem stranger torments in him sublimate.'

Within my heart this grievous weight descended
Hath slain that band of spirits which was bent
Heartward, that th' heart might by them be defended.
When the sad heart had summoned them they 'd left
Mine eyes of every other guard bereft
Till Rumour, courier through the mind, ran crying,
'Beauty within, Oyez! Within, is dying.
         On guard lest Beauty see your present state!'

BALLATA V

Veggio ne gli occhi de la donna mia
Un lume pien di spiriti d'Amore,
Che portano un piacer novo nel core,
Sì che vi desta d' allegrezza vita.

     Cosa m'avvien, quand' io le son presente,
Ch' i' i' non la posso a lo 'ntelletto dire:
Veder mi par de le sue labbia uscire
Una sì bella donna, che la mente
Comprender non la può che 'nmantenente
Ne nasce un' altra di bellezza nova.
Da la qual par, ch' una stella si mova,
E dica: Tua salute è dipartita.

     Là dove questa bella donna appare
S'ode una voce, che la vien davanti,
E par, che d'umiltà 'l suo nome canti
Sì dolcemente, che s'io 'l vo' contare,
Sento che 'l suo valor mi fa tremare;
E movonsi ne l'anima sospiri,
Che dicon: Guarda, se tu costei miri,
Vedrai la sua virtù nel ciel salita.

BALLATA V

Light do I see within my Lady's eyes
And loving spirits in its plenisphere
Which bear in strange delight on my heart's care
Till Joy's awakened from that sepulchre.

   That which befalls me in my Lady's presence
Bars explanations intellectual,
I seem to see a lady wonderful
Spring forth between her lips, one whom no sense
Can fully tell the mind of, and one whence
Another, in beauty, springeth marvellous,
From whom a star goes forth and speaketh thus:
'Now thy salvation is gone forth from thee.'

   There where this Lady's loveliness appeareth,
Is heard a voice which goes before her ways
And seems to sing her name with such sweet praise
That my mouth fears to speak what name she beareth,
And my heart trembles for the grace she weareth,
While far in my soul's deep the sighs astir
Speak thus: 'Look well! For if thou look on her,
Then shalt thou see her virtue risen in heaven.'

Vid. Introduction

BALLATA VI

La forte, e nova mia disaventura
M'ha disfatto nel core
Ogni dolce pensier, ch' i' avea d'Amore.

    Disfatta m' ha già tanto de la vita,
Che la gentil piacevol donna mia
Da l' anima distrutta s' è partita;
Sì ch'io non veggio là, dov' ella sia;
Non è rimasa in me tanta balia,
Ch'io de lo suo valore
Possa comprender ne la mente fiore.

    Vien, che m'uccide un sì gentil pensiero,
Che par, che dica, ch'io mai non la veggia,
Questo tormento dispietato e fiero,
Che struggendo m'incende ed amareggia;
Trovar non posso, a cui pietate chieggia,
Mercè di quel signore,
Che gira la fortuna del dolore.

    Pien d' ogni angoscia in loco di paura
Lo spirito de' l cor dolente giace,
Per la fortuna, che di me non cura,
Ch'ha volta morte dove assai mi spiace,
E dà speranza ch' è stata fallace,
Nel tempo, che si more,
M'ha fatto perder dilettevoli ore.

    Parole mie disfatte e paurose,
Dove di gir vi piace ve n'andate,
Ma sempre sospirando, e vergognose
Lo nome della mia donna chiamate;
Io pur rimango in tanta avversitate,
Che qual mira di fore
Vede la morte sotto 'l mio colore.

BALLATA VI

The harshness of my strange and new misventure
Hath in my mind distraught
The wonted fragrance of love's every thought.

Already is my life in such part shaken
That she, my gracious lady of delight,
Hath left my soul most desolate forsaken
And e'en the place she was, is gone from sight;
Till there rests not within me so much might
That my mind can reach forth
To comprehend the flower of her worth.

A noble thought is come well winged with death,
Saying that I shall ne'er see her again,
And this harsh torment, with no pity fraught,
Increaseth bitterness and in its strain
I cry, and find none to attend my pain,
While for the flame I feel,
I thank that lord who turns grief's fortune wheel.

Full of all anguish and within Fear's gates
The spirit of my heart lies sorrowfully,
Thanks to that Fortune who my fortune hates,
Who 'th spun death's lot where it most irketh me
And given hope that's ta'en in treachery,
Which ere it died aright
Had robbed me of mine hours of delight.

O words of mine foredone and full of terror,
Whither it please ye, go forth and proclaim
Grief. Throughout all your wayfare, in your error
Make ye soft clamour of my Lady's name,
While I downcast and fallen upon shame
Keep scant shields over me,
To whomso runs, death's colours cover me.

BALLATA VII

Era in pensier d'Amor, quand'io trovai
Due forosette nove;
L'una cantava: E' piove
Gioco d'Amore in nui.

Era la vista lor tanto soave,
Tanto quieta, cortese ed umile,
Ch'io dissi lor: Voi portate la chiave
Di ciascuna virtute alta, e gentile:
Deh forosette, non mi aggiate a vile:
Per lo colpo, ch'io porto,
Questo cor mi fu morto,
Poichè 'n Tolosa fui.

Elle con gli occhi lor si volser tanto,
Che vider come 'l core era ferito,
E come un spiritel nato di pianto
Era per mezzo de lo colpo uscito.
Poichè mi vider così sbigottito,
Disse l' una, che rise:
Guarda, come conquise
Gioia d'Amor costui.

Molto cortesemente mi rispose
Quella, che di me prima aveva riso,
Disse: La donna che nel cor ti pose
Con la forza d'Amor tutto 'l suo viso,
Dentro per gli occhi ti mirò sì fiso,
Ch'Amor fece apparire;
Se t' è grave il soffrire,
Raccomandati a lui.

Being in thought of love I came upon
Two damsels strange
Who sang 'The rains
Of love are falling, falling within us.'

So quiet in their modest courtesies
Their aspect coming softly on my vision
Made me reply, 'Surely ye hold the keys
O' the virtues noble, high, without omission.
Ah, little maids, hold me not in derision,
For the wound I bear within me
And this heart o' mine ha' slain me.
I was in Toulouse lately.'

And then toward me they so turned their eyes
That they could see my wounded heart's ill ease.
And how a little spirit born of sighs
Had issued forth from out the cicatrice.
Perceiving so the depth of my distress,
She who was smiling, said,
'Love's joy hath vanquished
This man. Behold how greatly!'

Then she who had first mocked me, in better part
Gave me all courtesy in her replies.
    She said, 'That Lady, who upon thine heart
Cut her full image, clear, by Love's device,
Hath looked so fixedly in through thine eyes
That she's made Love appear there;
If thou great pain or fear bear
Recommend thee unto him!'

L'altra pietosa piena di mercede,
Fatta di gioco in figura d'Amore
Disse: Il suo colpo, che nel cor si vede,
Fu tratto d' occhi di troppo valore;
Che dentro vi lassaro uno splendore,
Ch' i' nol posso mirare:
Dimmi, se ricordare
Di quegli occhi ti puoi?

A la dura quistione, e paurosa,
La qual mi fece questa forosetta,
Io dissi: E' mi ricorda ch' en Tolosa
Donna m'apparve accordellata e stretta,
La quale Amor chiamava La Mandetta:
Giunse sì presta e forte
Che 'nfin dentro alla morte
Mi colpir gli occhi sui.

Vanne a Tolosa, Ballatetta mia,
Ed entra quetamente a la Dorata,
Ed ivi chiama, che per cortesia
D'alcuna bella donna sia menata
Dinanzi a quella, di cui t' ho pregata;
E s' ella ti riceve,
Dille con voce leve:
Per mercè vegno a vui.

Then the other piteous, full of misericorde,
Fashioned for pleasure in love's fashioning:
'His heart's apparent wound, I give my word,
Was got from eyes whose power's an o'er great thing,
Which eyes have left in his a glittering
That mine can not endure.
Tell me, hast thou a sure
Memory of those eyes?'

To her dread question with such fears attended,
'Maid o' the wood,' I said, 'my memories render
Tolosa and the dusk and these things blended:
A lady in a corded bodice, slender
—Mandetta is the name Love's spirits lend her—
A lightening swift to fall,
And naught within recall
Save, Death! My wounds! Her eyes!'

(Envoi)
Speed Ballatet' unto Tolosa city
And go in softly 'neath the golden roof
And there cry out, 'Will courtesy or pity
Of any most fair lady, put to proof,
Lead me to her with whom is my behoof?'
Then if thou get *her* choice
Say, with a lowered voice,
'It is *thy* grace I seek here.'

BALLATA VIII

Gli occhi di quella gentil forosetta
Hanno distretta
        sì la mente mia
Ch'altro non chiama, che lei, nè disia.

    Ella mi fiere sì, quando la sguardo,
Ch' i' sento lo sospir tremar nel core.
Esce da gli occhi suoi, là ond' io ardo,
Un gentiletto spirito d'Amore,
Lo quale è pieno di tanto valore,
Che, quando giugne, l'anima va via,
Come colei che soffrir nol porria.

    Io sento poi gir fuor gli miei sospiri,
Quando la mente di lei mi ragiona:
E veggio piover per l'aer martiri,
Che traggon di dolor la mia persona,
Sì che ciascuna virtù m'abbandona
In guisa ch' i' non so là ov' i' mi sia:
Sol par che morte m'aggia in sua balìa.

    Sì mi sento disfatto, che mercede
Già non ardisco nel pensier chiamare;
Ch' i' truovo Amor, che dice: Ella si vede
Tanto gentil che non può 'mmaginare,
Ch' uom d' esto mondo l'ardisca mirare,
Che non convenga lui tremare in pria:
Ed io, s' i' la guardassi, ne morria.

    Ballata, quando tu sarai presente
A gentil donna, so che tu dirai
De la mia angoscia dolorosamente:
Dì: Quegli, che mi manda a voi, trae guai;
Però che dice che non spera mai
Trovar pietà di tanta cortesia,
Ch' a la sua donna faccia compagnia.

BALLATA VIII

The eyes of this gentle maid of the forest
Have set my mind in such bewilderment
That all my wistful thoughts on her are bent.

So doth she pierce me when mine eyes regard her
That I hear sighs a-trembling in my heart
As from her eyes aye sources of my ardour
The quaint small spirits of Amor forth-dart
From which small sprites such greater powers start
That when they reach me my faint soul is sent
Exhausted forth to swoon in banishment.

I feel how from my eyes the sighs forth-fare
When my mind reasoneth with me of her,
Till I see torments raining through the air.
Draggled by griefs, which I by these incur,
My every strength turns my abandoner,
And I know not what place I am toward,
Save that Death hath me in his castle-yard.

And I am so outworn that now for mercy
I am not bold to cry out even in thought,
And I find Love, who speaking saith of her, 'See,
She is not one whose image could be wrought.
Unto her presence no man could be brought
Who did not well to tremble for the daring.'
And I? Would swoon if I should meet her faring.

(Envoi)
Go! Ballad mine, and when thy journey has won
Unto my Lady's presence wonderful,
Speak of my anguish in some fitting fashion,
Sorrowfully thus, 'My sender is sorrowful,
Lo, how he saith, he hath no hope at all
Of drawing pity from such Courtesy
As keeps his Lady's gracious company.'

BALLATA IX

In un boschetto trovai pastorella
Più che la stella
        bella
          al mio parere.

    Capegli avea biondetti e ricciutelli,
E gli occhi pien d'amor, cera rosata;
Con sua verghetta pasturava agnelli;
E scalza, e di rugiada era bagnata;
Cantava come fosse innamorata,
Era adornata
        di tutto piacere.

    D' Amor la salutai immantenente,
E domandai, s'avesse compagnia;
Ed ella mi rispose dolcemente,
Che sola sola per lo bosco gia;
E disse: Sappi, quando l'augel pia,
Allor disia
        lo mio cor drudo avere.

Poichè mi disse di sua condizione,
E per lo bosco augelli udio cantare,
Fra me stesso dicea: Or è stagione
Di questa pastorella gioi' pigliare;
Mercè le chiesi, sol che di baciare,
E d'abbracciare
        fosse 'l suo volere.

    Per man mi prese d'amorosa voglia,
E disse che donato m'avea 'l core:
Menommi sotto una freschetta foglia,
Là dov' io vidi fior d'ogni colore;
E tanto vi sentio gioi' e dolzore,
Che Dio d'Amore
        mi parve ivi vedere.

BALLATA IX

In wood-way found I once a shepherdess,
More fair than stars are was she to my seeming.

Her hair was wavy somewhat, like a dull gold.
Eyes? Love-worn, and her face like some pale rose.
With a small twig she kept her lambs in hold,
And bare her feet were bar the dew-drop's gloze;
She sang as one whom mad love holdeth close,
And joy was on her for an ornament.

I greeted her in love without delaying:
'Hast thou companion in thy solitude?'
And she replied to me most sweetly, saying,
'Nay, I am quite alone in all this wood,
But when the birds 'gin singing in their coverts
My heart is fain that time to find a lover.'

As she was speaking thus of her condition
I heard the bird-song 'neath the forest shade
And thought me how 't was but the time's provision
To gather joy of this small shepherd maid.
Favour I asked her, but for kisses only,
And then I felt her pleasant arms upon me.

She held to me with a dear willfulness
Saying her heart had gone into my bosom,
She drew me on to a cool leafy place
Where I gat sight of every coloured blossom,
And there I drank in so much summer sweetness
Meseemed Love's god connived at its completeness.

BALLATA X

Posso de gli occhi miei novella dire,
La quale è tal, che piace sì al core,
Che di dolcezza ne sospira Amore.

Questo novo piacer, che 'l mio cor sente,
Fu tratto sol d'una donna veduta,
La quale è sì gentile ed avvenente,
E tanto adorna, che 'l cor la saluta:
Non è la sua biltate conosciuta
Da gente vile, che lo suo colore
Chiama intelletto di troppo valore.

Io veggio, che ne gli occhi suoi risplende
Una virtù d'amor tanto gentile,
Ch'ogni dolce piacer vi si comprende:
E muove allora un'anima sottile.
Rispetto de la quale ogni altra è vile;
E non si può di lei giudicar fore
Altro che dir: quest'e nuovo splendore.

Va Ballatetta, e la mia donna trova;
E tanto le dimanda di mercede,
Che gli occhi di pietà verso te mova
Per quel, che 'n lei ha tutta la sua fede;
E s'ella questa grazia ti concede,
Manda una voce d'allegrezza fore
Che mostri quella che t' ha facto onore.

BALLATA X

Now can I tell you tidings of mine eyes,
News which such pleasure to my heart supplyeth
That Love himself for glory of it sigheth.

This new delight which my heart drinketh in
Was drawn from nothing save a woman seen
Who hath such charm and a so courtly mien
And such fair fashion that the heart is fain
To greet her beauty, which nor base nor mean
Can know, because its hue and qualities demand
Intelligence in him who would understand.

I see Love grow resplendent in her eyes
With such great power and such noble thought
As hold therein all gracious ecstacies,
From them there moves a soul so subtly wrought
That all compared thereto are set at naught
And judgment of her speaks no truth save this:
'A splendour strange and unforeseen she is.'

(Envoi)
Go, Ballatetta, forth and find my Lady,
Ask if she have it this much of mercy ready,
This namely, that she turn her eyes toward thee?
Ask in his name whose whole faith rests in her,
And if she gracious, this much grace accord thee,
Offer glad-voiced incense of sweet savour
Proclaiming of whom thou receiv'st such favour.

BALLATA XI

Perch'io non spero di tornar già mai,
Ballatetta, in Toscana,
Va tu leggiera e piana
Dritta a la donna mia,
Che per sua cortesia
Ti fara molto onore.

　　　Tu porterai novelle de' sospiri,
Piene di doglia, e di molta paura;
Ma guarda che persona non ti miri,
Che sia nimica di gentil natura;
Che certo per la mia disavventura
Tu saresti contesa,
Tanto da lei ripresa,
Che mi sarebbe angoscia;
Dopo la morte poscia
Pianto e novel dolore.

　　　Tu senti Ballatetta, che la morte
Mi stringe sì, che vita m'abbandona;
E senti come 'l cor si sbatte forte
Per quel, che ciascun spirito ragiona;
Tant' e distrutta gia la mia persona,
Ch' i' non posso soffrire;
Se tu mi vuoi servire
Mena l'anima teco,
Molto di ciò ti preco,
Quando uscirà del core.

　　　Deh Ballatetta, a la tua amistate
Quest'anima, che triema, raccomando;
Menala teco nella sua pietate
A quella bella donna, a cui ti mando:

BALLATA XI

Because no hope is left me, Ballatetta,
Of return to Tuscany,
Light-foot go thou some fleet way
Unto my Lady straightway,
And out of her courtesy
Great honour will she do thee.

Tidings thou bearest with thee sorrow-fain
Full of all grieving, overcast with fear.
On guard! Lest any one see thee or hear,
Any who holds high nature in disdain,
For sure if so, to my increase of pain,
Thou wert made prisoner
And held afar from her,
Hereby new harms were given
Me and, after death even,
Dolour and griefs renewed.

Thou knowest, Ballatetta, that Death layeth
His hand upon me whom hath Life forsaken;
Thou knowest well how great a tumult swayeth
My heart at sound of her whom each sense crieth
Till all my mournful body is so shaken
That I cannot endure here,
Would'st thou make service sure here?
Lead forth my soul with thee
(I pray thee earnestly)
When it parts from my heart here.

Ah, Ballatetta, to thy friendliness,
I do give o'er this trembling soul's poor case.
Bring thou it there where her dear pity is,
And when thou hast found that Lady of all grace

Deh Ballatetta, dille sospirando,
Quando le se' presente:
Questa vostra servente
Vien per istar con vui,
Partita da colui,
Che fu servo d'Amore.

　　Tu voce sbigottita, e deboletta,
Ch' esci piangendo de lo cor dolente,
Con l'anima, e con questa Ballatetta
Va ragionando de la strutta mente,
Voi troverete una donna piacente
Di sì dolce intelletto,
Che vi sarà diletto
Starle davanti ognora:
Anima, e tu l' adora
Sempre nel suo valore.

Speak through thy sighs, my Ballad, with thy face
Low bowed, thy words in sum:
'Behold, thy servant is come
—This soul who would dwell with thee—
Asundered suddenly
From Him, Love's servitor.'

O smothered voice and weak that tak'st the road
Out from the weeping heart and dolorous,
Go, crying out my shatter'd mind's alarm,
Forth with my soul and this song piteous
Until thou find a lady of such charm,
So sweetly intelligent
That e'en thy sorrow is spent.
Take thy fast place before her.
And thou, Soul mine, adore her
Alway, with all thy might.

BALLATA XII

Quando di morte mi convien trar vita,
E di gravezza gioia,
Come di tanta noia,
Lo spirito d'Amore d'amar m'invita?

     Come m'invita lo mio cor d'amare?
Lasso, ch'è pien di doglia,
E da' sospir sì d'ogni parte priso,
Che quasi sol mercé non può chiamare;
E di virtù la spoglia
L'affanno che m'ha già quasi conquiso.
Canto, piacer con beninanza e riso,
Mi son doglia e sospiri;
Guardi ciascuno e miri,
Che morte m'è nel viso già salita.

     Amor, che nasce di simil piacere,
Dentro da'l cor si posa,
Formando di desio nova persona,
Ma fa la sua virtù 'n vizio cadere;
Sì ch'amar già non osa
Qual sente come servir guiderdona:
Dunque d'amar perchè meco ragiona?
Credo sol perchè vede,
Ch'io dimando mercede
A morte, ch'a ciascun dolor m'addita.

     Io mi posso biasmar di gran pesanza,
Più che nessun giammai:
Che morte dentro al cor mi tragge un core,
Che va parlando di crudele amanza,
Che ne' miei forti guai

BALLATA XII

If all my life be but some deathly moving,
Joy dragged from heaviness;
Seeing my deep distress
How doth Love's spirit call me unto loving?

How summon up my heart for dalliance?
When it is so sorrowful
And manacled by sighs so mournfully
That e'en the will for grace dare not advance?
Weariness over all
Spoileth that heart of power, despoiling me.
And song, sweet laughter and benignity
Are grown three grievous sighs,
Till all men's careless eyes
May see Death risen to my countenance.

Love that is born of loving like delight,
Within my heart sojourneth
And fashions a new person from desire
Yet toppleth down to vileness all his might,
So all love's daring spurneth
That man who knoweth service and its hire.
For Love, then why doth he of me inquire?
Only because he sees
Me cry on Death for ease,
While Death doth point me on toward all mischance.

And I can cry for Grief so heavily,
As hath man never,
For Grief drags to my heart a heart so sore
With wandering speech of her, who cruelly
Outwearieth me ever . . .!

M'affanna, laond' io perdo ogni valore.
Quel punto maledetto sia, ch'Amore
Nacque di tal maniera,
Che la mia vita fiera
Gli fu di tal piacere a lui gradita.

O Mistress, spoiler of my valour's store!
Accursed by the hour when Amor
Was born in such a wise
That my life in his eyes
Grew matter of pleasure and acceptable!

BALLATA XIII

Sol per pietà ti prego, giovinezza,
Che la dischiesta
                    Di mercè ti caglia,
Poi che la morte ha mosso la battaglia.

Questa dischiesta anima mia si trova
Sì sbigottita per lo spirto torto,
Che tu non curi, anzi sei fatta pruova,
E mostri bene sconoscenza scorto.
Tu sei nemico, ond' or prego colui,
Ch' ogni durezza muove, vince e taglia,
Ch' anzi a la fine mia mostri che vaglia.

Tu vedi ben, che l' aspra condizione
Ne' colpi di colei, che ha in odio vita,
Mi stringe in parte, ove umiltà si pone;
Sì che veggendo l' anima, ch' è in vita
Di dolenti sospir dicendo volta,
Ch'io veggio ben com' il valor si scaglia,
Deh prendati mercè sì, che in te saglia.

BALLATA XIII

For naught save pity do I pray thy youth
That thou have care for Mercy's castaway!
Lo, Death's upon me in his battle array!

And my soul finds him in his decadence
So over-wearied by that spirit wried
(For whom thou car'st not till his ways be tried,
Showing thyself thus wise in ignorance
To hold him hostile) that I pray that mover
And victor and slayer of every hard-wrought thing
That ere mine end he show him conquering.

Sith at his blows, who holds life in despite,
Thou seest clear how, in my barbed distress
He wounds me there where dwells my humbleness,
Till my soul living turneth in my sight
To speech, in words that grievous sighs o'ercover.
Until my eyes see worth's self wavering
Grant me thy mercies for my covering!

BALLATA XIV

I' prego voi che di dolor parlate
Che per virtù di nova pietate
Non disdegnate
                la mia pena udire.

Davanti agli occhi mei veggio lo core
Et l' anima dolente che s' ancide
Et muor d' un colpo che li diede amore
Entro 'n quel punto che madonna vide
Il suo gentile spirito che ride.
Quest' è collui che mi feste sentire
Questi mi dice: 'E ti conven morire:'

Se voi saveste come il cor si dole
Dentro alli vostri cuor voi tremereste,
Ch' amor mi dice si dolci parole
Che sospirando pietà chiamereste
Et sol di lui che voi intendereste
Ma non si po per me contar ne dire
Tanto e' l dolor che mi conven soffrire.

Lagrime scendon de la mente mia
Si tosto como questa doglia sente
Et van facendo per gli occhi una via
Per la qual passa il spirito dolente
Intra per l' aria si debolmente
Ch' oltre nol porria color discovrire
Nè imaginar s' i' ne porria morire.

BALLATA XIV

I pray ye gentles, ye who speak of grief,
Out of new clemency, for my relief
That ye disdain not to attend my pain.

I see my heart stand up before my eyes
While my self-torturing soul receiveth
Love's mortal stroke and in that moment dies,
Yea, in the very instant he perceiveth
Milady, and yet that smiling sprite who cleaveth
To her in joy, this very one is he
Who sets the seal of my mortality.

But should ye hear my sad heart's lamentation
Then would a trembling reach your heart's midmost.
For Love holds with me such sweet conversation
That Pity, by your sighs, ye would accost.
To all less keen than ye the sense were lost,
Nor other hearts could think soft nor speak loudly
How dire the throng of sorrows that enshroud me.

Yea from my mind behold what tears arise
As soon as it hath news of Her, Milady,
Forth move they making passage through the eyes
Wherethrough there goes a spirit sorrowing,
Which entereth the air so weak a thing
That no man else its place discovereth
Or deems it such an almoner of Death.

THE CANZONE

Donna mi priegha
                                        perch'i volglio dire
    D'un accidente
                            che sovente
                                                é fero
    Ed é si altero
                    ch'é chiamato amore

    Sicche chi l negha
                                possa il ver sentire
    Ond a'l presente
                            chonoscente
                                            chero
    Perch' i no spero
                        ch om di basso chore

    Atal ragione portj chonoscenza
        Chè senza
                            natural dimonstramento
    Non o talento
                        di voler provare
    Laove nascie e chì lo fá criare

    E qual è sua virtu e sua potenza
        L'essenza
                            e poi ciaschun suo movimento
    E'l piacimento
                        che'l fá dire amare
    E se hom per veder lo puó mostrare:—

CANZONE

Because a lady asks me, I would tell
Of an affect that comes often and is fell
And is so overweening: Love by name.

E'en its deniers can now hear the truth,
I for the nonce to them that know it call,
Having no hope at all
                            that man who is base in heart
Can bear his part of wit
                                into the light of it,

And save they know't aright from nature's source
I have no will to prove Love's course
                                            or say
Where he takes rest; who maketh him to be;
Or what his active *virtu* is, or what his force;

Nay, nor his very essence or his mode;
What his placation; why he is in verb,
Or if a man have might
        To show him visible to men's sight.

In quella parte
          dove sta memoria
Prende suo stato
          si formato
              chome
Diafan dal lume
          d'una schuritade

La qual da Marte
          viene e fá dimora
Elgli é creato
          e a sensato
              nome
D'alma chostume
          di chor volontade

Vien da veduta forma ches s'intende
   Che 'l prende
          nel possibile intelletto
Chome in subgetto
          locho e dimoranza
E in quella parte mai non a possanza

Perchè da qualitatde non disciende
   Risplende
          in sé perpetuale effecto
Non a diletto
          mà consideranza
Perche non pote laire simiglglianza:—

In memory's locus taketh he his state
Formed there in manner as a mist of light
Upon a dusk that is come from Mars and stays.
Love is created, hath a sensate name,
His modus takes from soul, from heart his will;

From form seen doth he start, that, understood,
Taketh in latent intellect—
As in a subject ready—
                        place and abode,

Yet in that place it ever is unstill,

Spreading its rays, it tendeth never down
By quality, but is its own effect unendingly
Not to delight, but in an ardour of thought
That the base likeness of it kindleth not.

Non é virtute
                    ma da questa vene
   Perfezione
                 ches si pone
                                tale
Non razionale
                  mà che si sente dicho

Fuor di salute
                  giudichar mantene
E l antenzione
                   per ragione
                                 vale
Discerne male
                  in chui é vizio amicho

Di sua virtu seghue ispesso morte

   Se forte
              la virtú fosse impedita
La quale aita
                 la contrara via
Nonche opposito natural sia

Mà quanto che da ben perfett e torte
   Per sorte
                 non po dir om ch abbia vita
Che stabilita
                 non a singnioria
A simil puó valer quant uom l obblia:-

136

It is not *virtu,* but perfection's source
Lying within perfection postulate
Not by the reason, but 'tis felt, I say.
Beyond salvation, holdeth its judging force,
Maintains intention reason's peer and mate;
Poor in discernment, being thus weakness' friend,
Often his power meeteth with death in the end

Be he withstayed
                        or from true course
                                        bewrayed

E'en though he meet not with hate
                                        or villeiny

Save that perfection fails, be it but a little;
Nor can man say he hath his life by chance
Or that he hath not stablished seigniory
Or loseth power, e'en lost to memory.

Lesser é quando
            lo valere a tanto
    Ch oltre misura
                di natura
                            torna
Poi non si addorna
                di riposo maj
Move changiando
                cholr riso in pianto
E lla fighura
            con paura
                        storna
Pocho soggiorna
                anchor di lui vedraj

Che n gente di valore il piu si trova
    La nova
                qualità move a sospirj

E vol ch om mirj
                in un formato locho
Destandos'ira la qual manda focho

Inmaginar nol puo hom che nol prova
    E non si mova
                    perch' a llui si tirj
E non si aggirj
                per trovarvi giocho
E certamente gran saver nè pocho:

Da ssimil tragge
                complessione e sghuardj
    Che fà parere
                lo piacere
                            piu certo

He comes to be and is when will's so great
It twists itself from out all natural measure;
Leisure's adornment puts he then never on,
Never thereafter, but moves changing state,
Moves changing colour, or to laugh or weep
Or wries the face with fear and little stays,

Yea, resteth little
               yet is found the most
Where folk of worth be host.

And his strange property sets sighs to move
And wills man look into unformed space
Rousing there thirst
               that breaketh into flame.

None can imagine love
               that knows not love;
Love doth not move, but draweth all to him;
Nor doth he turn
          for a whim
               to find delight
Nor to seek out, surely,
             great knowledge or slight.

Look drawn from like,
     delight maketh certain in seeming

Non puó choverto
       star quand è si giunto

Non giá selvagge
       la biltá son dardj
Ch a tal volere
     per temere
         sperto
Hom seghue merto
      spirito che punto

E Non si puó chonosciere per lo viso
  Chompriso
        biancho in tale obbietto chade
E chi ben aude
     forma non si vede
Perchè lo mena chi dallui procede

Fuor di cholore essere diviso
  Asciso
      mezzo schuro luce rade

Fuor d'ongni fraude
          dice dengno in fede
Chè solo da chostui nasce merzede:—

Tu puoj sichuramente gir chanzone
  Dove ti piace ch i t o sí ornata
  Ch assa lodata
        sará tua ragione
Dalle persone
     ch anno intendimento
Di star con l' altre tu non aj talento:

As it appears in the manuscript 'Ld,' Laurenziana 46-40 folio 32 verso, with a few errors corrected. Accents added from the Giuntine edition.

Nor can in covert cower,
                              beauty so near,
Not yet wild-cruel as darts,
So hath man craft from fear
                              in such his desire
To follow a noble spirit,
        edge, that is, and point to the dart,

Though from her face indiscernible;
He, caught, falleth
                              plumb on to the spike of the targe.
Who well proceedeth, form not seeth,
        following his own emanation.

There, beyond colour, essence set apart,
In midst of darkness light light giveth forth
Beyond all falsity, worthy of faith, alone
That in him solely is compassion born.

Safe may'st thou go my canzon whither thee pleaseth
Thou art so fair attired that every man and each
Shall praise thy speech
So he have sense or glow with reason's fire,
To stand with other
                              hast thou no desire.

ARNAUT DANIEL POEMS

PUBLISHERS' NOTE

Ezra Pound selected for translation the poems that best illustrated Arnaut's technical distinction, and arranged them in accordance with that intention. They were originally embodied, in this order, in an essay. More poems of Arnaut Daniel, added to this edition in 1970, will be found on pages 416–425.

III

Can chai la fueilla
Dels ausors entresims,
El freitz s' ergueilla
Don sechal vais' el vims,
Dels dous refrims
Vei sordezir la brueilla;
Mas ieu soi prims
D' amor, qui que s' en tueilla.

Tot quant es gela,
Mas ieu non puesc frezir,
C' amors novela
Mi fal cor reverdir;
Non dei fremir
C' Amors mi cuebr' em cela
Em fai tenir
Ma valor em cabdela.

Bona es vida
Pos joia la mante,
Que tals n' escrida
Cui ges no vai tan be;
No sai de re
Coreillar m' escarida,
Que per ma fe
Del mieills ai ma partida.

De drudaria
Nom sai de re blasmar,
C' autrui paria
Torn ieu en reirazar;
Ges ab sa par
No sai doblar m' amia,

III

When sere leaf falleth
    from the high forkèd tips,
And cold appalleth
    dry osier, haws and hips,
Coppice he strips
    of bird, that now none calleth.
Fordel[1] my lips
    in love have, though he galleth.

Though all things freeze here,
    I can naught feel the cold,
For new love sees, here
    my heart's new leaf unfold;
So am I rolled
    and lapped against the breeze here:
Love, who doth mould
    my force, force guarantees here.

Aye, life's a high thing,
    where joy's his maintenance,
Who cries 'tis wry thing
    hath danced never my dance,
I can advance
    no blame against fate's tithing
For lot and chance
    have deemed the best thing my thing.

Of love's wayfaring
    I know no part to blame,
All other pairing,
    compared, is put to shame,
Man can acclaim
    no second for comparing

[1] Preeminence.

C' una non par
Que segonda noill sia.

No vueill s' asemble
Mos cors ab autr' amor
Si qu' eu jail m' emble
Ni volval cap aillor;
Non ai paor
Que ja cel de Pontremble
N' aia gensor
De lieis ni que la semble.

Ges non es eroia
Cella cui soi amis!
De sai Savoia
Plus bella nos noiris;
Tals m' abelis
Don ieu plus ai de joia
Non ac Paris
D' Elena, cel de Troia.

Tan pareis genta
Cella quem te joios
Las gensors trenta
Vens de belas faisos!
Ben es razos
Doncas que mos chans senta,
Quar es tan pros
E de ric pretz manenta.

Vai t' en, chansos,
Denan lieis ti prezenta!
Que s' ill no fos
Noi meir' Arnautz s' ententa.

With her, no dame
      but hath the meaner bearing.

I'ld ne'er entangle
      my heart with other fere,
Although I mangle
      my joy by staying here
I have no fear
      that ever at Pontrangle
You'll find her peer
      or one that's worth a wrangle.

She'd ne'er destroy
      her man with cruelty,
'Twixt here 'n' Savoy
      there feeds no fairer she,
Than pleaseth me
      till Paris had ne'er joy
In such degree
      from Helena in Troy.

She's so the rarest
      who holdeth me thus gay,
The thirty fairest
      can not contest her sway;
'Tis right, par fay,
      thou know, O song that wearest
Such bright array,
      whose quality thou sharest.

Chançon, nor stay
      till to her thou declarest:
'Arnaut would say
      me not, wert thou not fairest.'

XVI

Ans quel eim reston de branchas
Sec ni despoillat de fuiolla
Farai, c' Amors m' o comanda,
Breu chansson de razon loigna.
Que gen m' a duoich de las artz de s' escola;
Tant sai quel cors fatz restar de suberna
E mos bous es pro plus correns que lebres.

Ab razos coindas e franchas
M' a mandat qu' ieu no m' en tuoilla
Ni non serva autra ni' n blanda,
Puois tant fai c' ab si m' acoigna;
Em di que flors noil semble de viola
Quis camja leu sitot nonca s' iverna,

Ans per s' amor sia laurs o genebres
    Dis: tu, c' aillors non t' estanchas
Per autra quit deing nit vuoilla,
Totz plaitz esquiva e desmanda
Sai e lai qui quet somoigna;
Gran son dan fai qui se meteus afola,
E tu no far failla don hom t' esquerna,
Mas apres Dieu lieis honors e celebres.

E tu, coartz, non t' afranchas
Per respeich c' amar not vuoilla;
Sec, s' il te fuig nit fai ganda,
Que greu er c' om noi apoigna
Qui s' afortis de preiar e no cola.
Qu' ieu passera part la palutz de Lerna
Com peregrins o lai per on cor Ebres.

148

XVI

Ere the winter recommences
And the leaf from bough is wrested,
On Love's mandate will I render
A brief end to long prolusion:
So well have I been taught his steps and paces
That I can stop the tidal-sea's inflowing.
My stot outruns the hare; his speed amazes.

Me he bade without pretences
That I go not, though requested;
That I make no whit surrender
Nor abandon our seclusion:
'Differ from violets, whose fear effaces
Their hue ere winter; behold the glowing
Laurel stays, stay thou. Year long the genet blazes.'

'You who commit no offences
'Gainst constancy; have not quested;
Assent not! Though a maid sent her
Suit to thee. Think you confusion
Will come to her who shall track out your traces?
And give your enemies a chance for boasts and crowing?
No! After God, see that she have your praises.'

Coward, shall I trust not defences!
Faint ere the suit be tested?
Follow! till she extend her
Favour. Keep on, try conclusion
For if I get in this naught but disgraces,
Then must I pilgrimage past Ebro's flowing
And seek for luck amid the Lernian mazes.

Provençal texts edited by U. A. Canello, published by M. Niemeyer, Halle, 1883.

S' ieu n' ai passatz pons ni planchas
Per lieis, cuidatz qu' ieu m' en duoilla?
Non eu, c' ab joi ses vianda
M' en sap far meizina coigna
Baisan tenen; el cors, sitot si vola,
Nois part de lieis quel capdella el governa.
Cors, on qu' ieu an, de lieis not loinz nit sebres!

    De part Nil entro c' a Sanchas
Gensser nois viest nis despuoilla,
Car sa beutatz es tant granda
Que semblariaus messoigna.
Bem vai d' amor, qu' elam baisa e m' acola,
E nom frezis freitz ni gels ni buerna,
Nim fai dolor mals ni gota ni febres.

    Sieus es Arnautz del cim tro en la sola
E senes lieis no vol aver Lucerna
Nil senhoriu del reion que cor Ebres.

If I've passed bridge-rails and fences,
Think you then that I am bested?
No, for with no food or slender
Ration, I'd have joy's profusion
To hold her kissed, and there are never spaces
Wide to keep me from her, but she'd be showing
In my heart, and stand forth before his gazes.

Lovelier maid from Nile to Sences
Is not vested nor divested,
So great is her bodily splendor
That you would think it illusion.
Amor, if she but hold me in her embraces,
I shall not feel cold hail nor winter's blowing
Nor break for all the pain in fever's dazes.

Arnaut hers from foot to face is,
He would not have Lucerne, without her, owing
Him, nor lord the land whereon the Ebro grazes.

IV

Lancan son passat li giure
E noi reman puois ni comba,
Et el verdier la flors trembla
Sus el entrecim on poma,
La flors e li chan eil clar quil
Ab la sazon doussa e coigna
M' enseignon c' ab joi m' apoigna,
Sai al temps de l' intran d' april.

Ben greu trob' om joi desliure,
C' a tantas partz volv e tomba
Fals' Amors, que no s' asembla
Lai on leiautatz asoma;
Qu' ieu non trob jes doas en mil
Ses falsa paraulla loigna,
E puois c' a travers non poigna
E no torne sa cartat vil.

Tuich li plus savi en vant biure
Ses muiol e ses retomba,
Cui ill gignosetz esclembla
La crin queil pend a la coma;
E plus pres li brui de l' auzil
On plus gentet s' en desloigna;
El fols cre mieills d' una moigna
Car a simple cor e gentil.

Ses fals' Amor cuidiei viure,
Mas ben vei c' un dat mi plomba
Quand ieu mieills vei qu' il m' o embla;
Car tuich le legat de Roma
No son jes de sen tant sotil,
Que na devisa Messoigna,

IV

When the frosts are gone and over,
And are stripped from hill and hollow,
When in close the blossom blinketh
From the spray where the fruit cometh,
  The flower and song and the clarion
Of the gay season and merry
Bid me with high joy to bear me
  Through days while April's coming on.

Though joy's right hard to discover,
Such sly ways doth false Love follow,
Only sure he never drinketh
At the fount where true faith hometh;
  A thousand girls, but two or one
Of her falsehoods over chary,
Stabbing whom vows make unwary
  Their tenderness is vilely done.

The most wise runs drunkest lover,
Sans pint-pot or wine to swallow,
If a whim her locks unlinketh,
One stray hair his noose becometh.
  When evasion's fairest shown,
Then the sly puss purrs most near ye.
Innocents at heart beware ye,
  When she seems colder than a nun.

See I thought so highly of her!
Trusted, but the game is hollow,
Not one won piece soundly clinketh;
All the cardinals that Rome hath,
  Yea, they all were put upon.
Her device is 'Slyly Wary.'

Que tant soaument caloigna,
Mens poiria falsar un fil.

Qui Amor sec, per tals liure:
Cogul tenga per colomba,
S' il l' o ditz ni ver li sembla
Fassail plan del Puoi de Doma;
Quan d' el plus prop es tant s' apil
Si col proverbis s' acoigna;
Sil trai l' uoill, el puois loil oigna,
Sofra e sega ab cor humil.

Ben conosc ses art d' escriure
Que es plan o que es comba,
Qu' ieu sai drut que si assembla
Don blasm' a leis, el col groma;
Qu'ieu n' ai ja perdut ric cortil
Car non vuoill gabs ab vergoigna
Ni blasme ab honor loigna,
Per que ieu loing son seignoril.

Bertran, non cre de sai lo Nil
Mais tant de fin joi m' apoigna
Tro lai on lo soleills ploigna,
Tro lai on lo soleills plovil.

Cunning are the snares they carry,
        Yet while they watched they'd be undone.

Whom Love makes so mad a rover,
'Ll take a cuckoo for a swallow,
If she say so, sooth! he thinketh
There's a plain where Puy-de-Dome is.
        Till his eyes and nails are gone,
He'll throw dice and follow fairly
—Sure as old tales never vary—
        For his fond heart he is foredone.

Well I know, sans writing's cover,
    What a plain is, what's a hollow.
I know well whose honor sinketh,
And who 'tis that shame consumeth.
        They meet. I lose reception.
'Gainst this cheating I'd not parry
Nor mid such false speech tarry,
        But from her lordship will be gone.

Coda

Sir Bertran,[1] sure no pleasure's won
Like this freedom naught so merry
'Twixt Nile 'n' where the suns miscarry
        To where the rain falls from the sun.

[1] Presumably De Born.

VIII

Autet e bas entrels prims fuoills
Son nou de flors li ram eil renc
E noi ten mut bec ni gola
Nuills auzels, anz braia e chanta
Cadahus
En son us:
Per joi qu' ai d' els e del tems
Chant, mas amors mi asauta
Quels motz ab lo son acorda.

Dieu o grazisc e a mos huoills,
Que per lor conoissensam venc.
Jois, qu' adreich auci e fola
L' ira qu' ieu n' agui e l'anta,
Er va sus,
Qui qu' en mus,
D' Amor don sui fis e frems;
C' ab lieis c' al cor plus m' azauta
Sui liatz ab ferma corda.

Merces, Amors, c' aras m' acuoills!
Tart mi fo, mas en grat m' o prenc,
Car si m' art dinz la meola
Lo fuocs non vuoill que s' escanta;
Mas pels us
Estauc clus
Que d' autrui joi fant greus gems
E pustell' ai' en sa gauta
Cel c' ab lieis si desacorda.

De bon' amor falsa l' escuoills,
E drutz es tornatz en fadenc,

VIII

Now high and low, where leaves renew,
Come buds on bough and spalliard pleach
And no beak nor throat is muted;
Auzel each in tune contrasted
Letteth loose
Wriblis[1] spruce.
Joy for them and spring would set
Song on me, but Love assaileth
Me and sets my words t' his dancing.

I thank my God and mine eyes too,
Since through them the perceptions reach.
Porters of joys that have refuted
Every ache and shame I've tasted;
They reduce
Pains, and noose
Me in Amor's corded net.
Her beauty in me prevaileth
Till bonds seem but joy's advancing.

My thanks, Amor, that I win through;
Thy long delays I naught impeach;
Though flame's in my marrow rooted
I'd not quench it, well 't hath lasted,
Burns profuse,
Held recluse
Lest knaves know our hearts are met,
Murrain on the mouth that aileth,
So he finds her not entrancing.

He doth in Love's book misconstrue,
And from that book none can him teach,

[1] Warblings.

Oui di qu' el parlar noil cola
Nuilla res quel cor creanta
De pretz jus;
Car enfrus
Es d' aco qu' eu mout ai crems;
E qui de parlar trassauta
Dreitz es qu'en la lengais morda.

Vers es qu' ieu l'am et es orguoills,
Mas ab jauzir celar loi tenc;
Qu' anc pos Sainz Pauls fetz pistola
Ni nuills hom dejus caranta
Non poc plus
Neis Jhesus
Far de tals, car totz absems
Als bos aips don es plus auta
Cella c' om per pros recorda.

Pretz e Valors, vostre capduoills
Es la bella c' ab sim retenc,
Qui m' a sol et ieu liei sola,
C' autra el mon nom atalanta;
Anz sui brus
Et estrus
Als autras el cor teing prems,
Mas pel sieu joi trepa e sauta:
No vuoill c' autra m'o comorda.

Arnautz ama e no di nems,
C' Amors l' afrena la gauta,
Que fols gabs no laill comorda.

Who saith ne'er's in speech recruited
Aught, whereby the heart is dasted.
Words' abuse
Doth traduce
Worth, but I run no such debt.
Right 'tis if man over-raileth
He tear tongue on tooth mischancing.[1]

That I love her, is pride, is true,
But my fast secret knows no breach.
Since Paul's writ was executed
Or the forty days first fasted,
Not Christus
Could produce
Her similar, where one can get
Charm's total, for no charm faileth
Her who's memory's enhancing.

Grace and valor, the keep of you
She is, who holds me, each to each,
She sole, I sole, so fast suited,
Other women's lures are wasted,
And no truce
But misuse
Have I for them, they're not let
To my heart, where she regaleth
Me with delights I'm not chancing.

Arnaut loves, and ne'er will fret
Love with o'er-speech. His throat quaileth,
Braggart voust is naught t'his fancy.

[1] This is nearly as bad in the original.

IX

I

L' aura amara
Fals bruoills brancutz
Clarzir
Quel doutz espeissa ab fuoills,
Els letz
Becs
Dels auzels ramencs
Ten balps e mutz,
Pars
E non-pars;
Per qu' eu m' esfortz
De far e dir
Plazers
A mains per liei
Que m' a virat bas d' aut,
Don tem morir
Sils afans no m' asoma.

II

Tant fo clara
Ma prima lutz
D' eslir
Lieis don crel cors los huoills,
Non pretz
Necs
Mans dos aigonencs;
D' autra s' esdutz
Rars

IX

I

The bitter air
Strips panoply
From trees
Where softer winds set leaves,
And glad
Beaks
Now in brakes are coy,
Scarce peep the wee
Mates
And un-mates.
      What gaud's the work?
      What good the glees?
What curse
I strive to shake!
Me hath she cast from high,
In fell disease
I lie, and deathly fearing.

II

So clear the flare
That first lit me
To seize
Her whom my soul believes;
If cad
Sneaks,
Blabs, slanders, my joy
Counts little fee
Baits

In this poem 'we have the chatter of birds in autumn, the onomatopoeia obviously depends upon the '-utz, -etz, -ences and -ortz' of the rhyme scheme, 17 of the 68 syllables of each strophe therein included . . . I have not been able to make more than a map of the relative positions in this canzo.'

Mos preiars,
Pero deportz
M' es adauzir
Volers,
Bos motz ses grei
De liei don tant m' azaut
Qu' al sieu servir
Sui del pe tro c' al coma.

III

Amors, gara,
Sui ben vengutz
C' auzir
Tem far sim desacuoills
Tals detz
Pecs
Que t' es mieills quet trencs;
Qu' ieu soi fis drutz
Cars
E non vars,
Mal cors ferms fortz
Mi fai cobrir
Mains vers;
C' ab tot lo nei
M' agr' ops us bais al chaut
Cor refrezir,
Que noi val autra goma.

IV

Si m' ampara
Cill cuim trahutz
D' aizir,
Si qu' es de pretz capduoills,
Dels quetz
Precs
C' ai dedinz a rencs,
L' er fort rendutz
Clars

And their hates.
　　　　I scorn their perk
　　　　And preen, at ease.
Disburse
Can she, and wake
Such firm delights, that I
Am hers, froth, lees
Bigod! from toe to earring.

III

Amor, look yare!
Know certainly
The keys:
How she thy suit receives;
Nor add
Piques,
'Twere folly to annoy.
I'm true, so dree
Fates;
No debates
　　　　Shake me, nor jerk.
　　　　My verities
Turn terse,
And yet I ache;
Her lips, not snows that fly
Have potencies
To slake, to cool my searing.

IV

Behold my prayer,
(Or company
Of these)
Seeks whom such height achieves;
Well clad
Seeks
Her, and would not cloy.
Heart apertly
States

163

Mos pensars;
Qu' eu fora mortz,
Mas fam sofrir
L' espers
Queill prec quem brei,
C' aissom ten let e baut;
Que d' als jauzir
Nom val jois una poma.

V

Doussa car', a
Totz aips volgutz,
Sofrir
M' er per vos mainz orguoills,
Car etz
Decs
De totz mos fadencs,
Don ai mains brutz
Pars
E gabars;
De vos nom tortz
Nim fai partir
Avers,
C' anc non amei
Ren tan ab meins d' ufaut,
Anz vos desir
Plus que Dieus cill de Doma.

VI

Erat para,
Chans e condutz,
Formir
Al rei qui t' er escuoills;
Car pretz,
Secs
Sai, lai es doblencs,
E mantengutz

Thought. Hope waits
  'Gainst death to irk:
  False brevities
And worse!
To her I raik,[1]
Sole her; all others' dry
Felicities
I count not worth the leering.

V

Ah, fair face, where
Each quality
But frees
One pride-shaft more, that cleaves
Me; mad frieks
(O' thy beck) destroy,
And mockery
Baits
Me, and rates.
  Yet I not shirk
  Thy velleities,
Averse
Me not, nor slake
Desire. God draws not nigh
To Dome,[2] with pleas
Wherein's so little veering.

VI

Now chant prepare,
And melody
To please
The king, who'll judge thy sheaves.
Worth, sad,
Sneaks
Here; double employ
Hath there. Get thee

[1] raik—haste precipitate.
[2] Our Lady of Poi de Dome? No definite solution of this reference yet found
H. and B. say: 'town of Périgord'. The same?

Dars
E manjars:
De joi lat portz,
Son anel mir,
Sil ders,
C' anc non estei
Jorn d' Aragon quel saut
Noi volgues ir,
Mas sai m' a' n clamat Roma.

Coda

Faitz es l' acortz
Qu' el cor remir
Totz sers
Lieis cui domnei
Ses parsonier Arnaut;
Qu' en autr' albir
N' es fort m' ententa soma.

Plates
Full, and cates,
      Gifts, go! Nor lurk
      Here till decrees
Reverse,
And ring thou take.
Straight t' Arago I'd ply
Cross the wide seas
But 'Rome' disturbs my hearing.

Coda

At midnight mirk,
In secrecies
I nurse
My served make[1]
In heart; nor try
My melodies
At other's door nor mearing.[2]

---

[1] Mate, fere, companion.
[2] Dante cites this poem in the second book of De Vulgari Eloquio with poems of his own, De Born's, and Cino Pistoija's.

En breu brisaral temps braus,
Eill bisa busina els brancs
Qui s' entreseignon trastuich
De sobreclaus rams de fuoilla;
Car noi chanta anzels ni piula
M' enseign' Amors qu' ieu fassa adonc
Chan que non er segons ni tertz
Ans prims d' afrancar cor agre.

Amors es de pretz la claus
E de proesa us estancs
Don naisson tuich li bon fruich,
S' es qui leialmen los cuoilla;
Q' un non delis gels ni niula
Mentre ques noiris el bon tronc;
Mas sil romp trefans ni culvertz
Peris tro leials lo sagre.

Faillirs esmendatz es laus;
Et eu sentim n' ams los flancs
Que mais n' ai d' amor ses cuich
Que tals qu' en parla eis n' orguoilla;
Que pieitz mi fal cor de friula.
Mentr' ellam fetz semblan embronc,
Mais volgr' ieu trair pena els desertz
On anc non ac d' auzels agre.

Bona doctrina e soaus
E cors clars, sotils e francs
M' an d' Amor al ferm conduich
De lieis don plus vuoill quem cuoilla;
Car sim fo fera et escriula
Er jauzen breviam temps lonc,

XI

Briefly bursteth season brisk,
Blasty north breeze racketh branch,
Branches rasp each branch on each
Tearing twig and tearing leafage,
     Chirms now no bird nor cries querulous;
So Love demands I make outright
A song that no song shall surpass
     For freeing the heart of sorrow.

Love is glory's garden close,
And is a pool of prowess staunch
Whence get ye many a goodly fruit
If true man come but to gather.
     Dies none frost-bit nor yet snowily,
For true sap keepeth off the blight
Unless knave or dolt there pass. . . .

.   .   .   .   .

The gracious thinking and the frank
Clear and quick perceiving heart
Have led me to the fort of love.

Qu'il m'es plus fina et ieu lieis certz
Que Talant' e Meleagre.

Tant dopti que per non-aus
Devenc sovens niers e blancs;
Si m' al sen desirs fors duich
No sap lo cors trep ois duoilla;
Mas Jois que d' esper m' afiula
M' encolpa car no la somonc;
Per qu' ieu sui d' est prec tant espertz
Non ai d' als talen neis magre.

Pensar de lieis m' es repaus,
E tragam ams los huoills crancs
S' a lieis vezer nols estuich;
El cor non crezatz qu' en tuoilla,
Car orars ni jocs ni viula
Nom pot de leis un travers jonc
Partir . . . C' ai dig? Dieus, tum somertz
Om peris el peleagre!

Arnautz vol sos chans sia ofertz
Lai on doutz motz mou en agre.

Finer she is, and I more loyal
Than were Atlanta and Meleager.

. . . . .

To think of her is my rest
And both of my eyes are strained wry
When she stands not in their sight,
Believe not the heart turns from her,
    For nor prayers nor games nor violing
Can move me from her a reed's breadth.

Notable for the opening bass onomatopoeia of the wind rowting in the autumn
branches. Arnaut may have caught his alliteration from the joglar engles.

XII

Doutz brais e critz,
Lais e cantars e voutas
Aug dels auzels qu' en lur latins fant precs
Quecs ab sa par, atressi cum nos fam
A las amigas en cui entendem;
E doncas ieu qu' en la genssor entendi
Dei far chansson sobre totz de bell' obra
Que noi aia mot fals mi rima estrampa.

Non fui marritz
Ni non presi destoutas
Al prim qu' intriei el chastel dinz los decs,
Lai on estai midonz, don ai gran fam
C' anc non l' ac tal lo nebotz Sain Guillem;
Mil vetz lo jorn en badaill em n' estendi
Per la bella que totas austras sobra
Tant cant val mais fis gaugz qu' ira ni rampa.

Ben fui grazitz
E mas paraulas coutas,
Per so que jes al chausir no fui pecs,
Anz volgui mais prendre fin aur que ram,
Lo jorn quez ieu e midonz nos baizem
Em fetz escut de son bel mantel endi
Que lausengier fals, lenga de colobra,
Non o visson, don tan mals motz escampa.

Dieus lo chauzitz,
Per cui foron assoutas
Las faillidas que fetz Longis lo cecs,
Voilla, sil platz, qu' ieu e midonz jassam

XII

Sweet cries and cracks
        and lays and chants inflected
By auzels who, in their Latin belikes,
Chirm each to each, even as you and I
Pipe toward those girls on whom our thoughts attract;
Are but more cause that I, whose overweening
Search is toward the noblest, set in cluster
Lines where no word pulls wry, no rhyme breaks gauges.

No culs de sacs
        nor false ways me deflected
When first I pierced her fort within its dykes,
Hers for whom my hungry insistency
Passes the gnaw whereby was Vivien wracked;[1]
Day-long I stretch, all times, like a bird preening,
And yawn for her, who hath o'er others thrust her
As high as true joy is o'er ire and rages.

Welcome not lax,
        and my words were protected
Not blabbed to other, when I set my likes
On her. Not brass but gold was 'neath the die.
That day we kissed, and after it she flacked
O'er me her cloak of indigo, for screening
Me from all culvertz' eyes, whose blathered bluster
Can set such spites abroad; win jibes for wages.

God who did tax
        not Longus' sin,[2] respected
That blind centurion beneath the spikes
And him forgave, grant that we two shall lie

[1] Vivien, strophe 2, nebotz Sain Guillem, an allusion to the romance, 'Enfances Vivien'.

[2] Longus, centurion in the crucifixion legend.

En lu chambra on amdui nos mandem
Uns rics convens don tan gran joi atendi,
Quel seu bel cors baisan rizen descobra
E quel remir contral lum de la lampa.

Ges rams floritz
De floretas envoutas
Cui fan tremblar auzelhon ab lurs becs
Non es plus frescs, per qu' ieu no volh Roam
Aver ses lieis ni tot Jherusalem;
Pero totz fis mas juntas a lim rendi,
Qu' en liei amar agr' ondral reis de Dobra
O celh cui es l' Estel' e Luna-pampa.

Bocca, que ditz?
Qu' eu crei quem auras toutas
Tals promessas don l' emperaire grecs
En for' onratz ol senher de Roam
Ol reis que ten Sur e Jerusalem;
Doncs ben sui fols que quier tan quem repend,
Ni eu d' Amor non ai poder quem cobra,
Ni savis es es nuls om qui joi acampa.

Los deschausitz
Ab las lengas esmoutas
Non dupt' ieu jes, sil seignor dels Galecs
An fag faillir, perqu' es dreitz s' o blasmam,
Que son paren pres romieu, so sabem,
Raimon lo filh al comte, et aprendi
Que greu faral reis Ferrans de pretz cobra
Si mantenen nol solv e nol escampa.

Eu l' agra vist, mas estiei per tal obra,
C' al coronar fui del bon rei d' Estampa.

Mos sobrecors, si tot grans sens lo sobra,
Tenga que ten, si non gaire nois ampa.

Within one room, and seal therein our pact,
Yes, that she kiss me in the half-light, leaning
To me, and laugh and strip and stand forth in the lustre
Where lamp-light with light limb but half engages.

The flowers wax
　　　　with buds but half perfected;
Tremble on twig that shakes when the bird strikes—
But not more fresh than she! No empery,
Though Rome and Palestine were one compact,
Would lure me from her; and with hands convening
I give me to her. But if kings could muster
In homage similar, you'd count them sages.

Mouth, now what knacks!
　　　　What folly hath infected
Thee? Gifts, that th' Emperor of the Salonikes
Or Lord of Rome were greatly honored by,
Or Syria's lord, thou dost from me distract;
O fool I am! to hope for intervening
From Love that shields not love! Yea, it were juster
To call him mad, who 'gainst his joy engages.

(*Political Postscript*)

The slimy jacks
　　　　with adders' tongues bisected,
I fear no whit, nor have; and if these tykes
Have led Galicia's king to villeiny—[1]
His cousin in pilgrimage hath he attacked—
We know—Raimon the Count's son—my meaning
Stands without screen.　The royal filibuster
Redeems not honor till he unbar the cages.

Coda

I should have seen it, but I was on such affair,
Seeing the true king crown'd here in Estampa.[2]

---

[1] King of the Galicians, Ferdinand II, King of Galicia, 1157-88, son of Berangere, sister of Raimon Berenger IV ('*quattro figlie ebbe*,' etc.) of Aragon, Count of Barcelona. His second son, Lieutenant of Provence, 1168.

[2] King crowned at Etampe, Phillipe August, crowned May 29, 1180, at age of 16. This poem might date Arnaut's birth as early as 1150.

V

Lanquan vei fueill' e flor e frug
Parer dels albres eill ramel,
Et aug lo chan que faun el brug
La ran' el riu, el bosc l' auzel,
Doncs mi fueilla em floris em fruch' Amors
El cor tan gen que la nueit me retsida
Quant autra gens dorm e pauz' e sojorna.

V

When I see leaf, and flower and fruit
    Come forth upon light lynd and bough,
And hear the frogs in rillet bruit,
    And birds quhitter in forest now,
Love inkirlie doth leaf and flower and bear,
And trick my night from me, and stealing waste it,
Whilst other wight in rest and sleep sojourneth.

XV

Sols sui qui sai lo sobrafan quem sortz
Al cor d' amor sofren per sobramar,
Car mos volers es tant ferms et entiers
C' anc no s' esduis de celliei ni s' estors
Cui encubic al prim vezer e puois:
Qu' ades ses lieis dic a lieis cochos motz,
Pois quan la vei non sai ,tant l' ai, que dire.

D' autras vezer sui secs e d' auzir sortz,
Qu' en sola lieis vei et aug et esgar;
E jes d' aisso noill sui fals plazentiers
Que mais la vol non ditz la bocal cors;
Qu' eu no vau tant chams, vauz ni plans ni puois
Qu' en un sol cors trob aissi bos aips totz:
Qu' en lieis los volc Dieus triar et assire.

Ben ai estat a maintas bonas cortz,
Mas sai ab lieis trob pro mais que lauzar
Mesura e sen et autres bos mestiers,
Beutat, joven, bos faitz e bels demors.
Gen l' enseignet Cortesia e la duois,
Tant a de si totz faitz desplazens rotz
De lieis no cre rens de ben si adire.

Nuills jauzimens nom fora breus ni cortz
De lieis cui prec qu'o vuoilla devinar,
Que ja per mi non o sabra estiers
Sil cors ses dirs nos presenta de fors;
Que jes Rozers per aiga que l' engrois
Non a tal briu c' al cor plus larga dotz
Nom fassa estanc d' amor, quand la remire.

Jois e solatz d' autram par fals e bortz,
C' una de pretz ab lieis nois pot egar,

XV

I only, and who elrische pain support
Know out love's heart o'er borne by overlove,
For my desire that is so firm and straight
And unchanged since I found her in my sight
And unturned since she came within my glance,
That far from her my speech springs up aflame;
Near her comes not. So press the words to arrest it.

I am blind to others, and their retort
I hear not. In her alone, I see, move,
Wonder . . . And jest not. And the words dilate
Not truth; but mouth speaks not the heart outright:
I could not walk roads, flats, dales, hills, by chance,
To find charm's sum within one single frame
As God hath set in her t' assay and test it.

And I have passed in many a goodly court
To find in hers more charm than rumor thereof . . .
In solely hers. Measure and sense to mate,
Youth and beauty learnèd in all delight,
Gentrice did nurse her up, and so advance
Her fair beyond all reach of evil name,
To clear her worth, no shadow hath oppresst it.

Her contact flats not out, falls not off short . . .
Let her, I pray, guess out the sense hereof
For never will it stand in open prate
Until my inner heart stand in daylight,
So that heart pools him when her eyes entrance,
As never doth the Rhone, fulled and untame,
Pool, where the freshets tumult hurl to crest it.

Flimsy another's joy, false and distort,
No paregale that she springs not above . . .

Quel sieus solatz es dels autres sobriers.
Ai si no l' ai! Las! Tant mal m' a comors!
Pero l' afans m' es deportz, ris e jois
Car en pensan sui de lieis lecs e glotz:
Ai Dieus, si ja' n serai estiers jauzire!

Anc mais, sous pliu, nom plac tant treps ni bortz
Ni res al cor tant de joi nom poc dar
Cum fetz aquel don anc feinz lausengiers
No s' esbrugic qu' a mi solses tresors . . .
Dic trop? Eu non, sol lieis non sia enois.
Bella, per dieu, lo parlar e la votz
Vuoill perdre enans que diga ren queus tire.

Ma chansos prec que nous sia enois,
Car si voletz grazir lo son els motz
Pauc preza Arnautz cui que plassa o que tire.

Her love-touch by none other mensurate.
To have it not? Alas! Though the pains bite
Deep, torture is but galzeardy and dance,
For in my thought my lust hath touched his aim.
God! Shall I get no more! No fact to best it!

No delight I, from now, in dance or sport,
Nor will these toys a tinkle of pleasure prove,
Compared to her, whom no loud profligate
Shall leak abroad how much she makes my right.
Is this too much? If she count not mischance
What I have said, then no. But if she blame,
Then tear ye out the tongue that hath expresst it.

The song begs you: Count not this speech ill chance,
But if you count the song worth your acclaim,
Arnaut cares lyt who praise or who contest it.

XVII

Sim fos Amors de joi donar tant larga
Cum ieu vas lieis d' aver fin cor e franc,
Ja per gran ben nom calgra far embarc,
Qu' er am tant aut quel pes mi poia em tomba;
Mas quand m' albir cum es de pretz al som
Mout m' en am mais car anc l' ausiei voler,
C' aras sai ieu que mos cors e mos sens
Mi farant far lor grat rica conquesta.

Pero s' ieu fatz lonc esper no m' embarga,
Qu' en tant ric luoc me sui mes e m' estanc
C' ab sos bels digz mi tengra de joi larc,
E segrai tant qu' om mi port a la tomba,
Qu' ieu non sui ges cel que lais aur per plom;
E pois en lieis nos taing c' om ren esmer
Tant li serai fis et obediens
Tro de s' amor, sil platz, baisan m' envesta.

Us bons respieitz mi reven em descarga
D' un doutz desir don mi dolon li flanc,
Car en patz prenc l' afan el sofr' el parc
Pois de beutat 'son las autras en comba,
Que la gensser par c' aia pres un tom
Plus bas de liei, qui la ve, et es ver;
Que tuig bon aip, pretz e sabers e sens
Reingnon ab liei, c' us non es meins ni' n resta.

E pois tant val, nous cujetz que s' esparga
Mos ferms volers ni qu' eisforc ni qu' eisbranc,
Car eu no sui sieus ni mieus si m' en parc,
Per cel Seignor queis mostret en colomba:
Qu' el mon non ha home de negun nom
Tant desires gran benanansa aver

XVII

Had Love as little need to be exhorted
To give me joy, as I to keep a frank
And ready heart toward her, never he'd blast
My hope, whose very height hath high exalted,
And cast me down . . . to think on my default,
And her great worth; yet thinking what I dare,
More love myself, and know my heart and sense
Shall lead me to high conquest, unmolested.

I am, spite long delay, pooled and contorted
And whirled with all my streams 'neath such a bank
Of promise, that her fair words hold me fast
In joy, and will, until in tomb I am halted.
As I'm not one to change hard gold for spalt,
And no alloy's in her, that debonaire
Shall hold my faith and mine obedience
Till, by her accolade, I am invested.

Long waiting hath brought in and hath extorted
The fragrance of desire; throat and flank
The longing takes me . . . and with pain surpassed
By her great beauty. Seemeth it hath vaulted
O'er all the rest . . . them doth it set in fault
So that whoever sees her anywhere
Must see how charm and every excellence
Hold sway in her, untaint, and uncontested.

Since she is such; longing no wise detorted
Is in me . . . and plays not the mountebank,
For all my sense is her, and is compassed
Solely in her; and no man is assaulted
(By God his dove!) by such desires as vault
In me, to have great excellence. My care

Cum ieu fatz lieis, e tenc a noncalens
Los enoios cui dans d' Amor es festa.

Na Mieills-de-ben, ja nom siatz avarga,
Qu' en vostr' amor me trobaretz tot blanc,
Qu' ieu non ai cor ni poder quem descarc
Del ferm voler que non hieis de retomba;
Que quand m' esveill ni clau los huoills de som
A vos m' autrei, quan leu ni vau jazer;
E nous cujetz queis merme mos talens,
Non fara jes, qu' aral sent en la testa.

Fals lausengier, fuocs las lengas vos arga
E que perdatz ams los huoills de mal cranc,
Que per vos son estraich cavail e marc,
Amor toletz c' ab pauc del tot non tomba;
Confondaus Dieus que ja non sapchatz com,
Queus fatz als drutz maldire e vil tener;
Malastres es queus ten, desconoissens,
Que peior etz qui plus vos amonesta.

Arnautz a faitz e fara loncs atens,
Qu' atenden fai pros hom rica conquesta.

On her so stark, I can show tolerance
To jacks whose joy 's to see fine loves uncrested.

Miels-de-Ben, have not your heart distorted
Against me now; your love has left me blank,
Void, empty of power or will to turn or cast
Desire from me . . . not brittle,[1] nor defaulted.
Asleep, awake, to thee do I exalt
And offer me. No less, when I lie bare
Or wake, my will to thee, think not turns thence,
For breast and throat and head hath it attested.

Pouch-mouthed blubberers, culrouns and aborted,
May flame bite in your gullets, sore eyes and rank
T' the lot of you, you've got my horse, my last
Shilling, too; and you'd see love dried and salted.
God blast you all that you can't call a halt!
God's itch to you, chit-cracks that overbear
And spoil good men, ill luck your impotence!!
More told, the more you've wits smeared and congested.

Coda
Arnaut has borne delay and long defence
And will wait long to see his hopes well nested.

[1] 'Brighter than glass, and yet as glass is, brittle.' The comparisons to glass went out of poetry when glass ceased to be a rare, precious substance. *Cf.* Passionate Pilgrim, III.

CATHAY

FOR THE MOST PART FROM THE CHINESE OF
RIHAKU, FROM THE NOTES OF THE LATE
ERNEST FENOLLOSA, AND THE
DECIPHERINGS OF THE
PROFESSORS MORI
AND ARIGA
(1915)

SONG OF THE BOWMEN OF SHU

Here we are, picking the first fern-shoots
And saying: When shall we get back to our country?
Here we are because we have the Ken-nin for our foemen,
We have no comfort because of these Mongols.
We grub the soft fern-shoots,
When anyone says 'Return', the others are full of sorrow.
Sorrowful minds, sorrow is strong, we are hungry and thirsty.
Our defence is not yet made sure, no one can let his friend return.
We grub the old fern-stalks.
We say: Will we be let to go back in October?
There is no ease in royal affairs, we have no comfort.
Our sorrow is bitter, but we would not return to our country.
What flower has come into blossom?
Whose chariot? The General's.
Horses, his horses even, are tired. They were strong.
We have no rest, three battles a month.
By heaven, his horses are tired.
The generals are on them, the soldiers are by them.
The horses are well trained, the generals have ivory arrows and
    quivers ornamented with fish-skin.
The enemy is swift, we must be careful.
When we set out, the willows were drooping with spring,
We come back in the snow,
We go slowly, we are hungry and thirsty,
Our mind is full of sorrow, who will know of our grief?

By Bunno
Reputedly 1100 B.C.

THE BEAUTIFUL TOILET

Blue, blue is the grass about the river
And the willows have overfilled the close garden.
And within, the mistress, in the midmost of her youth,
White, white of face, hesitates, passing the door.
Slender, she put forth a slender hand;

And she was a courtezan in the old days,
And she has married a sot,
Who now goes drunkenly out
And leaves her too much alone.

By Mei Sheng B.C. 140

THE RIVER SONG

This boat is of shato-wood, and its gunwales are cut magnolia,
Musicians with jewelled flutes and with pipes of gold
Fill full the sides in rows, and our wine
Is rich for a thousand cups.
We carry singing girls, drift with the drifting water,
Yet Sennin needs
A yellow stork for a charger, and all our seamen
Would follow the white gulls or ride them.
Kutsu's prose song
Hangs with the sun and moon.

King So's terraced palace
                              is now but barren hill,
But I draw pen on this barge
Causing the five peaks to tremble,
And I have joy in these words
                              like the joy of blue islands.
(If glory could last forever
Then the waters of Han would flow northward.)

And I have moped in the Emperor's garden, awaiting an order-
    to-write!
I looked at the dragon-pond, with its willow-coloured water
Just reflecting the sky's tinge,
And heard the five-score nightingales aimlessly singing.

The eastern wind brings the green colour into the island grasses at
    Yei-shu,
The purple house and the crimson are full of Spring softness.
South of the pond the willow-tips are half-blue and bluer,
Their cords tangle in mist, against the brocade-like palace.
Vine-strings a hundred feet long hang down from carved railings,
And high over the willows, the fine birds sing to each other, and
    listen,
Crying—'Kwan, Kuan', for the early wind, and the feel of it.
The wind bundles itself into a bluish cloud and wanders off.
Over a thousand gates, over a thousand doors are the sounds of
    spring singing,
And the Emperor is at Ko.
Five clouds hang aloft, bright on the purple sky,
The imperial guards come forth from the golden house with their
    armour a-gleaming.
The Emperor in his jewelled car goes out to inspect his flowers,
He goes out to Hori, to look at the wing-flapping storks,
He returns by way of Sei rock, to hear the new nightingales,
For the gardens at Jo-run are full of new nightingales,
Their sound is mixed in this flute,
Their voice is in the twelve pipes here.

By Ribaku
8th century A.D.

THE RIVER MERCHANT'S WIFE:
A LETTER

While my hair was still cut straight across my forehead
I played about the front gate, pulling flowers.
You came by on bamboo stilts, playing horse,
You walked about my seat, playing with blue plums.
And we went on living in the village of Chokan:
Two small people, without dislike or suspicion.

At fourteen I married My Lord you.
I never laughed, being bashful.
Lowering my head, I looked at the wall.
Called to, a thousand times, I never looked back.

At fifteen I stopped scowling,
I desired my dust to be mingled with yours
Forever and forever and forever.
Why should I climb the look out?

At sixteen you departed,
You went into far Ku-to-yen, by the river of swirling eddies,
And you have been gone five months.
The monkeys make sorrowful noise overhead.

You dragged your feet when you went out.
By the gate now, the moss is grown, the different mosses,
Too deep to clear them away!
The leaves fall early this autumn, in wind.
Th paired butterflies are already yellow with August
Over the grass in the West garden;
They hurt me. I grow older.
If you are coming down through the narrows of the river Kiang,
Please let me know beforehand,
And I will come out to meet you
　　　　　　　　　As far as Cho-fu-Sa.

By Ribaku

POEM BY THE BRIDGE AT TEN-SHIN

March has come to the bridge head,
Peach boughs and apricot boughs hang over a thousand gates,
At morning there are flowers to cut the heart,
And evening drives them on the eastward-flowing waters.
Petals are on the gone waters and on the going,
      And on the back-swirling eddies,
But to-day's men are not the men of the old days,
Though they hang in the same way over the bridge-rail.
The sea's colour moves at the dawn
And the princes still stand in rows, about the throne,
And the moon falls over the portals of Sei-go-yo,
And clings to the walls and the gate-top.
With head gear glittering against the cloud and sun,
The lords go forth from the court, and into far borders.
They ride upon dragon-like horses,
Upon horses with head-trappings of yellow metal,
And the streets make way for their passage.
      Haughty their passing,
Haughty their steps as they go in to great banquets,
To high halls and curious food,
To the perfumed air and girls dancing,
To clear flutes and clear singing;
To the dance of the seventy couples;
To the mad chase through the gardens.
Night and day are given over to pleasure
And they think it will last a thousand autumns,
      Unwearying autumns.
For them the yellow dogs howl portents in vain,
And what are they compared to the lady Riokushu,
      That was cause of hate!
Who among them is a man like Han-rei
      Who departed alone with his mistress,
With her hair unbound, and he his own skiffsman!

By Ribaku

THE JEWEL STAIRS' GRIEVANCE

The jewelled steps are already quite white with dew,
It is so late that the dew soaks my gauze stockings,
And I let down the crystal curtain
And watch the moon through the clear autumn.

By Rihaku

NOTE.—Jewel stairs, therefore a palace. Grievance, therefore there is something to complain of. Gauze stockings, therefore a court lady, not a servant who complains. Clear autumn, therefore he has no excuse on account of weather. Also she has come early, for the dew has not merely whitened the stairs, but has soaked her stockings. The poem is especially prized because she utters no direct reproach.

LAMENT OF THE FRONTIER GUARD

By the North Gate, the wind blows full of sand,
Lonely from the beginning of time until now!
Trees fall, the grass goes yellow with autumn.
I climb the towers and towers
to watch out the barbarous land:
Desolate castle, the sky, the wide desert.
There is no wall left to this village.
Bones white with a thousand frosts,
High heaps, covered with trees and grass;
Who brought this to pass?
Who has brought the flaming imperial anger?
Who has brought the army with drums and with
kettle-drums?
Barbarous kings.
A gracious spring, turned to blood-ravenous autumn,
A turmoil of wars-men, spread over the middle king-
dom,
Three hundred and sixty thousand,

And sorrow, sorrow like rain.
Sorrow to go, and sorrow, sorrow returning.
Desolate, desolate fields,
And no children of warfare upon them,
       No longer the men for offence and defence.
Ah, how shall you know the dreary sorrow at the
       North Gate,
With Rihaku's name forgotten,
And we guardsmen fed to the tigers.

                    By Rihaku

EXILES' LETTER

To So-Kin of Rakuyo, ancient friend, Chancellor of Gen.
Now I remember that you built me a special tavern
By the south side of the bridge at Ten-Shin.
With yellow gold and white jewels, we paid for songs and
    laughter
And we were drunk for month on month, forgetting the kings
    and princes.
Intelligent men came drifting in from the sea and from the west
    border,
And with them, and with you especially
There was nothing at cross purpose,
And they made nothing of sea-crossing or of mountain-crossing,
If only they could be of that fellowship,
And we all spoke out our hearts and minds, and without regret.
And then I was sent off to South Wei,
    smothered in laurel groves,
And you to the north of Raku-hoku,
Till we had nothing but thoughts and memories in common.
And then, when separation had come to its worst,
We met, and travelled into Sen-Go,
Through all the thirty-six folds of the turning and twisting waters,

Into a valley of the thousand bright flowers,
That was the first valley;
And into ten thousand valleys full of voices and pine-winds.
And with silver harness and reins of gold,
Out came the East of Kan foreman and his company.
And there came also the 'True man' of Shi-yo to meet me,
Playing on a jewelled mouth-organ.
In the storied houses of San-Ko they gave us more Sennin music,
Many instruments, like the sound of young phoenix broods.
The foreman of Kan Chu, drunk, danced
    because his long sleeves wouldn't keep still
With that music playing,
And I, wrapped in brocade, went to sleep with my head on his
    lap,
And my spirit so high it was all over the heavens,
And before the end of the day we were scattered like stars, or rain.
I had to be off to So, far away over the waters,
You back to your river-bridge.
And your father, who was brave as a leopard,
Was governor in Hei-Shu, and put down the barbarian rabble.
And one May he had you send for me,
        despite the long distance.
And what with broken wheels and so on, I won't say it wasn't
    hard going,
Over roads twisted like sheep's guts.
And I was still going, late in the year,
        in the cutting wind from the North,
And thinking how little you cared for the cost,
        and you caring enough to pay it.
And what a reception:
Red jade cups, food well set on a blue jewelled table,
And I was drunk, and had no thought of returning.
And you would walk out with me to the western corner of the
    castle,
To the dynastic temple, with water about it clear as blue jade,
With boats floating, and the sound of mouth-organs and drums,
With ripples like dragon-scales, going glass green on the water,

Pleasure lasting, with courtezans, going and coming without
    hindrance,
With the willow flakes falling like snow,
And the vermilioned girls getting drunk about sunset,
And the water, a hundred feet deep, reflecting green eyebrows
—Eyebrows painted green are a fine sight in young moonlight,
Gracefully painted—
And the girls singing back at each other,
Dancing in transparent brocade,
And the wind lifting the song, and interrupting it,
Tossing it up under the clouds.

       And all this comes to an end.
       And is not again to be met with.
I went up to the court for examination,
Tried Layu's luck, offered the Choyo song,
And got no promotion,
       and went back to the East Mountains
       White-headed.

And once again, later, we met at the South bridgehead.
And then the crowd broke up, you went north to San palace,
And if you ask how I regret that parting:
It is like the flowers falling at Spring's end
       Confused, whirled in a tangle.
What is the use of talking, and there is no end of
       talking,
There is no end of things in the heart.
I call in the boy,
Have him sit on his knees here
       To seal this,
And send it a thousand miles, thinking.

By Rihaku

FOUR POEMS OF DEPARTURE

Light rain is on the light dust
The willows of the inn-yard
Will be going greener and greener,
But you, Sir, had better take wine ere
*   your departure,*
For you will have no friends about you
When you come to the gates of Go.
*   (Rihaku or Omakitsu)*

Separation on the River Kiang

Ko-jin goes west from Ko-kaku-ro,
The smoke-flowers are blurred over the river.
His lone sail blots the far sky.
And now I see only the river,
    The long Kiang, reaching heaven.

Rihaku

Taking Leave of a Friend

Blue mountains to the north of the walls,
White river winding about them;
Here we must make separation
And go out through a thousand miles of dead grass.
Mind like a floating wide cloud,
Sunset like the parting of old acquaintances
Who bow over their clasped hands at a distance.
Our horses neigh to each other
    as we are departing.

Rihaku

Leave-taking Near Shoku

'*Sanso, King of Shoku, built roads*'

They say the roads of Sanso are steep,
Sheer as the mountains.
The walls rise in a man's face,
Clouds grow out of the hill
  at his horse's bridle.
Sweet trees are on the paved way of the Shin,
Their trunks burst through the paving,
And freshets are bursting their ice
  in the midst of Shoku, a proud city.

Men's fates are already set,
There is no need of asking diviners.

Rihaku

THE CITY OF CHOAN

The phoenix are at play on their terrace.
The phoenix are gone, the river flows on alone.
Flowers and grass
Cover over the dark path
  where lay the dynastic house of the Go.
The bright cloths and bright caps of Shin
Are now the base of old hills.

The Three Mountains fall through the far heaven,
The isle of White Heron
  splits the two streams apart.
Now the high clouds cover the sun
And I can not see Choan afar
And I am sad.

SOUTH-FOLK IN COLD COUNTRY

The Dai horse neighs against the bleak wind of Etsu,
The birds of Etsu have no love for En, in the north,
Emotion is born out of habit.
Yesterday we went out of the Wild-Goose gate,
To-day from the Dragon-Pen.[1]
Surprised. Desert turmoil. Sea sun.
Flying snow bewilders the barbarian heaven.

Lice swarm like ants over our accoutrements.
Mind and spirit drive on the feathery banners.
Hard fight gets no reward.
Loyalty is hard to explain.
Who will be sorry for General Rishogu,
            the swift moving,
Whose white head is lost for this province?

SENNIN POEM BY KAKUHAKU

The red and green kingfishers
            flash between the orchids and clover,
One bird casts its gleam on another.

Green vines hang through the high forest,
They weave a whole roof to the mountain,
The lone man sits with shut speech,
He purrs and pats the clear strings.
He throws his heart up through the sky,
He bites through the flower pistil
            and brings up a fine fountain.
The red-pine-tree god looks at him and wonders.

[1] *I.e.,* we have been warring from one end of the empire to the other, now east,
now west, on each border.

He rides through the purple smoke to visit the sennin,
He takes 'Floating Hill'[1] by the sleeve,
He claps his hand on the back of the great water sennin.

But you, you dam'd crowd of gnats,
Can you even tell the age of a turtle?

A BALLAD OF THE MULBERRY ROAD

The sun rises in south east corner of things
To look on the tall house of the Shin
For they have a daughter named Rafu,
      (pretty girl)
She made the name for herself: 'Gauze Veil',
For she feeds mulberries to silkworms.
She gets them by the south wall of the town.
With green strings she makes the warp of her
      basket,
She makes the shoulder-straps of her basket
      from the boughs of Katsura,
And she piles her hair up on the left side of her
      head-piece.
Her earrings are made of pearl,
Her underskirt is of green pattern-silk,
Her overskirt is the same silk dyed in purple,
And when men going by look on Rafu
      They set down their burdens,
They stand and twirl their moustaches.

(Fenollosa Mss., very early)

[1] Name of a sennin.

OLD IDEA OF CHOAN
BY ROSORIU

I

The narrow streets cut into the wide highway at
      Choan,
      Dark oxen, white horses,
      drag on the seven coaches with outriders.
The coaches are perfumed wood,
The jewelled chair is held up at the crossway,
Before the royal lodge:
A glitter of golden saddles, awaiting the princes;
They eddy before the gate of the barons.
The canopy embroidered with dragons
      drinks in and casts back the sun.
Evening comes.
      The trappings are bordered with mist.
The hundred cords of mist are spread through
      and double the trees,
Night birds, and night women,
Spread out their sounds through the gardens.

II

Birds with flowery wing, hovering butterflies
      crowd over the thousand gates,
Trees that glitter like jade,
      terraces tinged with silver,
The seed of a myriad hues,
A net-work of arbours and passages and covered ways,
Double towers, winged roofs,
      border the net-work of ways:
A place of felicitous meeting.
Riu's house stands out on the sky,
      with glitter of colour

CATHAY

As Butei of Kan had made the high golden lotus
      to gather his dews,
Before it another house which I do not know:
How shall we know all the friends
      whom we meet on strange roadways?

TO EM-MEI'S "THE UNMOVING CLOUD"

'Wet springtime,' says To-em-mei,
'Wet spring in the garden.'

I

The clouds have gathered, and gathered,
      and the rain falls and falls,
The eight ply of the heavens
      are all folded into one darkness,
And the wide, flat road stretches out.
I stop in my room toward the East, quiet, quiet,
I pat my new cask of wine.
My friends are estranged, or far distant,
I bow my head and stand still.

II

Rain, rain, and the clouds have gathered,
The eight ply of the heavens are darkness,
The flat land is turned into river.
      'Wine, wine, here is wine!'
I drink by my eastern window.
I think of talking and man,
And no boat, no carriage, approaches.

III

The trees in my east-looking garden
      are bursting out with new twigs,
They try to stir new affection,

CATHAY

And men say the sun and moon keep on moving
   because they can't find a soft seat.
The birds flutter to rest in my tree,
   and I think I have heard them saying,
'It is not that there are no other men
But we like this fellow the best,
But however we long to speak
He can not know of our sorrow.'

T'ao Yuan Ming
A.D. 365-427

THE SEAFARER

From the Anglo-Saxon

THE SEAFARER

From the Anglo-Saxon

May I for my own self song's truth reckon,
Journey's jargon, how I in harsh days
Hardship endured oft.
Bitter breast-cares have I abided,
Known on my keel many a care's hold,
And dire sea-surge, and there I oft spent
Narrow nightwatch nigh the ship's head
While she tossed close to cliffs. Coldly afflicted,
My feet were by frost benumbed.
Chill its chains are; chafing sighs
Hew my heart round and hunger begot
Mere-weary mood. Lest man know not
That he on dry land loveliest liveth,
List how I, care-wretched, on ice-cold sea,
Weathered the winter, wretched outcast
Deprived of my kinsmen;
Hung with hard ice-flakes, where hail-scur flew,
There I heard naught save the harsh sea
And ice-cold wave, at whiles the swan cries,
Did for my games the gannet's clamour,
Sea-fowls' loudness was for me laughter,
The mews' singing all my mead-drink.
Storms, on the stone-cliffs beaten, fell on the stern
In icy feathers; full oft the eagle screamed
With spray on his pinion.
                    Not any protector
May make merry man faring needy.
This he little believes, who aye in winsome life
Abides 'mid burghers some heavy business,
Wealthy and wine-flushed, how I weary oft
Must bide above brine.

Neareth nightshade, snoweth from north,
Frost froze the land, hail fell on earth then,
Corn of the coldest. Nathless there knocketh now
The heart's thought that I on high streams
The salt-wavy tumult traverse alone.
Moaneth alway my mind's lust
That I fare forth, that I afar hence
Seek out a foreign fastness.
For this there's no mood-lofty man over earth's midst,
Not though he be given his good, but will have in his youth greed;
Nor his deed to the daring, nor his king to the faithful
But shall have his sorrow for sea-fare
Whatever his lord will.
He hath not heart for harping, nor in ring-having
Nor winsomeness to wife, nor world's delight
Nor any whit else save the wave's slash,
Yet longing comes upon him to fare forth on the water.
Bosque taketh blossom, cometh beauty of berries,
Fields to fairness, land fares brisker,
All this admonisheth man eager of mood,
The heart turns to travel so that he then thinks
On flood-ways to be far departing.
Cuckoo calleth with gloomy crying,
He singeth summerward, bodeth sorrow,
The bitter heart's blood. Burgher knows not—
He the prosperous man—what some perform
Where wandering them widest draweth.
So that but now my heart burst from my breastlock,
My mood 'mid the mere-flood,
Over the whale's acre, would wander wide.
On earth's shelter cometh oft to me,
Eager and ready, the crying lone-flyer,
Whets for the whale-path the heart irresistibly,
O'er tracks of ocean; seeing that anyhow
My lord deems to me this dead life
On loan and on land, I believe not
That any earth-weal eternal standeth

Save there be somewhat calamitous
That, ere a man's tide go, turn it to twain.
Disease or oldness or sword-hate
Beats out the breath from doom-gripped body.
And for this, every earl whatever, for those speaking after—
Laud of the living, boasteth some last word,
That he will work ere he pass onward,
Frame on the fair earth 'gainst foes his malice,
Daring ado, . . .
So that all men shall honour him after
And his laud beyond them remain 'mid the English,
Aye, for ever, a lasting life's-blast,
Delight 'mid the doughty.
                              Days little durable,
And all arrogance of earthen riches,
There come now no kings nor Caesars
Nor gold-giving lords like those gone.
Howe'er in mirth most magnified,
Whoe'er lived in life most lordliest,
Drear all this excellence, delights undurable!
Waneth the watch, but the world holdeth.
Tomb hideth trouble. The blade is layed low.
Earthly glory ageth and seareth.
No man at all going the earth's gait,
But age fares against him, his face paleth,
Grey-haired he groaneth, knows gone companions,
Lordly men, are to earth o'ergiven,
Nor may he then the flesh-cover, whose life ceaseth,
Nor eat the sweet nor feel the sorry,
Nor stir hand nor think in mid heart,
And though he strew the grave with gold,
His born brothers, their buried bodies
Be an unlikely treasure hoard.

'NOH' PLAYS

1916

PART I

INTRODUCTION

The life of Ernest Fenollosa was the romance par excellence of modern scholarship. He went to Japan as a professor of economics. He ended as Imperial Commissioner of Arts. He had unearthed treasure that no Japanese had heard of. It may be an exaggeration to say that he had saved Japanese art for Japan, but it is certain that he had done as much as any one man could have to set the native art in its rightful pre-eminence and to stop the apeing of Europe. He had endeared himself to the government and laid the basis for a personal tradition. When he died suddenly in England the Japanese government sent a warship for his body, and the priests buried him within the sacred enclosure at Miidera. These facts speak for themselves.

His present reputation in Europe rests upon his 'Epochs of Chinese and Japanese Art.' In America he is known also for his service to divers museums. His work on Japanese and Chinese literature has come as a surprise to the scholars. It forms, I think, the basis for a new donation, for a new understanding of 'the East'. For instance, as I look over that section of his papers which deals with the Japanese Noh, having read what others have written in English about these plays, I am in a position to say definitely that Professor Fenollosa knew more of the subject than any one who has yet written in our tongue.

The Noh is unquestionably one of the great arts of the world, and it is quite possibly one of the most recondite.

In the eighth century of our era the dilettante of the Japanese court established the tea cult and the play of 'listening to incense'.[1]

In the fourteenth century the priests and the court and the players all together produced a drama scarcely less subtle.

[1] Vide Brinkley, Oriental Series, vol. iii.

For 'listening to incense' the company was divided into two parties, and some arbiter burnt many kinds and many blended sorts of perfume, and the game was not merely to know which was which, but to give to each one of them a beautiful and allusive name, to recall by the title some strange event of history or some passage of romance or legend. It was a refinement in barbarous times, comparable to the art of polyphonic rhyme, developed in feudal Provence four centuries later, and now almost wholly forgotten.

The art of allusion, or this love of allusion in art, is at the root of the Noh. These plays, or eclogues, were made only for the few; for the nobles; for those trained to catch the allusion. In the Noh we find an art built upon the god-dance, or upon some local legend of spiritual apparition, or, later, on gestes of war and feats of history; an art of splendid posture, of dancing and chanting and of acting that is not mimetic. It is, of course, impossible to give much idea of the whole of this art on paper. One can only trace out the words of the text and say that they are spoken, or half-sung and chanted, to a fitting and traditional accompaniment of movement and colour, and that they are themselves but half shadows. Yet, despite the difficulties of presentation, I find these words very wonderful, and they become intelligible if, as a friend says, 'you read them all the time as though you were listening to music.'

If one has the habit of reading plays and imagining their setting, it will not be difficult to imagine the Noh stage—different as it is from our own or even from Western mediaeval stages— and to feel how the incomplete speech is filled out by the music or movement. It is a symbolic stage, a drama of masks—at least they have masks for spirits and gods and young women. It is a theatre of which both Mr. Yeats and Mr. Craig may approve. It is not, like our theatre, a place where every fineness and subtlety must give way; where every fineness of word or of word-cadence is sacrificed to the 'broad effect'; where the paint must be put on with a broom. It is a stage where every subsidiary art is bent precisely upon holding the faintest shade of a difference; where the poet may even be silent while the gestures consecrated by four centuries of usage show meaning.

INTRODUCTION

'We work in pure spirit,' said Umewaka Minoru, through whose efforts the Noh survived the revolution of 1868, and the fall of the Tokugawa.

Minoru was acting in the Shogun's garden when the news of Perry's arrival stopped the play. Without him the art would have perished. He restored it through poverty and struggle, 'living in a poor house, in a poor street, in a kitchen, selling his clothes to buy masks and costumes from the sales of bankrupt companies, and using "kaiyu" for rice.'

The following prospectus from a programme of one of his later performances (March 1900) will perhaps serve to show the player's attitude toward the play.

PROGRAMME ANNOUNCEMENT

Our ancestor was called Umegu Hiogu no Kami Tomotoki. He was the descendant in the ninth generation of Tachibana no Moroye Sadaijin, and lived in Umedzu Yamashiro, hence his family name. After that he lived in Oshima, in the province of Tamba, and died in the fourth year of Ninwa. Moroye's descendant, the twenty-second after Tomotoki, was called Hiogu no Kami Tomosato. He was a samurai in Tamba, as his fathers before him. The twenty-eighth descendant was Hiogu no Kami Kagehisa. His mother dreamed that a Noh mask was given from heaven; she conceived, and Kagehisa was born. From his childhood Kagehisa liked music and dancing, and he was by nature very excellent in both of these arts. The Emperor Gotsuchi Mikado heard his name, and in January in the 13th year of Bunmei he called him to his palace and made him perform the play Ashikari. Kagehisa was then sixteen years old. The Emperor admired him greatly and gave him the decoration (Monsuki) and a curtain which was purple above and white below, and he gave him the honorific ideograph 'waka' and thus made him change his name to Umewaka. By the Emperor's order, Ushoben Fugiwara no Shunmei sent the news of this and the gifts to Kagehisa. The letter of the Emperor, given at that time, is still in our house. The curtain was, unfortunately, burned in the great fire of Yedo on the 4th of March in the third year of Bunka.

Kagehisa died in the second year of Kioroku and after him the family of Umewaka became professional actors of Noh. Hironaga, the thirtieth descendant of Umewaka Taiyu Rokuro, served Ota Nobunaga,[1] And he was given a territory of 700 koku in Tamba. And he died in Nobunaga's battle, Akechi. His son, Taiyu Rokuro Ujimori, was called to the palace of Tokugawa Iyeyasu in the fourth year of Keicho, and given a territory of 100 koku near his home in Tamba. He died in the third year of Kambun. After that the family of Umewaka served the Tokugawa shoguns with Noh for generation after generation down to the revolution of Meiji (1868). These are the outlines of the genealogy of my house.

This is the 450th anniversary of Tomosato, and so to celebrate him and Kagehisa and Ujimori, we have these performances for three days. We hope that all will come to see them.

The head of the performance is the forty-fifth of his line, the Umewaka Rokoro, and is aided by Umewaka Manzaburo.

(Dated.) In the 33rd year of Meiji, 2nd month.

You see how far this is from the conditions of the Occidental stage. Pride of descent, pride in having served dynasties now extinct, fragments of ceremony and religious ritual, all serve at first to confuse the modern person, and to draw his mind from the sheer dramatic value of Noh.

Some scholars seem to have added another confusion. They have not understood the function of the individual plays in the performance, and have thought them fragmentary, or have complained of imperfect structure. The Noh plays are often quite complete in themselves; certain plays are detachable units, comprehensible as single performances, and without annotation or comment. Yet even these can be used as part of the Ban-gumi, the full Noh programme. Certain other plays are only 'formed' and intelligible when considered as part of such a series of plays. Again, the texts or libretti of certain other plays, really complete in themselves, seem to us unfinished, because their final scene depends more upon the dance than on the words. The following section of Professor Fenollosa's notes throws a good deal of light

[1] Nobunaga died in 1582.

on these questions. It is Notebook J, Section I, based on the authority of Mr. Taketi Owada, and runs as follows:

'In the time of Tokugawa (A.D. 1602 to 1868), Noh became the music of the Shogun's court and it was called O-no, the pro- gramme O-no-gumi, the actor O-no-yakusha, and the stage O-no-butai, with honorific additions. The first ceremony of the year, Utai-zome, was considered very important at the court. In the palaces of the daimyos, also, they had their proper ceremonies. This ceremony of Utai-zome began with the Ashikaga shoguns (in the fourteenth century). At that time on the fourth day of the first month, Kanze (the head of one of the five chartered and hereditary companies of court actors) sang a play in Omaya, and the Shogun gave him jifuku ("clothes of the season"), and this became a custom. In the time of Toyotomi, the second day of the first month was set apart for the ceremony. But in the time of Tokugawa, the third day of the first month was fixed "eternally" as the day for Utai-zome. On that day, at the hour of "tori no jō" (about 5 a.m.), the Shogun presented himself in a large hall in Hon-Maru (where the imperial palace now is), taking with him the San-ke, or three relative daimyos, the ministers, and all the other daimyos and officials, all dressed in the robes called "noshime-kami-shimo". And the "Tayus" (or heads) of the Kanze and Komparu schools of acting come every year, and the Tayus of Hosho and Kita on alternate years, and the Waki actors, that is, the actors of second parts, and the actors of Kiogen or farces, and the hayashikata ("cats," or musicians) and the singers of the chorus, all bow down on the verandah of the third hall dressed in robes called "suo," and in hats called "yeboshi".

And while the cup of the Shogun is poured out three times, Kanze sings the "Shikai-nami" passage from the play of Taka- sago, still bowing. Then the plays Oi-matsu, Tōbuku, and Takasago are sung with music, and when they are over the Shogun gives certain robes, called the "White-aya," with crimson lining, to the three chief actors, and robes called "ori- kami" to the other actors. Then the three chief actors put on the new robes over their "suos" and begin at once to dance the Dance of the Match of Bows and Arrows. And the chant that accompanies it is as follows:

The chief actor sings—

"Shakuson, Shakuson!" (Buddha, Buddha!)

And the chorus sings this rather unintelligible passage—

"Taking the bow of Great Love and the arrow of Wisdom, he awakened Sandoku from sleep. Aisemmyō-o displayed these two as the symbols of IN and YO.[1] Monju (another deity) appeared in the form of Yo-yu and caught the serpent, Kishu-ja, and made it into a bow. From its eyes he made him his arrows.[2]

"The Empress Jingō of our country defeated the rebels with these arrows and brought the peace of Ciyo-shun to the people. O Hachiman Daibosatsu, Emperor Ojin, War-god Yumi-ya, enshrined in Iwashimidzu, where the clear water-spring flows out! O, O, O! This water is water flowing forever."'

This 'yumi-ya' text cannot be used anywhere save in this ceremony at the Shogun's court, and in the 'Takigi-No' of the Kasuga temple at Nara (where a few extra lines are interpolated).

When the above chant and dance are finished, the Shogun takes the robe 'Kataginu' from his shoulders and throws it to the samurai in attendance. The samurai hands it to the minister, who walks with it to the verandah and presents it to the Taiyu of Kanze very solemnly. Then all the daimyos present take off their 'kata-ginus' and give them to the chief actors, and thus ends the ceremony of Utai-zome. The next day the tays, or chief actors, take the robes back to the daimyos and get money in exchange for them.

There are performances of Noh lasting five days at the initiations, marriages, and the like, of the Shoguns; and at the Buddhist memorial services for dead Shoguns for four days. There are performances for the reception of imperial messengers from Kyoto, at which the actors have to wear various formal costumes. On one day of the five-day performances the town people of the eight hundred and eight streets of Yedo are admitted, and they are

---

[1] In and yo are divisions of metric, and there is a Pythagorean-like symbolism attached to them.

[2] The serpent is presumably the sky, and the stars the eyes made into arrows.

marshalled by the officers of every street. The nanushi, or street officers, assemble the night before by the gates of Ote and Kikyo, and each officer carries aloft a paper lantern bearing the name of his street. They take sake and refreshments and wait for the dawn. It looks like a place on fire, or like a camp before battle.

The Kanze method of acting was made the official style of the Tokugawa Shoguns, and the tayus, or chief actors, of Kanze were placed at the head of all Noh actors. To the Kanze tayu alone was given the privilege of holding one subscription performance, or Kanjin-No, during his lifetime, for the space of ten days. And for this performance he had the right to certain dues and levies on the daimyos and on the streets of the people of Yedo. The daimyos were not allowed to attend the common theatre, but they could go to the Kanjin-No. (Note that the common theatre, the place of mimicry and direct imitation of life, has always been looked down upon in Japan. The Noh, the symbolic and ritual stage, is a place of honour to actor and audience alike.) The daimyos and even their wives and daughters could see Kanjin-No without staying behind the blinds. Programmes were sold in the streets, and a drum was beaten as a signal, as is still done to get an audience for the wrestling matches.

The privilege of holding one subscription performance was later granted to the Hosho company also.

BAN-GUMI

In the performance of Utai, or Noh, the arrangement of pieces for the day is called 'Ban-gumi'. 'Gumi' means a setting in order, and 'Ban' is derived from the old term 'Ban-no-mai', which was formerly used when the two kinds of mai, or dancing, the Korean 'u-ho' and the Chinese 'sa-ho', were performed one after the other.

Now the Ka-den-sho, or secret book of Noh, decrees that the arrangement of plays shall be as follows:

'A "Shugen" must come first. And Shugen, or congratulatory pieces, are limited to Noh of the Gods (that is, to pieces connected with some religious rite), because this country of the rising sun is the country of the gods. The gods have guarded the country from

Kami-yo (the age of the gods) down to the time of the present reign. So in praise of them and in prayer we perform first this Kami-No.

The Shura, or battle-piece, comes second, for the gods and emperors pacified this country with bows and arrows; therefore, to defeat and put out the devils, we perform the Shura. (That is to say, it is sympathetic magic.)

Kazura, or Onna-mono, "wig-pieces", or pieces for females, come third. Many think that any Kazura will do, but it must be a "female Kazura", for after battle comes peace, or Yu-gen, mysterious calm, and in time of peace the cases of love come to pass. Moreover, the battle-pieces are limited to men; so we now have the female piece in contrast like in and yo (the different divisions of the metric, before mentioned).

The fourth piece is Oni-No, or the Noh of spirits. After battle comes peace and glory, but they soon depart in their turn. The glory and pleasures of man are not reliable at all. Life is like a dream and goes with the speed of lightning. It is like a dewdrop in the morning; it soon falls and is broken. To suggest these things and to lift up the heart for Buddha (to produce "Bodai-shin") we have this sort of play after the Onna-mono, that is, just after the middle of the programme, when some of the audience will be a little tired. Just to wake them out of their sleep we have these plays of spirits ("Oni"). Here are shown the struggles and the sins of mortals, and the audience, even while they sit for pleasure, will begin to think about Buddha and the coming world. It is for this reason that Noh is called Mu-jin-Kyo, the immeasurable scripture.[1]

Fifth comes a piece which has some bearing upon the moral duties of man, Jin, Gi, Rei, Chi, Shin; that is, Compassion, Righteousness, Politeness, Wisdom, and Faithfulness. This fifth piece teaches the duties of man here in this world as the fourth piece represents the results of carelessness to such duties.

Sixth comes another Shugen, or congratulatory piece, as

[1] These pieces are the most interesting because of their profound and subtle psychology and because of situations entirely foreign to our Western drama, if not to our folk-lore and legend.

conclusion to the whole performance, to congratulate and call down blessings on the lords present, the actors themselves, and the place. To show that though the spring may pass, still there is a time of its return, this Shugen is put in again just as at the beginning.'

This is what is written in the Ka-den-sho. Then some one, I think Mr. Owada, comments as follows:

'Though it is quite pedantic in wording, still the order of the performance is always like this. To speak in a more popular manner, first comes the Noh of the Divine Age (Kamiyo); then the battle-piece; then the play of women; fourth, the pieces which have a very quiet and deep interest, to touch the audience to their very hearts; fifth, the pieces which have stirring or lively scenes; and, sixth, pieces which praise the lords and the reign.

This is the usual order. When we have five pieces instead of six, we sing at the end of the performance the short passage from the play Takasago, beginning at "Senshuraku wa tami wo nade," "Make the people glad with the joy of a Thousand Autumns." (From the final chorus of Takasago.) This is called the "adding Shugen." But if in the fifth piece there are phrases like "Medeta kere" or "Hisashi kere"—"Oh, how happy!" or "O everlasting," —then there is no necessity to sing the extra passage. In performances in memory of the dead, Tsuizen-No, they sing short passages from Toru and Naniwa.

Though five or six pieces are the usual number, there can be more or even fewer pieces, in which case one must use the general principles of the above schedule in designing and arranging the programme.'

I think I have quoted enough to make clear one or two points.

First: There has been in Japan from the beginning a clear distinction between serious and popular drama. The merely mimetic stage has been despised.

Second: The Noh holds up a mirror to nature in a manner very different from the Western convention of plot. I mean the Noh performance of the five or six plays in order presents a complete service of life. We do not find, as we find in Hamlet, a certain situation or problem set out and analysed. The Noh service presents, or symbolizes, a complete diagram of life and recurrence.

The individual pieces treat for the most part known situations, in a manner analogous to that of the Greek plays, in which we find, for instance, a known Oedipus in a known predicament.

Third: As the tradition of Noh is unbroken, we find in the complete performance numerous elements which have disappeared from our Western stage; that is, morality plays, religious mysteries, and even dances—like those of the mass—which have lost what we might call their dramatic significance.

Certain texts of Noh will therefore be interesting only to students of folk-lore or of comparative religion. The battle-pieces will present little of interest, because Chansons de Geste are pretty much the same all the world over. The moralities are on a par with Western moralities, for ascetic Buddhism and ascetic Christianity have about the same set of preachments. These statements are general and admit of numerous exceptions, but the lover of the stage and the lover of drama and of poetry will find his chief interest in the psychological pieces, or the Plays of Spirits; the plays that are, I think, more Shinto than Buddhist. These plays are full of ghosts, and the ghost psychology is amazing. The parallels with Western spiritist doctrines are very curious. This is, however, an irrelevant or extraneous interest, and one might set it aside if it were not bound up with a dramatic and poetic interest of the very highest order.

I think I can now give a couple of texts, without much more preface than saying that the stage is visible from three sides. It is reached by a bridge which is divided into three sections by three real pine trees which are small and in pots. There is one scene painted on the background. It is a pine tree, the symbol of the unchanging. It is painted right on the back of the stage, and, as this cannot be shifted, it remains the same for all plays.

A play very often represents some one going a journey. The character walks along the bridge or about the stage, announces where he is and where he is going, and often explains the meaning of his symbolic gestures, or tells what the dance means, or why one is dancing.

INTRODUCTION

Thus, in Sotoba Komachi, a play by Kiyotsugu, two priests are going from Koyosan to Kioto, and in Settsu they meet with Ono no Komachi; that is to say, they meet with what appears to be an old woman sitting on a roadside shrine—though she is really the wraith of Ono, long dead.

EZRA POUND

SOTOBA KOMACHI

ONO

When I was young I had pride
And the flowers in my hair
Were like spring willows.
I spoke like the nightingales, and now am old,
Old by a hundred years, and wearied out.
I will sit down and rest.

THE WAKI

[one of the priests, is shocked at her impiety and says]

It is near evening; let us be getting along. Now will you look at that beggar. She is sitting on a sotoba (a carved wooden devotional stick, or shrine). Tell her to come off it and sit on some proper thing.

ONO

Eh, for all your blather it has no letters on it, not a smudge of old painting. I thought it was only a stick.

WAKI

Is it only a stick or a stump? May be it had once fine flowers—in its time, in its time; and now it is a stick, to be sure, with the blessed Buddha cut in it.

ONO

Oh, well then, I'm a stump, too, and well buried, with a flower at my heart. Go on and talk of the shrine.

The Tsure, in this case the second priest, tells the legend of the shrine, and while he is doing it, the Waki notices something strange about the old hag, and cries out—

Who are you?

Ono

I am the ruins of Ono,
The daughter of Ono no Yoshizane.

Waki and Tsure
(together)

How sad a ruin is this:
Komachi was in her day a bright flower;
She had the blue brows of Katsura;
She used no powder at all;
She walked in beautiful raiment in palaces.
Many attended her verse in our speech
And in the speech of the foreign court.

[*That is, China.*]

White of winter is over her head,
Over the husk of her shoulders;
Her eyes are no more like the colour on distant mountains.
She is like a dull moon that fades in the dawn's grip.
The wallet about her throat has in it a few dried beans,
A bundle is wrapped on her back, and on her shoulder is a
    basket of woven roots;
She cannot hide it at all.
She is begging along the road;
She wanders, a poor, daft shadow.

[*I cannot quite make out whether the priest is still sceptical, and thinks
he has before him merely an old woman who thinks she is Komachi. At
any rate, she does not want commiseration, and replies.*]

Ono

Daft! Will you hear him? In my own young days I had a hundred letters from men a sight better than he is. They came like rain-drops in May. And I had a high head, may be, that time. And I sent out no answer. You think because you see me alone now that I was in want of a handsome man in the old days, when Shosho came with the others—Shii no Shocho of Fukakusa [Deep Grass] that came to me in the moonlight and in the dark night and in the nights flooded with rain, and in the black face of the wind and in the wild swish of the snow. He came as often as the melting drops fall from the eaves, ninety-nine times, and he died. And his ghost is about me, driving me on with the madness.

Umewaka Minoru acted Ono in this play on March 8, 1899. It is quite usual for an old actor, wearing a mask, to take the part of a young woman. There is another play of Ono Shosho called Kayoi Komachi, 'Komachi Going'; it is by a Minoru, and Umewaka acted it on November 19, 1899; and it was followed by Suma Genji. I shall give both of these plays complete without further comment.

TECHNICAL TERMS IN NOH

Shite (pronounced '*Sch'tay*'): The hero or chief character.
Tsure: The follower of the hero.
Waki: Guest or guests, very often a wandering priest.
Waki no tsure, or *Wadzure:* Guest's attendant.
Tomo: An insignificant attendant.
Kogata: A very young boy.
Kiogenshi: Sailor or servant.
Hannya: An evil spirit.

The speaking part of Noh is called 'Kataru', the singing parts, 'Utai'.

KAYOI KOMACHI[1]

The Scene is in Yamashiro

CHARACTERS

SHITE, SHOSHO, the ghost of ONO NO KOMACHI's lover.
WAKI, or subsidiary character, a priest.
TSURE, Ono no Komachi.

WAKI

I am a priest in the village of Yase. And there's an odd little woman comes here every day with fruit and fuel. If she comes to-day I shall ask her who she is.

TSURE

(*announcing herself to the audience*)

I am a woman who lives out about Itchiharano. There are many rich houses in Yase, and I take fruit and wood to them, and there's where I'm going now.

WAKI

Then you are the woman. What sort of fruit have you there?

TSURE

I've nuts and kaki and chestnuts and plums and peaches, and big and little oranges, and a bunch of tachibana, which reminds me of days that are gone.

WAKI

Then that's all right—but who are you?

[1] The crux of the play is that Shosho would not accept Buddhism, and thus his spirit and Ono's are kept apart. There is nothing like a ghost for holding to an idée fixe. In Nishikigi, the ghosts of the two lovers are kept apart because the woman had steadily refused the hero's offering of charm sticks. The two ghosts are brought together by the piety of a wandering priest. Mr. Yeats tells me that he has found a similar legend in Arran, where the ghosts come to a priest to be married.

KAYOI KAMACHI

Tsure

(*To herself.*) I can't tell him that now. (*To him.*) I'm just a woman who lives out by Ichihara-no-be, in all that wild grass there.   [*So saying she disappears.*

Waki

That's queer. I asked her her name. She won't tell me. She says she's just a woman from Ichihara, and then she's gone like a mist. If you go down by Ichihara you can hear the wind in the Susuki bushes as in the poem of Ono no Komachi's, where she says, 'Ono, no I will not tell the wind my name is Ono, as long as Susuki has leaves.' I dare say it is she or her spirit. I will go there the better to pray for her.

Chorus

(*announcing the action and change of scene*)

So he went out of his little cottage in the temple enclosure. He went to Ichihara and prayed.

Tsure

(*her voice heard from the furze bush, speaking to the priest*)

There's a heap of good in your prayers; do you think you could bring me to Buddha?

Shite

(*the spirit of* Shosho)

It's an ill time to do that. Go back. You move in ill hours.

Tsure

I say they were very fine prayers. I will not come back without a struggle.

Shite

I've a sad heart to see you looking up to Buddha, you who left me alone, I diving in the black rivers of hell. Will soft prayers be a comfort to you in your quiet heaven, you who know that I'm alone in that wild, desolate place? To put you away from me! That's all he has come for, with his prayers. Will they do any good to my sort?

227

TSURE

O dear, you can speak for yourself, but my heart is clear as new moonlight.

CHORUS

See, she comes out of the bush.

> [*That is, the spirit has materialized.*]

SHITE

Will nothing make you turn back?

TSURE

Faith is like a wild deer on the mountain. It will not stop when you call it.

SHITE

Then I'll be the dog of your Buddha; I will not be beaten away from you.

TSURE

How terrible, how terrible his face is![1]

CHORUS

See, he has caught at her sleeve.

WAKI

(*This apparently trivial speech of the* WAKI'S *arrests them. It is most interesting in view of the 'new' doctrine of the suggestibility or hypnotizability of ghosts. The* WAKI *says merely:*) Are you Ono no Komachi? And you, Shosho? Did you court her a hundred nights? Can you show this?

> [*Then they begin the dance of this Noh, the image of the coming of* SHOSHO.]

TSURE

I did not know you had such deep thirst for me.

SHITE

You deceived me by telling me to drive out a hundred nights. I thought you meant it. I took my carriage and came.

---

[1] Shosho is not by any means bringing a humble and contrite heart to his conversion.

Tsure

I said, 'Change your appearance, or people will see you and talk.'

Shite

I changed my carriage. Though I had fresh horses in Kohata, I even came barefoot.

Tsure

You came in every sort of condition.

Shite

It was not such a dark way by moonlight.

Tsure

You even came in the snow.

Shite

I can, even now, seem to be shaking it off my sleeves.

> [*This movement is developed into a dance.*]

Tsure

In the evening rain.

Shite

That devil in your rain was my invisible terror.

Tsure

On the night there was no cloud——

Shite

I had my own rain of tears; that was the dark night, surely.

Tsure

The twilight was always my terror.

Shite

She will wait for the moon, I said, but she will never wait for me.

Chorus

The dawn! oh, the dawn is also a time of many thoughts.

Shite

Yes, for me.

CHORUS

Though the fowls crow, though the bells ring, and though the night shall never come up, it is less than nothing to her.

SHITE

With many struggles——

CHORUS

—I went for ninety-nine nights. And this is the hundredth night. This night is the longing fulfilled. He hurries. What is he wearing?

SHITE

His kasa is wretched; it is a very poor cloak, indeed.

CHORUS

His hat is in tatters.

SHITE

His under-coat is in rags.

[*All this refers both to* SHOSHO'S *having come disguised, and being now in but the tatters of some sort of astral body. Then presumably a light shows in his spirit, as probably he had worn some rich garment under his poor disguise.*]

CHORUS

He comes in the dress with patterns;
He comes oversprinkled with flowers.
It is Shosho!

SHITE

In a garment with many folds.

CHORUS

The violet-coloured hakama. He thought she would wait for his coming.

SHITE

I hurried to her as now.

CHORUS

(*speaking for* SHOSHO'S *thoughts*)

Though she only asks me to drink a cup of moonlight, I will not take it. It is a trick to catch one for Buddha.

CHORUS

(in a final statement)

Both their sins vanished. They both became pupils of Buddha, both Komachi and Shosho.

––––––––––

The final dance means that the lovers are spirits fluttering in the grass.

This eclogue is very incomplete. Ono seems rather like Echo, and without the last two lines of the chorus one could very well imagine her keeping up her tenzone with Shosho until the end of time.

In the performance of November 19, as stated before, this play was followed by Manzaburo's Suma Genji (Genji at Suma).

I must ask the reader to suspend his judgment of the dramatic values of such plays until he has read Nishikigi and some of the longer eclogues, at least some of those in which the utai or libretto set by itself conveys a fuller sense of the meaning.[1]

––––––––––

[1] Several Noh, including the Awoi-na-Uye, had, by 1939, been recorded on sound-film, which is the only medium capable of conveying any true idea of the whole art, unless one can see it properly done in Japan.

SUMA GENJI

CHARACTERS

SHITE, an old wood-cutter, who is an apparition of the hero,
   GENJI, as a sort of place-spirit, the spirit of the seashore at
   Suma.

WAKI, FUJIWARA, a priest with a hobby for folk-lore, who is
   visiting sacred places.

SECOND SHITE, or the SHITE in his second manner or apparition,
   GENJI's spirit appearing in a sort of glory of waves and
   moonlight.

WAKI

(announcing himself)

I, Fujiwara no Okinori,
Am come over the sea from Hiuga;
I am a priest from the shinto temple at Miyazaki,
And, as I lived far afield,
I could not see the temple of the great god at Ise;
And now I am a-mind to go thither,
And am come to Suma, the sea-board.
Here Genji lived, and here I shall see the young cherry,
The tree that is so set in the tales——

SHITE

And I am a wood-cutter of Suma.
I fish in the twilight;
By day I pack wood and make salt.
Here is the mount of Suma.
There is the tree, the young cherry.[1]

   And you may be quite right about Genji's having lived here.
That blossom will flare in a moment.[2]

---

[1] It must be remembered that the properties and scene are not representational but
symbolic, the hero-actor simply says in effect, 'Pretend that that is the tree and that
the mountain'.

[2] There is here the double-entente. The blossom will really come out: it is a day of
anniversary or something of that kind; also Genji will appear in his proper glory, as
the audience knows, though the Waki does not.

SUMA GENJI

WAKI

I must find out what that old man knows. (*To* SHITE.) Sir, you seem very poor, and yet you neglect your road; you stop on your way home, just to look at a flower. Is that the tree of the stories?

SHITE

I dare say I'm poor enough; but you don't know much if you're asking about that tree, 'Is it the fine tree of Suma?'

WAKI

Well, *is* it the tree? I've come on purpose to see it.

SHITE

What! you really have come to see the cherry-blossom, and not to look at Mount Suma?

WAKI

Yes; this is where Genji lived, and you are so old that you ought to know a lot of stories about him.

CHORUS
(*telling out* GENJI's *thoughts*)

If I tell over the days that are gone,
My sleeves will wither.[1]
The past was at Kiritsubo;
I went to the lovely cottage, my mother's,
But the emperor loved me.

I was made esquire at twelve, with the hat. The soothsayers unrolled my glories.[2] I was called Hikaru Genji. I was chujo in Hahakigi province. I was chujo in the land of the maple-feasting.[3] At twenty-five I came to Suma, knowing all sorrow of seafare, having none to attend my dreams, no one to hear the old stories.

Then I was recalled to the city. I passed from office to office. I was naidaijin in Miwotsukushi, I was dajodaijin in the lands of Otome, and daijotenno in Fufi no Uraba; for this I was called Hikam Kimi.

[1] That is, this present manifestation in the shape of an old man will fade.
[2] The 'soothsayer' is literally 'the physiognomist from Corea'.
[3] Chujo, naidaijin, etc. are names for different grades of office.

WAKI

But tell me exactly where he lived. Tell me all that you know about him.

SHITE

One can't place the exact spot; he lived all along here by the waves. If you will wait for the moonlight you might see it all in a mist.

CHORUS

He was in Suma in the old days——

SHITE

(*stepping behind a screen or making some sign of departure, he completes the sentence of the chorus*)

—but now in the aery heaven.

CHORUS

(*to* WAKI)

Wait and the moon will show him.
That woodman is gone in the clouds.

WAKI

That 'woodman' was Genji himself, who was here talking live words. I will wait for the night. I will stay here to see what happens. (*Announcing his act.*[1]) Then Fujiwara no Okinori lay down and heard the waves filled with music.

SCENE II *begins with the appearance of the* SECOND SHITE, *that is to say, a bright apparition of* GENJI *in supernatural form.*

GENJI

How beautiful this sea is! When I trod the grass here I was called 'Genji the gleaming', and now from the vaulting heaven I reach down to set a magic on mortals. I sing of the moon in this

---

[1] The characters often give their own stage directions or explain the meaning of their acts, as in the last line here.

shadow, here on this sea-marge of Suma. Here I will dance Sei-kai-ha, the blue dance of the sea waves.

[*And then he begins to dance.*]

CHORUS
(*accompanying and describing the dance*)

The flower of waves-reflected
Is on his white garment;
That pattern covers the sleeve.
The air is alive with flute-sounds,
With the song of various pipes
The land is a-quiver,
And even the wild sea of Suma

Is filled with resonant quiet.
Moving in clouds and in rain,
The dream overlaps with the real;
There was a light out of heaven,
There was a young man at the dance here;
Surely it was Genji Hikaru,
It was Genji Hikaru in spirit.

GENJI

My name is known to the world;
Here by the white waves was my dwelling;
But I am come down out of sky
To put my glamour on mortals.

CHORUS

Gracious is the presence of Genji,
It is like the feel of things at Suma.

GENJI
(*referring also to a change in the dance*)

The wind is abated.

CHORUS

A thin cloud——

GENJI

—clings to the clear-blown sky.
It seems like the spring-time.

CHORUS

He came down like Brahma, Indra, and the Four Kings visiting
    the abode of Devas and Men.[1]
He, the soul of the place.[2]
He, who seemed but a woodman,
Flashed with the honoured colours,
He the true-gleaming.
Blue-grey is the garb they wear here,
Blue-grey he fluttered in Suma;
His sleeves were like the grey sea-waves;
They moved with curious rustling,
Like the noise of the restless waves,
Like the bell of a country town
'Neath the nightfall.

———————

I dare say the play, Suma Genji, will seem undramatic to some
people the first time they read it. The suspense is the suspense of
waiting for a supernatural manifestation—which comes. Some
will be annoyed at a form of psychology which is, in the West,
relegated to spiritistic séances. There is, however, no doubt that
such psychology exists. All through the winter of 1914-15 I
watched Mr. Yeats correlating folk-lore (which Lady Gregory
had collected in Irish cottages) and data of the occult writers,
with the habits of charlatans of Bond Street. If the Japanese
authors had not combined the psychology of such matters with
what is to me a very fine sort of poetry, I would not bother about it.

The reader will miss the feel of suspense if he is unable to put

[1] The Four Kings, i.e. of the four points of the compass. Devas (spirits) and
Men occupy the position immediately below the Gods.

[2] More precisely 'He became the place'. You can compare this with Buckle, or
Jules Romains' studies in unanimism.

himself in sympathy with the priest eager to see 'even in a vision' the beauty lost in the years, 'the shadow of the past in bright form'. I do not say that this sympathy is easily acquired. It is too unusual a frame of mind for us to fall into it without conscious effort. But if one can once get over the feeling of hostility, if one can once let himself into the world of the Noh, there is undoubtedly a new beauty before him. I have found it well worth the trial, and can hope that others will also.

The arrangement of five or six Noh into one performance explains, in part, what may seem like a lack of construction in some of the pieces; the plays have, however, a very severe construction of their own, a sort of musical construction.

When a text seems to 'go off into nothing' at the end, the reader must remember 'that the vagueness or paleness of words is made good by the emotion of the final dance', for the Noh has its unity in emotion. It has also what we may call Unity of Image.[1] At least, the better plays are all built into the intensification of a single Image: the red maple leaves and the snow flurry in Nishikigi, the pines in Takasago, the blue-grey waves and wave pattern in Suma Genji, the mantle of feathers in the play of that name, Hagoromo.

When it comes to presenting Professor Fenollosa's records of his conversations with Umewaka Minoru, the restorer of Noh, I find myself much puzzled as to where to begin. I shall, however, plunge straight into the conversation of May 15, 1900, as that seems germane to other matters already set forth in this excerpt, preceding it only by the quaint record of an earlier meeting, December 20, 1898, as follows:

'Called on old Mr. Umewaka with Mr. Hirata. Presented him with large box of eggs. He thanked me for presenting last Friday 18 yen to Takeyo for my six lessons, which began on November 18. I apologized to him for the mistake of years ago, thanked him for his frankness, his reticence to others, and his kindness in allow-

[1] This intensification of the Image, this manner of construction, is very interesting to me personally, as an Imagiste, for we Imagistes knew nothing of these plays when we set out in our own manner. These plays are also an answer to a question that has several times been put to me: 'Could one do a long Imagiste poem, or even a long poem in vers libre?'

ing me to begin again with him, asked him to receive 15 yen as a present in consideration of his recent help.

He was very affable, and talked with me for about $1\frac{1}{2}$ hours. He asked me to sing, and I sang "Hansakaba". He praised me, said everything was exactly right and said that both he and Takeyo considered my progress wonderful; better than a Japanese could make. He said I was already advanced enough to sing in a Japanese company.[2]

Mosse and I are the only foreigners who have ever been taught Noh, and I am the only foreigner now practising it.

We spoke much of the art of it, I giving him a brief account of Greek drama. He already knew something about opera.

He said the excellence of Noh lay in emotion, not in action or externals. Therefore there were no accessories, as in the theatres. "Spirit" (tamashii) was the word he used. The pure spirit was what it (Noh) worked in, so it was higher than other arts. If a Noh actor acted his best, Umewaka could read his character. The actor could not conceal it. The spirit must out, the "whole man," he said. Therefore he always instructed his sons to be moral, pure and true in all their daily lives, otherwise they could not become the greatest actors.

He spoke much about the (popular) theatre, of its approximation of Noh when he was about thirteen years old. The present Danjuro's father and his troop disguised themselves and came to the performance of Kanjin Noh, from which they were normally excluded. This was the one opportunity for the public to see Noh, it is (as said elsewhere) the single benefit performance allowed to each master Noh actor. Other actors were excluded.

Then it was that Ichikawa, having seen these Noh plays, imitated them in the famous "Kanjiinjo", which the present Danjuro still plays as one of his 18 special pieces. Under the present regime, the popular actors have access to the Noh plays, and the popular plays have imitated them still further. Almost all forms of music and recitation have now (1898) taken more or less of their style from Noh.

[1] This is in Fenollosa's diary, not in a part of a lecture or in anything he had published, so there is no question of its being an immodest statement.

Noh has been a purification of the Japanese soul for 400 years. Kobori Enshu classified the fifteen virtues of Noh, among which he counted mental and bodily health as one, calling it "Healing without medicine".

"Dancing is especially known, by its circulation of the blood, to keep off the disease of old age."

Now Minoru and his sons occasionally go to Danjuro's theatre. He spoke much about the Shogun's court. When a Noh actor was engaged by the Shogun he had to sign long articles to the effect that he would never divulge even to his wife or his relatives any of the doings or descriptions of things in the palace, also that he would not visit houses of pleasure or go to the theatre. If caught doing these things he was severely punished. Occasionally a Noh actor would go to the theatre in disguise.

With the exception of the Kanjin Noh, common people could not, at that time, see the Noh, but a very few were occasionally let in to the monthly rehearsals.'

The notes for May 15, 1900, begin as follows:

'He (Minoru) says that Mitsuni (a certain actor) has learning and great Nesshin, or technique, but that, after all the technique is learned, the great difficulty is to grasp the spirit of the piece.

He always tells the newspaper men to-day not to write criticisms of Noh. They can criticize the popular theatre, for there even the plots may change, and amateurs can judge it. But in Noh everything comes down by tradition from early Tokugawa days and cannot be judged by any living man, but can only be followed faithfully.[1]

Although there is no general score for actors and cats (i.e. the four musicians who have sat at the back of the Noh stage for so many centuries that no one quite knows what they mean or how they came there), there is in the hands of the Taiyu, or actor-manager, a roll such as he (Minoru) himself has, which gives general directions, not much detail. This contains only the ordinary text, with no special notations for singing, but for the dances

---

[1] This is not so stupid as it seems; we might be fairly grateful if some private or chartered company had preserved the exact Elizabethan tradition for acting Shakespeare.

there are minute diagrams showing where to stand, how far to go forward, the turns in a circle, the turns to right or left, how far to go with the right or left foot, how many steps, eyes right, eyes left, what mask and what clothes are to be worn, the very lines in which the clothes must hang, and the exact position of the arms. There are drawings of figures naked for old men, women, girls, boys, ghosts, and all kinds of characters sitting and standing; they show the proper relation of limbs and body. Then there are similar drawings of the same figures clothed.

But one cannot trust merely to such a set of instructions. There is a great deal that must be supplied by experience, feeling, and tradition, and which has always been so supplied. Minoru feels this so strongly that he has not yet shown the rolls to his sons, for fear it might make them mechanical.

"KUDEN" (TRADITION)

A book of this sort has been handed down by his ancestors from early Tokugawa days, but it is only a rough draft. He has written a long supplement on the finer points, but has shown it to no one. One should not trust to it, either. Such fine things as Matsukaze, the pose for looking at the moon, or at the dawn, or at the double reflection of the moon in two tubs, and all the details of business cannot be written down; at such places he writes merely "kuden" (tradition), to show that this is something that can be learned only from a master. Sometimes his teacher used to beat him with a fan when he was learning.

Relying on record plus such tradition, we can say with fair certitude that there has been no appreciable change in Noh since the early days of Tokugawa (that is to say, since the beginning of the seventeenth century, or about the end of Shakespeare's lifetime).

Kuden, or this feeling for the traditional intensity, is not to be gained by mere teaching or mimicry, or by a hundred times trying; but it must be learned by a grasp of the inner spirit. In a place, for instance, where a father comes to his lost son, walks three steps forward, pats him twice on the head and balances his stick, it is very difficult to get all this into grace and harmony, and it certainly cannot be written down or talked into a man by word of mouth.

Imitation must not be wholly external. There is a tradition of a young actor who wished to learn Sekidera Komachi, the most secret and difficult of the three plays, which alone are so secret that they were told and taught only by father to eldest son. He followed a fine old woman, eighty years of age, in the street and watched her every step. After a while she was alarmed and asked him why he was following her. He said she was interesting. She replied that she was too old. Then he confessed that he was an ambitious Noh actor and wanted to play Komachi.

An ordinary woman would have praised him, but she did not. She said it was bad for Noh, though it might be good for the common theatre, to imitate facts. For Noh he must feel the thing as a whole, from the inside. He would not get it copying facts point by point. All this is true.

You must lay great stress upon this in explaining the meaning and esthetics of the Noh.

There is a special medium for expressing emotion. It is the voice.

Each pupil has his own voice; it cannot be made to imitate the voice of an old woman or a spirit (oni). It must remain always the same, his own; yet with that one individual voice of his he must so express himself as to make it clear that it is the mentality of an old woman, or whatever it happens to be, who is speaking.

It is a Noh saying that "The heart is the form."

COSTUMES

There is a general tradition as to costumes. Coloured garments cannot be interchanged for white. The general colour is a matter of record, but not the minute patterns, which may be changed from time to time. It is not necessary that one dress should be reserved for one particular character in one particular piece. Even in Tokugawa days there was not always a costume for each special character. Some were used for several parts and some were unique; so also were the masks.

The general colour and colour-effect of the dress cannot be

changed: say it were small circular patterns on a black ground, this must remain, but the exact flower or ornament inside the circles may vary. The length and cut of the sleeve could not be altered, but only the small details of the pattern. The size of the pattern might be changed just a little.

MASKS

The hannia, or daemonic masks, are different. The hannia in Awoi no Uye is lofty in feeling; that of Dojoji is base. They are very different. The masks of Shunkan, Semimaru, Kagekiyo, and Yoroboshi cannot be used for any other parts. Kontan's mask can be used for several parts, as, for example, the second shite in Takasago. Of course if one has only one hannia mask one must use it for all hannia, but it is better not to do so. The Adachigahara hannia is the lowest in feeling.

Fifty years ago they tried to copy the old masks exactly. The Shogun had Kanze's masks copied even to the old spots. Now it is difficult to get good sculptors.

Turning the head is very difficult, for the actor must be one piece with the mask.

An ordinary mask is worth 30 yen; a great one, 200. At first one cannot distinguish between them. But the longer you look at a good mask the more charged with life it becomes. A common actor cannot use a really good mask. He cannot make himself one with it. A great actor makes it live.'

MUSIC

In the notes for a conversation of May 6, there are the following remarks about the singing or chanting [the Noh texts are part in prose and part in verse; some parts are sung and some spoken, or one might better say, intoned]:

'The importance of the music is in its intervals [he seems to mean intervals between beats, i.e. rhythm intervals, not "intervals" of pitch]. It is just like the dropping of rain from the eaves.

The musical bar is a sort of double bar made up of five notes and seven notes, or of seven notes and then seven more notes, the fourteen notes being sung in the same time as the twelve first ones.

The division of seven syllables is called "yo", that of five is called "in"; the big drum is called "yo", and the small drum "in". The seven syllables are the part of the big drum, the five syllables are the part of the small drum—but if they come in succession it is too regular; so sometimes they reverse and the big drum takes the "in" part and the small drum the "yo".

The head of the chorus naturally controls the musicians. The chorus is called "kimi", or lord, and the "cats", or musicians, are called "subjects". When Minoru acts as head of the chorus, he says he can manage the "cats" by a prolonging or shortening of sounds. [This is obscure, but apparently each musician has ideas of his own about tempo.]

The "cats" must conform to him. The chorus is subject to the shite, or chief actor. A certain number of changes may have crept into the tradition. The art consists in not being mechanical. The "cats", the chorus, and the shite "feel out their own originality", and render their own emotions. Even during the last fifteen years some changes may have crept in unconsciously. Even in Tokugawa days there never was any general score bringing all the parts under a single eye. There is not and never has been any such score. There are independent traditions. [NOTE.—The privileges of acting as "cats" and as waki were hereditary privileges of particular families, just as the privilege of acting the chief parts pertained to the members of the five hereditary schools.] Minoru and other actors may know the parts [he means here the musical air] instinctively or by memory; no one has ever written them down. Some actors know only the arias of the few pieces of which they are masters.

Each "cat" of each school has his own traditions. When he begins to learn, he writes down in his note-book a note for each one of the twelve syllables. Each man has his own notation, and he has a more or less complete record to learn from. These details are never told to any one. The ordinary actors and chorus singers do not know them.

In singing, everything depends on the most minute distinction between "in" and "yo". Minoru was surprised to hear that this was not so in the West. In "yo" there must be "in", and in "in", "yo". This adds breadth and softness, "haba" he calls it.' [1]

THE STAGE

The stage is, as I have said, a platform open on three sides and reached by a bridge from the green-room. The notes on the conversation of June 2 run as follows:

'They have Hakama Noh in summer. The general audience does not like it, but experts can see the movements better as the actors sometimes wear no upper dress at all, and are naked save for the semi-transparent hakama. New servants are surprised at it.

Mr. Umewaka Minoru has tried hard not to change any detail of the old customs. In recent times many have urged him to change the lights, but he prefers the old candles. They ask him to modernize the text and to keep the shite from sitting in the middle [of the stage? or of the play?], but he won't.

A pupil of his, a wood-dealer, says that a proper Noh stage could not be built now, for it is all of hinoten. The floor is in twenty pieces, each of which would now cost 250 yen. There must be no knots in the pillars, and all the large pillars and cross pieces are of one piece. This would cost enormously now even if it were possible at all.

Awoyama Shimotsuke no Kami Roju built this stage [the one now used by Minoru] for his villa in Aoyama more than forty years ago; it was moved to its present site in the fourth year of Meiji (1872). The daimyo sold it to a curio dealer from whom Umewaka Minoru bought it. Shimotsuke was some relation to the daimyo of Bishu, in Owari, and so he got the timbers for nothing. The best timber comes from Owari. So the stage had cost only the carpenter's wages (2000 yen?). Now the wood alone would cost 20,000 to 40,000 yen, if you could get it at all. You couldn't contract for it.

---

[1] This looks like a sort of syncopation. I don't know enough about music to consider it musically with any fullness, but it offers to the student of metric most interesting parallels, or if not parallels, suggestions for comparison with sapphics and with some of the troubadour measures (notably those of Arnaut Daniel), the chief trouble being that Professor Fenollosa's notes at this point are not absolutely lucid.

The form of the stage was fixed in the time of Hideyoshi and Iyeyasu. In Ashikaga (fourteenth century) the performances were in Tadasu ga wara, and the stage was open on all sides. The bridge came to the middle of one side (apparently the back) where the pine tree now is. The stage was square, as it now is, with four pillars. The audience surrounded it in a great circle "like Sumo" [whatever that may mean]. They had a second story or gallery and the Shogun sat in front. The roof was as it now is.

The roof should not be tiled, but should be like the roof of the shinto temples in Ise. Shimotsuke had had a tiled roof because he was afraid of fire. People had said that he (Minoru) was mad to set up a Noh stage [at the time when he was starting to revive the performance]; so he had made the roof small and inconspicuous to attract less notice.

Under the stage are set five earthen jars, in the space bounded by the pillars, to make the sound reverberate—both the singing and the stamping.[1] There are two more jars under the musicians' place and three under the bridge. This has been so since early Tokugawa times. The ground is hollowed out under the stage to the depth of four feet.[2]

The jars are not set upright, as this would obstruct the sound. They are set at 45 degrees. Sometimes they are hung by strings and sometimes set on posts. Minoru's are on posts.

Some jars are faced right and some left; there is a middle one upright. Minoru says it is just like a drum, and that the curve of the jars has to be carefully made. The larger the jars the better.

Hideyoshi or Iyeyasu put the back on the stage. It is made of a double set of boards in order to throw the sound forward. They didn't like having the sound wasted. This innovation was, on that score, aesthetic.

"Social and palace" reasons have in some measure determined the form of the stage.

The floor is not quite level, but slopes slightly forward. The art

[1] This stamping dates from the time when some mythological person danced on a tub to attract the light-goddess.

[2] The stage is in the open. Minoru says elsewhere, 'Snow is worst for it blows on the stage and gets on the feet'.

of stage-building is a secret of "daiko". It is as difficult to build a Noh stage as to build a shinto temple, and there are no proper Noh stages built now.

The painting of the pine tree on the back is most important. It is a congratulatory symbol of unchanging green and strength.

On some stages they have small plum flowers, but this is incorrect; there should be no colour except the green. The bamboo is the complement of the pine. To paint these trees well is a great secret of Kano artists. When skilfully painted, they set off the musicians' forms.

The three real little pine trees along the bridge are quite fixed; they symbolize heaven, earth, and man. The one for heaven is nearest the stage, and then comes the one which symbolizes man. They are merely symbols like the painted pine tree. Sometimes when a pine is mentioned the actors look toward it.

The measurements of the stage have not changed since early Tokugawa days. It should be three ken square, but this measurement is sometimes taken inside, sometimes outside the pillars.

There is no special symbolism in the bridge; it is merely a way of getting across. The length was arbitrary under the Ashikaga; later it was fixed by rule. At the Shogun's court the bridge was 13 ken long, and one needed a great voice to act there. The middle palace bridge was 7 ken. Minoru's bridge is 5 ken. The bridge must be an odd number of ken, like 13, or like the "in" and "yo" numbers (7 and 5). The width is 9 "shaken" outside and 8 inside the pillars.'

PART II

The reader, having perused thus far in patience or in impatience, will probably want to know what came of it all. Does the present Noh, saved from the ashes of the revolution, justify so minute an examination of its past? Believing, as I do, that the Noh is a very great art, I can heartily say that it does. I give here several further specimens of the text or libretto. The reader must remember that the words are only one part of this art. The words are fused with the music and with the ceremonial dancing. One must read or 'examine' these texts 'as if one were listening to music'. One must build out of their indefiniteness a definite image. The plays are at their best, I think, an image; that is to say, their unity lies in the image—they are built up about it as the Greek plays are built up about a single moral conviction. The Greek plays are elaborate presentations of some incident of a story well known; so also the Japanese plays rely upon a certain knowledge of past story or legend. They present some more vivid hour or crisis. The Greek plays are troubled and solved by the gods; the Japanese are abounding in ghosts and spirits. Often the spirit appears first in some homely guise, as, in Catholic legend, we find Christ appearing as a beggar.

The spirit seems often an old man or old woman rapt in meditation. In Kumasaka we come upon a simple recluse. The plot is as follows:

The pilgrim priest is asked to pray for some anonymous soul. His interlocutor's hut has in it no shrine, no single picture of Buddha, nothing but a spear and an iron mace. The owner of the hut alludes to himself as 'this priest'. His gospel is the very simple one of protecting travellers from neighbouring bandits.

Suddenly both he and his hut disappear (vide the comments of the chorus). The pilgrim, however, having begun his prayer for the unknown dead man, goes on with the service.

He is rewarded. The second act opens with the reappearance of the spirit in splendid array. He is the spirit of Kumasaka, remembering the glory of his days, meditating upon them, upon his bowmen and deeds of arms. The final passage is the Homeric presentation of combat between him and the young boy, Ushiwaka. But note here the punctilio. Kumasaka's spirit returns to do justice to the glory of Ushiwaka and to tell of his own defeat. All this is symbolized in the dance climax of the play, and is told out by the chorus.

KUMASAKA

A play in two Acts, by Ujinobu, adopted son of Motokiyo

CHARACTERS

A PRIEST.

FIRST SHITE, or HERO, the apparition of KUMASAKA in the form of an old priest.

SECOND SHITE, the apparition of KUMASAKA in his true form.

CHORUS. This chorus sometimes speaks what the chief characters are thinking, sometimes it describes or interprets the meaning of their movements.

PLOT.—The ghost of Kumasaka makes reparation for his brigandage by protecting the country. He comes back to praise the bravery of the young man who had killed him in single combat.

PRIEST

Where shall I rest, wandering weary of the world? I am a city-bred priest, I have not seen the east counties, and I've a mind to go there. Crossing the hills, I look on the lake of Omi, on the woods of Awatsu. Going over the long bridge at Seta, I rested a night at Noji, and another at Shinohara, and at the dawn I came to the green field, Awono in Miwo. I now pass Akasaka at sunset.

SHITE

(in the form of an old priest)

I could tell that priest a thing or two.

PRIEST

Do you mean me? What is it?

SHITE

A certain man died on this day. I ask you to pray for him.

PRIEST

All right; but whom shall I pray for?

SHITE

I will not tell you his name, but his grave lies in the green field beyond that tall pine tree. He cannot enter the gates of Paradise, and so I ask you to pray.

PRIEST

But I do not think it is right for me to pray unless you tell me his name.

SHITE

No, no; you can pray the prayer, Ho kai shujo biodo ri aku; that would do.

PRIEST

(*praying*)

Unto all mortals let there be equal grace, to pass from this life of agony by the gates of death into law; into the peaceful kingdom.

SHITE

(*saying first a word or two*)

If you pray for him,——

CHORUS

(*continuing the sentence*)

——If you pray with the prayer of 'Exeat' he will be thankful, and you need not then know his name. They say that prayer can be heard for even the grass and the plants, for even the sand and the soil here; and they will surely hear it, if you pray for an unknown man.

SHITE

Will you come in? This is my cottage.

PRIEST

This is your house? Very well, I will hold the service in your house; but I see no picture of Buddha nor any wooden image in this cottage—nothing but a long spear on one wall and an iron stick in place of a priest's wand, and many arrows. What are these for?

SHITE

(*thinking*)

Yes, this priest is still in the first stage of faith. (*Aloud.*) As you see, there are many villages here: Tarui, Awohaka, and Akasaka. But the tall grass of Awo-no-gahara grows round the roads between them, and the forest is thick at Koyasu and Awohaka, and many robbers come out under the rains. They attack the baggage on horseback, and take the clothing of maids and servants who pass here. So I go out with his spear.

PRIEST

That's very fine, isn't it?

CHORUS

You will think it very strange for a priest to do this, but even Buddha has the sharp sword of Mida, and Aizen Miowa has arrows, and Tamon, taking his long spear, throws down the evil spirits.

SHITE

The deep love——

CHORUS

—is excellent. Good feeling and keeping order are much more excellent than the love of Bosatsu. 'I think of these matters and know little of anything else. It is from my own heart that I am lost, wandering. But if I begin talking I shall keep on talking until dawn. Go to bed, good father, I will sleep too.'

He seemed to be going to his bedroom, but suddenly his figure disappeared, and the cottage became a field of grass. The priest passes the night under the pine trees.

PRIEST

I cannot sleep out the night. Perhaps if I held my service during the night under this pine tree——

[*He begins his service for the dead man.*]

PART SECOND

SECOND SHITE

There are winds in the east and south; the clouds are not calm in the west; and in the north the wind of the dark evening blusters; and under the shade of the mountain——

CHORUS

——there is a rustling of boughs and leaves.

SECOND SHITE

Perhaps there will be moonshine to-night, but the clouds veil the sky; the moon will not break up their shadow. 'Have at them!' 'Ho, there!' 'Dash in!' That is the way I would shout, calling and ordering my men before and behind, my bowmen and horsemen. I plundered men of their treasure, that was my work in the world, and now I must go on; it is sorry work for a spirit.

PRIEST

Are you Kumasaka Chohan? Tell me the tale of your years.

SECOND SHITE
(now known as KUMASAKA)

There were great merchants in Sanjo, Yoshitsugu, and Nobutaka; they collected treasure each year; they sent rich goods up to Oku. It was then I assailed their trains. Would you know what men were with me?

PRIEST

Tell me the chief men; were they from many a province?

KUMASAKA

There was Kakusho of Kawachi, there were the two brothers Suriharitaro; they have no rivals in fencing.[1]

PRIEST

What chiefs came to you from the city?

KUMASAKA

Emon of Sanjo, Kozari of Mibu.

[1] 'Omoteuchi', face-to-face attack.

KUMASAKA

PRIEST

In the fighting with torches and in mêlée——

KUMASAKA

—they had no equals.

PRIEST

In northern Hakoku?

KUMASAKA

Were Aso no Matsuwaka and Mikune no Kuro.

PRIEST

In Kaga?

KUMASAKA

No, Chohan was the head there. There were seventy comrades who were very strong and skilful.

CHORUS

While Yoshitsugu was going along in the fields and on the mountains, we set many spies to take him.

KUMASAKA

Let us say that he is come to the village of Akasaka. This is the best place to attack him. There are many ways to escape if we are defeated, and he has invited many guests and has had a great feast at the inn.

PRIEST

When the night was advanced the brothers Yoshitsugu and Nobutaka fell asleep.

KUMASAKA

But there was a small boy with keen eyes, about sixteen or seventeen years old, and he was looking through a little hole in the partition, alert to the slightest noise.

PRIEST

He did not sleep even a wink.

KUMASAKA

We did not know it was Ushiwaka.

PRIEST

It was fate.

KUMASAKA

The hour had come.

PRIEST

Be quick!

KUMASAKA

Have at them!

CHORUS

(describing the original combat, now symbolized in the dance)

At this word they rushed in, one after another. They seized the torches; it seemed as if gods could not face them. Ushiwaka stood unafraid; he seized a small halberd and fought like a lion in earnest, like a tiger rushing, like a bird swooping. He fought so cleverly that he felled the thirteen who opposed him; many were wounded besides. They fled without swords or arrows. Then Kumasaka said, 'Are you the devil? Is it a god who has struck down these men with such ease? Perhaps you are not a man. However, dead men take no plunder, and I'd rather leave this truck of Yoshitsugu's than my corpse.' So he took his long spear and was about to make off——

KUMASAKA

——But Kumasaka thought——

CHORUS

(taking it up)

——What can he do, that young chap, if I ply my secret arts freely? Be he god or devil, I will grasp him and grind him. I will offer his body as sacrifice to those whom he has slain. So he drew back, and holding his long spear against his side, he hid himself behind the door and stared at the young lad. Ushiwaka beheld him, and holding his bill at his side, he couched at a little distance. Kumasaka waited likewise. They both waited, alertly; then Kumasaka stepped forth swiftly with his left foot, and struck out with the long spear. It would have run through an iron wall. Ushiwaka parried it lightly, swept it away, left volted. Kumasaka followed and again lunged out with the spear, and Ushiwaka parried the spear-blade quite lightly. Then Kumasaka turned the edge of his spear-blade towards Ushiwaka and slashed at him, and Ushiwaka leaped to the right. Kumasaka lifted his spear and the two weapons were twisted together. Ushiwaka drew back his blade. Kumasaka swung with his spear. Ushiwaka led up and stepped in shadow.

Kumasaka tried to find him, and Ushiwaka slit through the back-chink of his armour; this seemed the end of his course, and he was wroth to be slain by such a young boy.

KUMASAKA

Slowly the wound——

CHORUS

——seemed to pierce; his heart failed; weakness o'ercame him.

KUMASAKA

At the foot of this pine tree——

CHORUS

——he vanished like a dew.

And so saying, he disappeared among the shades of the pine tree at Akasaka, and night fell.

SHOJO

This little dance-plan or eclogue is, evidently, one of the 'opening or closing pieces in praise of the gods or the reign.' It is merely a little service of praise to the wine-spirit. It is quite easy to understand, from such a performance as this, why one meets travellers who say, 'Noh? I've seen Noh Dances; I know nothing about Noh Plays.'

WAKI

I am a man called Kofu in a village by Yosu,[1] which is at the foot of Kane Kinzan in China, and because of my filial deference I dreamed a strange dream. And the dream told me that if I would sell saké in the street by Yosu I should be rich. I obeyed. Time passed. I am rich. And this is the strange thing about it: whenever I go to the market, there's the same man comes to drink saké. No matter how much he drinks, his face shows no change. It is curious. When I asked his name, he said, 'Shojo'. A shojo is a monkey. I waited for him where the river runs out at Jinyo, clipping chrysanthemum petals into the saké. I waited for him before moon-rise.

CHORUS

This is chrysanthemum water. Give me the cup. I take it and look at a friend.

HERO

O saké!

CHORUS

Saké is a word well in season. Saké is best in autumn.

HERO

Though autumn winds blow——

CHORUS

——I am not cold at all.

[1] Yosu, i.e. Yang-tze.

SHOJO

HERO

I will put cotton over——

CHORUS

—the white chrysanthemum flowers
To keep in the smell.
Now we'll take saké.

HERO

The guests will also see——

CHORUS

—the moon and the stars hung out.

HERO

This place is by Jinyo.

CHORUS

The feast is on the river.

HERO

(*who is in reality* SHOJO)

Shojo will dance now.

CHORUS

The thin leaves of ashi, the leaves of the river reeds, are like flute-notes. The waves are like little drums.

HERO

The voice sounds clear through the shore-winds.

CHORUS

It is the sound of autumn.

HERO

You are welcome. I have made this jar full of saké. Take it. It will never run dry.

CHORUS

No, it will never be empty—the saké of bamboo leaves; although you drink from the lasting cup of the autumn, the autumn evening remains ever the same.

The moon fades out of the river, and the saké weighs down my blood.

And I am shaking and falling; I lie down filled with wine, and I dream; and, awaking, I find the saké still flowing from the jar of Shojo, from the magical fountain.

TAMURA

This play is to be regarded as one of those dealing with the 'pacification of the country and the driving out of evil spirits', although one might perhaps look upon it as a ceremonial play for the Temple founded by Tamura, or even less exactly a ghost play.

The notes are in fragments, or rather there are several long cuts, which do not, however, obscure the outline or structure of the play.

CHARACTERS

HERO, first apparition, a boy ('doji' or temple servant).
TAMURA MARO, second apparition.
WAKI, a priest.

(The opening may be thus summarized: The Waki comes on and says that he is going to Kioto to see the sights. It is spring, and he comes from Kiyomidzu. Sakura are blooming. He wants to ask questions about the place. The boy comes on, describes the flowers, and says that the light of the goddess Kwannon has made them brighter than usual. The Waki asks him who he is 'to be standing there in the shade and sweeping up the fallen petals.')

WAKI
Are you the flower-keeper?

BOY
I am a man who serves the 'Jinnushi Gongen'. I always sweep in blossom season—so you may call me the flower-keeper, or the honorary servant; but, whatever name you use, you should think of me as some one of rank, though I am concealed in humble appearance.

WAKI
Yes, you look that. Will you tell me about this temple?

BOY

This temple is called Seisuiji; it was founded by Tamura Maro. In Kojimadera of Yamato there was a priest named Kenshin. He was always wishing to see the true light of Kwannon. And one time he saw a golden light floating on the Kotsu River. And he was going toward it, when he met an old man who said to him, 'I am Gioye Koji, and you must seek out a certain patron and put up a great temple.'

And the old man went off to the East, and he was Kwannon. And the patron was Maro, Sakanouye no Tamura Maro.

CHORUS

In this pure water, Kwannon with a thousand hands gives blessing. She blesses this land and this people.

WAKI

Well, I have met some one interesting. Can you tell me of other places about here?

BOY

The peak to the south is Nakayama Seikanji.

WAKI

And what is that temple to the northward where they are ringing the nightfall bell?

BOY

That is the temple of Ashino-o. Look! the moon is lifting itself over Mount Otoba,[1] and lights the cherry flowers. You must look!

WAKI

It is an hour outweighing much silver.

[*The* BOY *and the* PRIEST *together recite the Chinese poem*)

One moment of this spring night is worth a full thousand gold bars.

The flowers have a fine smell under the moon.[2]

(*There is a break here in the notes. There should follow a chorus about cherries under the moon*)

---

[1] Otoba, 'sounding-wings'.
[2] Two lines from a poem by the Chinese poet Su Shih, A.D. 1036-1101.

TAMURA

CHORUS

Having seen these things with you, I know you are out of the common. I wonder what your name is.

BOY

If you want to discover my name, you must watch what road I take. You must see to what I return.

CHORUS

We cannot know the far or near of his route.

BOY

I go into the mountains.

CHORUS

He said: 'Watch my path'. And he went down in front of the Jinnushi Gongen temple, and to Tamura-do. He opened the door and went in.

END OF PART ONE

II

WAKI

I have watched all night under the cherries. I do service beneath the full moon.

[*He performs a service.*

HERO

(*in his second apparition, no longer the boy, but* TAMURA MARO)
That is a very blessed scripture. Just because you have droned it over, I am able to come here and speak with the traveller. This is the blessing of Kwannon.

WAKI

How strange! A man appears, lit up by the light of the flowers. What are you?

TAMURA

To be open, I am none other than Saka-no-Uye Tamura Maro, out of the time of Heijo Tenno. I conquered the eastern wild men, beat down their evil spirit, and was an honest servant to my Emperor by the grace of this temple's Buddha.

(Here there follows a passage in which he describes his battles)

CHORUS

The Emperor bade me beat down the evil spirits in Suzuka in Ise, and to set the capital of that country in peace. I drew up my forces, and then, before I set out, I came to this Kwannon and prayed.

TAMURA

And then a strange sign appeared.

CHORUS

Having faith in the true smile of Kwannon, he went swiftly to war, out past Osaka to the forest Awadzu. He passed Ishiyamaji, and, thinking it one of the gods of Kiyomidzu, he prayed on the long bridge of Seta, as he was come nigh to Ise.

CHORUS

(changing from narrative of the journey to description)

There the plum-trees were blossoming. All the scene showed the favour of Kwannon and the virtue of the Emperor.

Then there was a great noise of evil voices, a shaking of mountains.

TAMURA

(excitedly, as if amid the original scene)

Hear ye the evil spirits! Once in the reign of Tenshi, the evil spirit who served the bad minister Chikata died, and Chikata fell. But you are near to Suzukayama; you are easy to kill.

CHORUS

Look to the sea of Ise, on the pine-moor of Anono the evil spirits rain their black clouds. They pour down fires of iron; they move like ten thousand footmen; they are piled like the mountains.

TAMURA

Look forth on the carnage!

TAMURA

Chorus

The battle! Senju Kwannon pours lights on our banner. Her lights fly about in the air. She holds in her thousand hands the bow of 'Great Mercy'. Hers are the arrows of wisdom. Fly forth her thousand arrows. They harry the spirits; they fall in a swirl of hail. The spirits are dead from her rain.

How Great is the Mercy of Kwannon![1]

[1] Tamura Maro had a special devotion to the Kwannon of the Seisui Temple. Her image, thousand-handed with an arrow in each hand, was woven on his battle banners.

FOREWORD TO TSUNEMASA

The Noh, especially the Noh of spirits, abounds in dramatic situations, perhaps too subtle and fragile for our western stage, but none the less intensely dramatic. Kumasaka is martial despite the touch of Buddhism in the opening scene, where the spirit is atoning for his past violence.

Tsunemasa is gentle and melancholy. It is all at high tension, but it is a psychological tension, the tension of the séance. The excitement and triumph are the nervous excitement and triumph of a successful ritual. The spirit is invoked and appears.

The parallels with Western spiritist doctrines are more than interesting. Note the spirit's uncertainty as to his own success in appearing. The priest wonders if he really saw anything. The spirit affirms that 'The body was there if you saw it.'

As to the quality of poetry in this work: there is the favoured youth, soon slain; the uneasy-blood-stained and thoughtless spirit; there are the lines about the caged stork crying at sunset, and they are as clear as Dante's.

'Era già l' ora che volge il disio.'

TSUNEMASA

Priest

I am Sodzu Giokei, keeper of the temple of Ninnaji. Tajima no Kami Tsunemasa, of the house of Taira, was loved by the Emperor when he was a boy, but he was killed in the old days at the battle of the West Seas. And this is the Seizan lute that the Emperor gave him before that fighting. I offer this lute to his spirit in place of libation; I do the right service before him.

[*They perform a service to the spirit of Tsunemasa.*

264

PRIEST

Although it is midnight I see the form of a man, a faint form, in the light there. If you are spirit, who are you?

SPIRIT

I am the ghost of Tsunemasa. Your service has brought me.

PRIEST

Is it the ghost of Tsunemasa? I perceive no form, but a voice.

SPIRIT

It is the faint sound alone that remains.

PRIEST

O! But I saw the form, really.

SPIRIT

It is there if you see it.

PRIEST

I can see.

SPIRIT

Are you sure that you see it, really?

PRIEST

O, do I, or do I not see you?

CHORUS

Changeful Tsunemasa, full of the universal unstillness, looked back upon the world. His voice was heard there, a voice without form. None might see him, but he looked out from his phantom, a dream that gazed on our world.

PRIEST

It is strange! Tsunemasa! The figure was there and is gone, only the thin sound remains. The film of a dream, perhaps! It was a reward for this service.

SPIRIT

When I was young I went into the court. I had a look at life then. I had high favour. I was given the Emperor's biwa.[1] That is

[1] Lute.

the very lute you have there. It is the lute called 'Seizan'. I had it when I walked through the world.

CHORUS

It is the lute that he had in this world, but now he will play Buddha's music.

PRIEST

Bring out what stringed lutes you possess, and follow his music.

SPIRIT

And I will lead you unseen.

[*He plays.*

PRIEST

Midnight is come; we will play the 'midnight-play', Yaban-raku.

SPIRIT

The clear sky is become overclouded; the rain walks with heavier feet.

PRIEST

They shake the grass and the trees.

SPIRIT

It was not the rain's feet. Look yonder.

CHORUS

A moon hangs clear on the pine-bough. The wind rustles as if flurried with rain. It is an hour of magic. The bass strings are something like rain; the small strings talk like a whisper. The deep string is a wind voice of autumn; the third and the fourth strings are like the crying stork in her cage, when she thinks of her young birds toward nightfall. Let the cocks leave off their crowing. Let no one announce the dawn.

SPIRIT

A flute's voice has moved the clouds of Shushinrei. And the phoenix came out from the cloud; they descend with their playing. Pitiful, marvellous music! I have come down to the world. I have resumed my old playing. And I was happy here. All that is soon over.

PRIEST

Now I can see him again, the figure I saw here; can it be Tsunemasa?

SPIRIT

It's a sorry face that I make here. Put down the lights if you see me.

CHORUS

The sorrow of the heart is a spreading around of quick fires. The flames are turned to thick rain. He slew by the sword and was slain. The red wave of blood rose in fire, and now he burns with that flame. He bade us put out the lights; he flew as a summer moth.

> His brushing wings were a storm.
> His spirit is gone in the darkness.

PART III

FENOLLOSA ON THE NOH

The Japanese people have loved nature so passionately that they have interwoven her life and their own into one continuous drama of the art of pure living. I have written elsewhere[1] of the five Acts into which this life-drama falls, particularly as it reveals itself in the several forms of their visual arts. I have spoken of the universal value of this special art-life, and explained how the inflowing of such an Oriental stream has helped to revitalize Western Art, and must go on to assist in the solution of our practical educational problems. I would now go back to that other key, to the blossoming of Japanese genius, which I mentioned under my account of the flower festivals, namely, the national poetry, and its rise, through the enriching of four successive periods, to a vital dramatic force in the fifteenth century. Surely literature may be as delicate an exponent of a nation's soul as is art; and there are several phases of Oriental poetry, both Japanese and Chinese, which have practical significance and even inspiration for us in this weak, transitional period of our Western poetic life.

We cannot escape, in the coming centuries, even if we would, a stronger and stronger modification of our established standards by the pungent subtlety of Oriental thought, and the power of the condensed Oriental forms. The value will lie partly in relief from the deadening boundaries of our own conventions. This is no new thing. It can be shown that the freedom of the Elizabethan mind, and its power to range over all planes of human experience, as in Shakespeare, was, in part, an aftermath of Oriental contacts—in the Crusades, in an intimacy with the Mongols such as Marco Polo's, in the discovery of a double sea-passage to Persia and India, and in the first gleanings of the Jesuit missions to Asia.

[1] *Epochs of Chinese and Japanese Art*, by Ernest Fenollosa. London: Heinemann, 1911.

Still more clearly can it be shown that the romantic movement in English poetry, in the later eighteenth century and the early nineteenth, was influenced and enriched, though often in a subtle and hidden way, by the beginnings of scholarly study and translation of Oriental literature. Bishop Percy, who afterwards revived our knowledge of the mediaeval ballad, published early in the 1760's the first appreciative English account of Chinese poetry; and Bishop Hood wrote an essay on the Chinese theatre, seriously comparing it with the Greek. A few years later Voltaire published his first Chinese tragedy, modified from a Jesuit translation; and an independent English version held the London stage till 1824. Moore, Byron, Shelley, and Coleridge were influenced by the spirit, and often by the very subject, of Persian translations; and Wordsworth's 'Intimations of Immortality' verges on the Hindoo doctrine of reincarnation. In these later days India powerfully reacts upon our imagination through an increasingly intimate knowledge . . .

I

A form of drama, as primitive, as intense, and almost as beautiful as the ancient Greek drama at Athens, still exists in the world. Yet few care for it, or see it.[1] In the fifth century before Christ the Greek drama arose out of the religious rites practised in the festivals of the God of Wine. In the fifteenth century after Christ, the Japanese drama arose out of religious rites practised in the festivals of the Shinto gods, chiefly the Shinto god of the Kasuga temple at Nara. Both began by a sacred dance, and both added a sacred chorus sung by priests. The transition from a dance chorus to drama proper consisted, in both cases, in the evolving of a solo part, the words of which alternate in dialogue with the chorus. In both the final form of drama consists of a few short scenes, wherein two or three soloists act a main theme, whose deeper meaning is interpreted by the poetical comment of the chorus. In both the speech was metrical, and involved a clear organic structure of separate lyrical units. In both music played

---

[1] The Noh has been 'popularized' since Fenollosa wrote this.

an important part. In both action was a modification of the dance. In both rich costumes were worn; in both, masks. The form and tradition of the Athenian drama passed over into the tradition of the ancient Roman stage, and died away in the early middle ages fourteen centuries ago. It is dead, and we can study it from scant records only. But the Japanese poetic drama is alive to-day, having been transmitted almost unchanged from one perfected form reached in Kioto in the fifteenth century.

It has been said that all later drama has been influenced by the Greek; that the strolling jugglers and contortionists, who wandered in troupes over Europe in the middle ages, constitute an unbroken link between the degenerate Roman actors and the miracle plays of the church, which grew into the Shakespearean drama. It is even asserted that, as the Greek conquest gave rise to a Greco-Buddhist form of sculpture on the borders of India and China, Greek dramatic influence entered also into the Hindoo and Chinese drama, and eventually into the Noh of Japan. But the effect of foreign thought on the Noh is small in comparison with that of the native Shinto influences. It is as absurd to say that the Noh is an offshoot of Greek drama as it would be to say that Shakespeare is such an offshoot.

There is, however, beside the deeper analogy of the Japanese Noh with Greek plays, an interesting secondary analogy with the origin of Shakespeare's art. All three had an independent growth from miracle plays—the first from the plays of the worship of Bacchus, the second from the plays of the worship of Christ, the third from the plays of the worship of the Shinto deities and of Buddha. The plays that preceded Shakespeare's in England were acted in fields adjoining the churches, and later in the courtyards of nobles. The plays that preceded the Noh, and even the Noh themselves, were enacted, first in the gardens of temples or on the dry river-beds adjoining the temples, and later in the courtyards of the daimio. On the other hand, the actual modus of the Shakespearean drama is practically dead for us. Occasional revivals have to borrow scenery and other contrivances unknown to the Elizabethan stage, and the continuity of professional tradition has certainly been broken. But in the Japanese Noh, though it arose one hundred years before Shakespeare, this continuity has never been broken. The same plays are to-day enacted in the same manner as then; even the leading actors of to-day are blood descendants of the very men who created this drama 450 years ago.

This ancient lyric drama is not to be confounded with the modern realistic drama of Tokio, with such drama, for instance, as Danjuro's. This vulgar drama is quite like ours, with an elaborate stage and scenery, with little music or chorus, and no masks; with nothing, in short, but realism and mimetics of action. This modern drama, a ghost of the fifth period, arose in Yedo some 300 years ago. It was an amusement designed by the common people for themselves, and was written and acted by them. It therefore corresponds to the work of Ukiyo-ye in painting, and more especially to the colour prints; and a large number of these prints reproduce characters and scenes from the people's theatre.

As the pictorial art of the fifth period was divisible into two parts—that of the nobility, designed to adorn their castles, and that of the common people, printed illustration,—so has the drama of the last 200 years been twofold, that of the lyric Noh, preserved pure in the palaces of the rich; and that of the populace, running to realism and extravagance in the street theatres. To-day, in spite of the shock and revolution of 1868, the former, the severe and poetic drama, has been revived, and is enthusiastically studied by cultured Japanese. In that commotion the palaces of the daimios, with their Noh stages, were destroyed, the court troupes of actors were dispersed. For three years after 1868 performances ceased entirely. But Mr. Umewaka Minoru, who had been one of the soloists in the Shogun's central troupe, kept guard over the pure tradition, and had many stage directions or 'tenets' preserved in writing along with the texts. In 1871 he bought an ex-daimio's stage for a song, set it up on the banks of the Sumida river in Tokio, and began to train his sons. Many patient pupils and old actors flocked to him; the public began their patronage; he bought up collections of costumes and masks at sales of impoverished nobles; and now his theatre is so thronged that boxes have to be engaged a week beforehand, and five other theatres have been built in Tokio. . . .

For the last twenty years I have been studying the Noh, under the personal tuition of Umewaka Minoru and his sons, learning by actual practice the method of the singing and something of the acting; I have taken down from Umewaka's lips invaluable oral traditions of the stage as it was before 1868; and have prepared, with his assistance and that of native scholars, translations of some fifty of the texts.

II

The art of dance has played a richer part in Chinese and Japanese life than it has in Europe. In prehistoric days, when men or women were strongly moved, they got up and danced. It was as natural a form of self-expression as improvised verse or song, and was often combined with both. But the growing decorum of a polite society tended to relegate this dancing to occasions of special inspiration and to professional dancers. These occasions were roughly of two sorts—formal entertainments at Court and religious ceremonial. The former, which survives to this day in the Mikado's palace, represented the action of historic heroes, frequently warriors posturing with sword and spear. This was accompanied by the instrumental music of a full orchestra. The religious ceremonial was of two sorts—the Buddhist miracle plays in the early temples and the god dances of the Shinto.

The miracle plays represented scenes from the lives of saints and the intervention of Buddha and Bodhisattwa in human affairs. Like the very earliest forms of the European play, these were pantomimic, with no special dramatic text, save possibly the reading of appropriate scripture. The Japanese miracle plays were danced with masks; and the temples of Nara are still full of these masks, which date from the eighth century. It is clear that many popular and humorous types must have been represented; and it is barely possible that these were remotely derived, through Greco-Buddhist channels, from the masks of Greek low comedy. In these plays the god is the chief actor, sometimes in dramatic relation to a human companion. The god always wears a mask.

The solo part is established; and herein the play differs from the Greek, where the original rite was performed by a group of priests, or (in the comedy) by goats or fauns.

The most certainly Japanese element of the drama was the sacred dance in the Shinto temples. This was a kind of pantomime, and repeated the action of a local god on his first appearance to men. The first dance, therefore, was a god dance; the god himself danced, with his face concealed in a mask. Here is a difference between the Greek and Japanese beginnings. In Greece the chorus danced, and the god was represented by an altar. In Japan the god danced alone.

The ancient Shinto dance or pantomime was probably, at first, a story enacted by the local spirit, as soloist—a repetition, as it were, of the original manifestation. Shintoism is spiritism, mild, nature-loving, much like the Greek. A local spirit appeared to men in some characteristic phase. On the spot a Shinto temple was built, and yearly or monthly rites, including pantomime, perpetuated the memory of the event. Such things happened all over the country; and thus thousands of different stories were perpetuated in the dances—hence the wealth of primitive material. The thing can be seen to-day in every village festival. Even in great cities like Tokio, every district maintains its primitive village spirit-worship, that of some tutelary worthy who enacts the old story once a year on a specially made platform raised in the street, about which the people of the locality congregate. The plays are generally pantomime without text.

In the Shinto dance the soloist has no chorus. He performs some religious act of the spirit, though this is often turned into rude comedy. This dance takes the form of a dignified pantomime. It is not an abstract kicking or whirling, not a mere dervish frenzy, but is full of meaning, representing divine situations and motions, artistically, with restraint and with the chastening of a conventional beauty, which makes every posture of the whole body—head, trunk, hands, and feet—harmonious in line, and all the transitions from posture to posture balanced and graceful in line. A flashlight glimpse across such a dance is like a flashlight of sculpture; but the motion itself, like a picture which moves in colour, is like the art of music. There is an orchestral accompaniment of flutes, drums, and cymbals, slow, fast, low, passionate, or accented, that makes a natural ground-tone. Akin to these are the moving street pageants, which are like early European pageants, or even those of to-day in Catholic countries.

Thus the three sources of the Noh, all belonging to the first period, are, in the order of their influence, (1) the Shinto god dance, (2) the warrior court dance, (3) the Buddhist sacred pantomime.

As the old Chinese court dances were modified in the aristocratic life of the second period, it was natural that lovers of poetry should begin to add poetical comment to the entertainment. Thus the next step consisted in the addition of a text for a chorus to sing during the solo dance. They were already used to accompany their verses with the lute.

In the first of the five periods, Japanese lyric poetry reached its height. It was quite different from the Chinese, as the language is polysyllabic, the sentences long and smooth, the tone gently contemplative. About the year 900, when the capital had been removed to Kioto, the longer and straggling verse structure went out of fashion. A tense stanzaic form had come into almost universal use. This fashion may be referred to Chinese influence. Rhyme, however, was not introduced. The lines, usually of five or seven syllables, are rich and sonorous. Soon afterwards the passion for composing and reciting this Japanese poetry became so powerful among the educated classes, especially in the cultured aristocracy at Kioto, where men and women met on equal terms, that the old court entertainments of dance and music had to be modified to admit the use of poetic texts. At first the nobles themselves, at their feasts or at court ceremonies, sang in unison songs composed for the occasion. The next step was to write songs appropriate to the dances; finally the chorus of nobles became a trained chorus, accompanied by court musicians. Thus by the end of the ninth century there was a body of performers definitely associated with the court, with a minister in charge of it. There were two divisions. The composition of the texts and the composition of the music and dances were allotted to different persons. At this stage the old Chinese subjects fell into the background, and subjects of Japanese historical interest, or of more national and lyric nature, were substituted.

Thus arose the court entertainment called Saibara, which ceased to be practised after the twelfth century. Most of the details of it are hopelessly lost, though a few texts remain from a manuscript collection compiled about the year 900. The music and dance are utterly lost, except so far as we can discern a trace of what they must have been, in the later practices of the Noh. It is interesting to find that the very names of some of the pieces in Saibara are identical with those used in Noh five centuries later. The Saibara pieces are very short, much like the lyric poems of the day; and they are often so lyrical or so personal as hardly to suggest how they may have been danced. It is also uncertain whether these brief texts were repeated over and over, or at intervals during the long dance, or whether they were a mere introduction to a dance which elaborated their thought.[1] The following Saibara will serve as example:

> O white-gemmed camelia and you jewel willow,
> Who stand together on the Cape of Takasago!
> This one, since I want her for mine,
> That one, too, since I want her for mine—
> Jewel willow!
> I will make you a thing to hang my cloak on,
> With its tied-up strings, with its deep-dyed strings.
> Ah! what have I done?
> There, what is this I am doing?
> O what am I to do?
> Mayhap I have lost my soul!
> But I have met
> The lily flower,
> The first flower of morning.

[1] Professor Fenollosa, in an earlier half-sentence which I have omitted, would seem to underestimate the effect of the dance on European art forms. It was from the May-day dance and dance-songs that the Provençal poetry probably arose. By stages came strophe and antistrophe tenzone, the Spanish loa and entremes. See also W. P. Ker, 'English Mediaeval Literature', pp. 79 et seq., for the spread of the dance through Europe and the effect on the lyric forms. Compare also the first Saibara given in the text with the Provençal 'A l'entrada del temps clar'.

This new combination of dance and song soon spread from the court ceremonies to the religious rites of the god dances in the Shinto temples, not, however, to the Buddhist, which were too much under the influence of Hindu and Chinese thought to care for Japanese verse. In Shinto dances the subject was already pure Japanese and fit for Japanese texts; and it may very well have occurred to some priest, in one of the thousand Shinto matsuris (festivals) going on all over the land, to sing a poem concerning the subject of the dance. By the end of the ninth century, in the second period, this custom had become common in the great Shinto festivals, in the Mikado's private chapel, and at Kasuga. The texts were sung by a trained chorus, and here is a second difference from the line of Greek advance. In Greece the chorus not only sang but danced; in Japan the chorus did not dance or act, but was merely contemplative, sitting at the side. The songs so sung were called Kagura.

A few examples of these ancient Shinto texts for Kagura have come down to us. They are not exactly prayers; they are often lovely poems of nature, for, after all, these Shinto gods were a harmless kind of nature spirit clinging to grottoes, rivers, trees, and mountains. It is curious to note that the structure of the texts is always double, like the Greek strophe and antistrophe. They were probably sung by a double chorus; and this is doubtless the basis of the alternation or choric dialogue.

Here is a kagura, sung by a priestess to her wand:

Strophe As for this mitegura,
      As for this mitegura,
      It is not mine at all;
      It is the mitegura of a god,
      Called the Princess Toyooka,
      Who lives in heaven,
      The mitegura of a god,
      The mitegura of a god.

Antistrophe O how I wish in vain that I could turn myself into a
      mitegura,

That I might be taken into the hand of the Mother of
the Gods,
That I might come close to the heart of a god, close
to the heart of a god!

III

We have now come to the point where we can deal with this
mass of playwriting as literature. The plays are written in a
mixture of prose and verse. The finest parts are in verse; ordinary
conversation lapses into prose; the choruses are always in verse.

It appears that the first period of Japanese civilization supplied
the chance elements for the Noh, that is, the dances and certain
attitudes of mind. The second period supplied the beginnings of
literary texts. The third period, dating from the end of the twelfth
century, is marked by the rise of the military classes and supplied
naturally a new range of dramatic motives. The land was filled
with tales of wild achievement and knight-errantry and with a
passionate love for individuality, however humble. The old court
customs and dances of the supplanted nobles were kept up solely
in the peaceful enclosures of the Shinto temples. New forms of
entertainment arose. Buddhism threw away scholarship and
mystery, and aimed only at personal salvation. As in contemporary Europe, itinerant monks scoured the country, carrying inspiration from house to house. Thus arose a semi-epic literature, in
which the deeds of martial heroes were gathered into several great
cycles of legend, like the Carolingian and the Arthurian cycles in
Europe. Such were the Heike epic, the Soga cycle, and a dozen
others. Episodes from these were sung by individual minstrels to
the accompaniment of a lute. One of the most important effects
of this new epic balladry was to widen greatly the scope of
motives acceptable for plays.

As for comedy, another movement was growing up in the
country, from farmers' festivals, the spring sowing of the rice, and
the autumn reaping. These were at first mere buffooneries or
gymnastic contests arranged by the villagers for their amusement.
They were called Dengaku, a rice-field music. Later, professional
troupes of Dengaku jugglers and acrobats were kept by the

daimios in their palaces, and eventually by the authorities of the Buddhists and Shinto temples, in order to attract crowds to their periodic festivals. Such professional troupes began to add rude country farces to their stock of entertainments, at first bits of coarse impromptu repartee, consisting of tricks by rustics upon each other, which were probably not out of harmony with some of the more grotesque and comic Shinto dances. About the twelfth and thirteenth centuries these two elements of comedy—the rustic and the sacred—combined at the Shinto temples, and actors were trained as a permanent troupe. Such farces are called Kiogen. In the later part of the fourteenth century, towards the end, that is, of the third period, Dengaku troupes of Shinto dancers advanced to the incorporating of more tragic subjects, selected from the episodes of the balladry. The god dancer now became, sometimes, a human being, the hero of a dramatic crisis—sometimes even a woman, interchanging dialogue with the chorus, as the two ancient Shinto choruses had sung dialogue in the Kagura.

It was not till the fourth period of Japanese culture, that is to say, early in the fifteenth century, when a new Buddhist civilization, based upon contemplative and poetic insight into nature had arisen, that the inchoate Japanese drama, fostered in the Shinto temples, could take on a moral purpose and a psychologic breadth that should expand it into a vital drama of character. The Shinto god dance, the lyric form of court poetry, the country farces, and a full range of epic incident, in short, all that was best in the earlier Japanese tradition, was gathered into this new form, arranged and purified.

The change came about in this way. The Zen parish priests summoned up to Kioto the Dengaku troupe from Nara, and made it play before the Shogun. The head actor of this Nara troupe, Kwan, took the new solo parts, and greatly enlarged the scope of the music of the other acting. During the lifetime of his son and grandson, Zei and On, hundreds of new plays were created. It is a question to what extent these three men, Kwan, Zei, and On, were the originators of the texts of these new dramas, and how far the Zen priests are responsible. The lives of the former are even more obscure than is Shakespeare's. No full account exists of their work. We have only stray passages from contemporary notebooks relating to the great excitement caused by their irregular performances. A great temporary circus was erected on the dry bed of the Kamo river, with its storeys divided into boxes for each noble family, from the Emperor and the Shogun downwards. Great priests managed the show, and used the funds collected for building temples. The stage was a raised open circle in the centre, reached by a long bridge from a dressing-room outside the circus.

We can now see why, even in the full lyric drama, the god dance remains the central feature. All the slow and beautiful postures of the early dramatic portion invariably lead up to the climax of the hero's dance (just as the Greek had planned for the choric dances). This often comes only at the end of the second act, but sometimes also in the first. Most plays have two acts. During the closing dance the chorus sings its finest passages, though it will have been already engaged many times in dialogue with the soloist. Its function is poetical comment, and it carries the mind beyond what the action exhibits to the core of the spiritual meaning. The music is simple melody, hardly more than a chant, accompanied by drums and flutes. There is thus a delicate adjustment of half a dozen conventions appealing to eye, ear, or mind, which produces an intensity of feeling such as belongs to no merely realistic drama. The audience sits spellbound before the tragedy, bathed in tears; but the effect is never one of realistic horror, rather of a purified and elevated passion, which sees divine purpose under all violence.

The beauty and power of Noh lie in the concentration. All elements—costume, motion, verse, and music—unite to produce a single clarified impression. Each drama embodies some primary human relation or emotion; and the poetic sweetness or poignancy of this is carried to its highest degree by carefully excluding all such obtrusive elements as a mimetic realism or vulgar sensation might demand. The emotion is always fixed upon idea, not upon personality. The solo parts express great types of human character, derived from Japanese history. Now it is brotherly love, now love to a parent, now loyalty to a master, love of husband and wife, of mother for a dead child, or of jealousy or anger, of self-mastery in battle, of the battle passion itself, of the clinging of a ghost to the scene of its sin, of the infinite compassion of a Buddha, of the sorrow of unrequited love. Some one of these intense emotions is chosen for a piece, and, in it, elevated to the plane of universality by the intensity and purity of treatment. Thus the drama became a storehouse of history, and a great moral force for the whole social order of the Samurai.

After all, the most striking thing about these plays is their marvellously complete grasp of spiritual being. They deal more with heroes, or even we might say ghosts, than with men clothed in the flesh. Their creators were great psychologists. In no other drama does the supernatural play so great, so intimate a part. The types of ghosts are shown to us; we see great characters operating under the conditions of the spirit-life; we observe what forces have changed them. Bodhisattwa, devas, elementals, animal spirits, hungry spirits or pseta, cunning or malicious or angry devils, dragon kings from the water world, spirits of the moonlight, the souls of flowers and trees, essences that live in wine and fire, the semi-embodiments of a thought—all these come and move before us in the dramatic types.

These types of character are rendered particularly vivid to us by the sculptured masks. Spirits, women, and old men wear masks; other human beings do not. For the 200 plays now extant, nearly 300 separate masks are necessary in a complete list of properties. Such variety is far in excess of the Greek types, and immense vitality is given to a good mask by a great actor, who acts up to it until the very mask seems alive and displays a dozen turns of emotion. The costumes are less carefully individualized. For the hero parts, especially for spirits, they are very rich, of splendid gold brocades and soft floss-silk weaving, or of Chinese tapestry stitch, and are very costly. In Tokugawa days (1602–1868) every rich daimio had his own stage, and his complete collection of properties. The dancing is wonderful—a succession of beautiful poses which make a rich music of line. The whole body acts together, but with dignity. Great play is given to the sleeve, which is often tossed back and forth or raised above the head. The fan also plays a great part, serving for cup, paper, pen, sword, and a dozen other imaginary stage properties. The discipline of the actor is a moral one. He is trained to revere his profession, to make it a sacred act thus to impersonate a hero. He yields himself up to possession by the character. He acts as if he knew himself to be a god, and after the performance he is generally quite exhausted.

IV

In Dojoji a girl is in love with a priest, who flees from her and takes shelter under a great bronze temple bell, which falls over him. Her sheer force of desire turns her into a dragon, she bites the top of the bell, twists herself about the bell seven times, spits flame from her mouth, and lashes the bronze with her tail. Then the bell melts away under her, and the priest she loves dies in the molten mass. In Kumasaka the boy-warrior, Ushiwaka, fights a band of fifteen giant robbers in the dark. They fight with each other also. One by one, and two by two, they are all killed. At one time all are dancing in double combat across stage and bridge. The Noh fencing with spear and sword is superb in line. In the conventional Noh fall, two robbers, facing, who have killed each other with simultaneous blows, stand for a moment erect and stiff, then slowly fall over backward, away from each other, as stiff as logs, touching the stage at the same moment with head and heel.

In the play of Atsumori there is an interesting ghost, taken from the epic cycle of the Yoritomo. Atsumori was a young noble of the Heike family who was killed in one of Yoshitsumi's decisive battles. The priest who opens the final scene tells the story thus:

'I am one who serves the great Bishop Homeri Shonini in Kurodain temple. And that little one over there is the child of Atsumori, who was killed at Ichinotani. Once when the Shonini was going down to the Kamo river, he found a baby about two years old in a tattered basket under a pine tree. He felt great pity for the child, took it home with him, and cared for it tenderly. When the boy had grown to be ten years of age and was lamenting that he had no parents, the Shonini spoke about the matter to an audience which came to his preaching. Then a young woman came up, and cried excitedly, "This must be my child." On further enquiry he found it was indeed the child of the famous Atsumori. The child, having heard all this, is most desirous to see the image of his father, even in a dream, and he has been praying devoutly to this effect at the shrine of Kamo Miojin for seven days. To-day the term is up for the fulfilment of his vow, so I am taking him down to Kamo Miojin for his last prayer. Here we are at Kamo. Now, boy! pray well!'

During his prayer the boy hears a voice which tells him to go to the forest of Ikuta; and thither the priest and the boy journey. On arrival they look about at the beauty of the place, till suddenly nightfall surprises them. 'Look here, boy, the sun has set! What, is that a light yonder? Perhaps it may be a house? We will go to take lodging there.' A straw hut has been set at the centre of the stage. The curtain in front of it is now withdrawn, and the figure of a very young warrior is disclosed, in a mask, and wearing a dress of blue, white, and gold. He begins to speak to himself:

'Gowun! Gowun! The five possessions of man are all hollow. Why do we love this queer thing—body? The soul which dwells in agony flies about like a bat under the moon. The poor bewildered ghost that has lost its body whistles in the autumn wind.'

They think him a man, but he tells them he has had a half-hour's respite from hell. He looks wistfully at the boy, who wishes to seize him, and cries, 'Flower child of mine, left behind in the world, like a favourite carnation, how pitiful to see you in those black sleeves!' Then the spirit dances with restraint, while the chorus chants the martial scene of his former death. 'Rushing like two clouds together they were scattered in a whirlwind.' Suddenly he stops, looks off the stage, and stamps, shouting:

Who is that over there? A messenger from hell?
Yes, why do you stay so late? King Enma is angry.

Then the grim warriors frantically rush across the stage like Valkyrie, and Atsumori is forced to fight with a spear in a tremendous mystic dance against them. This is a vision of his torment transferred to earth. Exhausted and bleeding he falls; the hell fires vanish; and crying out, 'Oh, how shameful that you should see me thus,' he melts away from the frantic clutches of the weeping boy.

Among the most weird and delicately poetic pieces is Nishikigi, in which the hero and heroine are the ghosts of two lovers who died unmarried a hundred years before. Their spirits are in the course of the play united near a hillside grave where their bodies had long lain together. This spiritual union is brought about by the piety of a priest. Action, words, and music are vague and ghostly shadows. The lover, as a young man, had waited before the girl's door every night for months, but she, from ignorance or coquetry, had refused to notice him. Then he died of despair. She repented of her cruelty and died also.

The play opens with the entrance of the travelling priest, who has wandered to the ancient village of Kefu in the far north of the island. He meets the two ghosts in ancient attire. At first he supposes them to be villagers. He does not seem to notice their dress, or, if he does, he apparently mistakes it for some fashion of the province. Then the two ghosts sing together, as if muttering to themselves:

We are entangled—whose fault was it, dear?—tangled up as the grass patterns are tangled in this coarse cloth, or that insect which lives and chirrups in dried seaweed. We do not know where are to-day our tears in the undergrowth of this eternal wilderness. We neither wake nor sleep, and passing our nights in a sorrow, which is in the end a vision, what are these scenes of spring to us? This thinking in sleep of some one who has no thought for you, is it more than a dream? And yet surely it is the natural way of love. In our hearts there is much and in our bodies nothing, and we do nothing at all, and only the waters of the river of tears flow quickly.

Then the priest says:

'It is strange, seeing these town-people here. I might suppose them two married people; and what the lady gives herself the trouble of carrying might be a piece of cloth woven from birds' feathers, and what the man has is a sword, painted red. It is indeed queer merchandise.'

Gradually they tell him the story—they do not say at first that it is their own story. Two people had lived in that village, one of whom had offered the nishikigi, the charm-sticks, the 'crimson tokens of love,' night after night for three years. That was the man, of course; and the girl, apparently oblivious, had sat inside her house, weaving long bands of cloth. They say that the man was buried in a cave and all his charm-sticks with him. The priest says it will be a fine tale for him to tell when he gets home, and says he will go see the tomb, to which they offer to guide him. Then the chorus for the first time sings:

'The couple are passing in front and the stranger behind, having spent the whole day until dusk, pushing aside the rank grass from the narrow paths about Kefu. Where, indeed, for them is that love-grave? Ho! you farmer there, cutting grass upon the hill, tell me clearly how I am to get on further. In this frosty night, of whom shall we ask about the dews on the wayside grass?'

Then the hero, the man's ghost, breaks in for a moment: 'Oh how cold it is in these evening dusks of autumn!' And the chorus resumes:

'Storms, fallen leaves, patches of the autumn showers clogging the feet, the eternal shadow of the long-sloped mountain, and, crying among the ivies on the pine tree, an owl! And as for the love-grave, dyed like the leaves of maple with the tokens of by-gone passion, and like the orchids and chrysanthemums which hide the mouth of a fox's hole, they have slipped into the shadow of the cave; this brave couple has vanished into the love-grave.'

After an interval, for the changing of the spirits' costumes, the second act begins. The priest cannot sleep in the frost, and thinks he had better pass the night in prayer. Then the spirits in masks steal out, and in mystic language, which he does not hear, try to thank him for his prayer, and say that through his pity the love promise of incarnations long perished is now just realized, even in dream. Then the priest says:

'How strange! That place, which seemed like an old grave, is now lighted up from within, and has become like a human dwelling, where people are talking and setting up looms for spinning, and painted sticks. It must be an illusion!'

Then follows a wonderful loom song and chorus, comparing

284

the sound of weaving to the clicking of crickets; and in a vision is seen the old tragic story, and the chorus sings that 'their tears had become a colour.' 'But now they shall see the secret bride-room.' The hero cries, 'And we shall drink the cup of meeting.' Then the ghostly chorus sings a final song:

> How glorious the sleeves of the dance
> That are like snow-whirls.

But now the wine-cup of the night-play is reflecting the first hint of the dawn. Perhaps we shall feel awkward when it becomes really morning. And like a dream which is just about to break, the stick and the cloth are breaking up, and the whole place has turned into a deserted grave on a hill, where morning winds are blowing through the pines.

ERNEST FENOLLOSA
(? about 1906)

NISHIKIGI[1]

A Play in two Acts, by Motokiyo

CHARACTERS

THE WAKI, a priest.
THE SHITE, or HERO, ghost of the lover.
TSURE, ghost of the woman; they have both been long dead, and
    have not been united.
A CHORUS.

PART FIRST

WAKI

There never was anybody heard of Mt. Shinobu but had a
kindly feeling for it; so I, like any other priest that might want to
know a little bit about each one of the provinces, may as well be
walking up here along the much-travelled road.

I have not yet been about the east country, but now I have set
my mind to go as far as the earth goes, and why shouldn't I, after
all? seeing that I go about with my heart set upon no particular
place whatsoever, and with no other man's flag in my hand, no
more than a cloud has. It is a flag of the night I see coming down
upon me. I wonder now, would the sea be that way, or the little
place Kefu that they say is stuck down against it.

SHITE AND TSURE

Times out of mind am I here setting up this bright branch, this
silky wood with the charms painted in it as fine as the web you'd
get in the grass-cloth of Shinobu, that they'd be still selling you
in this mountain.

SHITE
(*to* TSURE)

Tangled, we are entangled. Whose fault was it, dear? tangled
up as the grass patterns are tangled in this coarse cloth, or as the

---

[1] The 'Nishikigi' are wands used as a love-charm. 'Hosonuno' is the name of a
local cloth which the woman weaves.

little Mushi that lives on and chirrups in dried seaweed. We do not know where are to-day our tears in the undergrowth of this eternal wilderness. We neither wake nor sleep, and passing our nights in a sorrow which is in the end a vision, what are these scenes of spring to us? this thinking in sleep of some one who has no thought of you, is it more than a dream? and yet surely it is the natural way of love. In our hearts there is much and in our bodies nothing, and we do nothing at all, and only the waters of the river of tears flow quickly.

CHORUS

Narrow is the cloth of Kefu, but wild is that river, that torrent of the hills, between the beloved and the bride.

The cloth she had woven is faded, the thousand one hundred nights were night-trysts watched out in vain.

WAKI

(not recognizing the nature of the speakers)

Strange indeed, seeing these town-people here,
They seem like man and wife,
And the lady seems to be holding something
Like a cloth woven of feathers,
While he has a staff or a wooden sceptre
Beautifully ornate.
Both of these things are strange;
In any case, I wonder what they call them.

TSURE

This is a narrow cloth called 'Hosonuno,'
It is just the breadth of the loom.

SHITE

And this is merely wood painted,
And yet the place is famous because of these things.
Would you care to buy them from us?

WAKI

Yes, I know that the cloth of this place and the lacquers are famous things. I have already heard of their glory, and yet I still wonder why they have such great reputation.

TSURE

Well now, that's a disappointment. Here they call the wood 'Nishikigi,' and the woven stuff 'Hosonuno', and yet you come saying that you have never heard why, and never heard the story. Is it reasonable?

SHITE

No, no, that is reasonable enough. What can people be expected to know of these affairs when it is more than they can do to keep abreast of their own?

BOTH

(to the PRIEST)

Ah well, you look like a person who has abandoned the world; it is reasonable enough that you should not know the worth of wands and cloths with love's signs painted upon them, with love's marks painted and dyed.

WAKI

That is a fine answer. And you would tell me then that Nishi-kigi and Hosonuno are names bound over with love?

SHITE

They are names in love's list surely. Every day for a year, for three years come to their full, the wands, Nishikigi, were set up, until there were a thousand in all. And they are in song in your time, and will be. 'Chidzuka' they call them.

TSURE

These names are surely a byword.
As the cloth Hosonuno is narrow of weft,
More narrow than the breast,
We call by this name any woman
Whose breasts are hard to come nigh to.
It is a name in books of love.

SHITE

'Tis a sad name to look back on.

TSURE

A thousand wands were in vain.
A sad name, set in a story.

SHITE

A seed pod void of the seed,
We had no meeting together.

TSURE

Let him read out the story.

CHORUS

At last they forget, they forget.
The wands are no longer offered,
The custom is faded away.
The narrow cloth of Kefu
Will not meet over the breast.
'Tis the story of Hosonuno,
This is the tale:
These bodies, having no weft,
Even now are not come together.
Truly a shameful story,

A tale to bring shame on the gods.
Names of love,
Now for a little spell,
For a faint charm only,
For a charm as slight as the binding together
Of pine-flakes in Iwashiro,
And for saying a wish over them about sunset,
We return, and return to our lodging.
The evening sun leaves a shadow.

WAKI

Go on, tell out all the story.

SHITE

There is an old custom of this country. We make wands of mediation and deck them with symbols and set them before a gate when we are suitors.

TSURE

And we women take up a wand of the man we would meet with, and let the others lie, although a man might come for a hundred nights, it may be, or for a thousand nights in three years, till there were a thousand wands here in the shade of this mountain. We know the funeral cave of such a man, one who had watched out the thousand nights; a bright cave, for they buried him with all his wands. They have named it the 'Cave of the many charms.'

WAKI

I will go to that love-cave,
It will be a tale to take back to my village.
Will you show me my way there?

SHITE

So be it, I will teach you the path.

TSURE

Tell him to come over this way.

BOTH

Here are the pair of them
Going along before the traveller.

CHORUS

We have spent the whole day until dusk
Pushing aside the grass
From the overgrown way at Kefu,
And we are not come to the cave.
O you there, cutting grass on the hill,
Please set your mind on this matter.
  'You'd be asking where the dew is
  'While the frost's lying here on the road.
  'Who'd tell you that now?'
Very well, then, don't tell us,
But be sure we will come to the cave.

SHITE

There's a cold feel in the autumn.
Night comes. . . .

CHORUS

And storms; trees giving up their leaf,
Spotted with sudden showers.
Autumn! our feet are clogged
In the dew-drenched, entangled leaves.
The perpetual shadow is lonely,
The mountain shadow is lying alone.
The owl cries out from the ivies
That drag their weight on the pine.
Among the orchids and chrysanthemum flowers
The hiding fox is now lord of that love-cave,
Nishidzuka,
That is dyed like the maple's leaf.
They have left us this thing for a saying.
That pair have gone into the cave.

[*Sign for the exit of* SHITE *and* TSURE.

PART SECOND

(The Waki has taken the posture of sleep. His respectful visit
to the cave is beginning to have its effect.)

WAKI
(*restless*)

It seems that I cannot sleep
For the length of a pricket's horn.
Under October wind, under pines, under night!
I will do service to Butsu.

[*He performs the gestures of a ritual.*

TSURE

Aïe, honoured priest!
You do not dip twice in the river
Beneath the same tree's shadow
Without bonds in some other life.

291

Hear soothsay,
Now is there meeting between us,
Between us who were until now
In life and in after-life kept apart.
A dream-bridge over wild grass,
Over the grass I dwell in.
O honoured! do not awake me by force.
I see that the law is perfect.

SHITE
(*supposedly invisible*)

It is a good service you have done, sir,
A service that spreads in two worlds,
And binds up an ancient love
That was stretched out between them.
I had watched for a thousand days.
I give you largess,
For this meeting is under a difficult law.
And now I will show myself in the form of Nishikigi.
I will come out now for the first time in colour.

CHORUS

The three years are over and past:
All that is but an old story.

SHITE

To dream under dream we return.
Three years. . . . And the meeting comes now!
This night has happened over and over,
And only now comes the tryst.

CHORUS

Look there to the cave
Beneath the stems of the Suzuki.
From under the shadow of the love-grass,
See, see how they come forth and appear
For an instant. . . . Illusion!

NISHIKIGI

Shite

There is at the root of hell
No distinction between princes and commons;
Wretched for me! 'tis the saying.

Waki

Strange, what seemed so very old a cave
Is all glittering-bright within,
Like the flicker of fire.
It is like the inside of a house.
They are setting up a loom,
And heaping up charm-sticks. No,
The hangings are out of old time.
Is it illusion, illusion?

Tsure

Our hearts have been in the dark of the falling snow,
We have been astray in the flurry.
You should tell better than we
How much is illusion,
You who are in the world.
We have been in the whirl of those who are fading.

Shite

Indeed in old times Narihira said
(And he has vanished with the years),
'Let a man who is in the world tell the fact.'
It is for you, traveller,
To say how much is illusion.

Waki

Let it be a dream, or a vision,
Or what you will, I care not.
Only show me the old times over-past and snowed under;
Now, soon, while the night lasts.

Shite

Look, then, for the old times are shown,
Faint as the shadow-flower shows in the grass that bears it;
And you've but a moon for lanthorn.

TSURE

The woman has gone into the cave.
She sets up her loom there
For the weaving of Hosonuno,
Thin as the heart of Autumn.

SHITE

The suitor for his part, holding his charm-sticks,
Knocks on a gate which was barred.

TSURE

In old time he got back no answer,
No secret sound at all
Save . . .

SHITE

. . . the sound of the loom.

TSURE

It was a sweet sound like katydids and crickets,
A thin sound like the Autumn.

SHITE

It was what you would hear any night.

TSURE

Kiri.

SHITE

Hatari.

TSURE

Cho.

SHITE

Cho.

CHORUS
(*mimicking the sound of crickets*)

Kiri, hatari, cho, cho,
Kiri, hatari, cho, cho.
The cricket sews on at his old rags,

With all the new grass in the field; sho,
Churr, isho, like the whirr of a loom: churr.

CHORUS
(antistrophe)
Let be, they make grass-cloth in Kefu,
Kefu, the land's end, matchless in the world.

SHITE
That is an old custom, truly,
But this priest would look on the past.

CHORUS
The good priest himself would say:
Even if we weave the cloth, Hosonuno,
And set up the charm-sticks
For a thousand, a hundred nights;
Even then our beautiful desire will not pass,
Nor fade nor die out.

SHITE
Even to-day the difficulty of our meeting is remembered,
And is remembered in song.

CHORUS
That we may acquire power,
Even in our faint substance.
We will show forth even now,
And though it be but in a dream,
Our form of repentance.
       [*Explaining the movement of the* SHITE *and* TSURE
There he is carrying wands,
And she had no need to be asked.
See her within the cave,
With a cricket-like noise of weaving.
The grass-gates and the hedge are between them,
That is a symbol.
Night has already come on.

[*Now explaining the thoughts of the man's spirit.*

Love's thoughts are heaped high within him,
As high as the charm-sticks,
As high as the charm-sticks, once coloured,
Now fading, lie heaped in this cave;
And he knows of their fading. He says:
I lie, a body, unknown to any other man,
Like old wood buried in moss.
It were a fit thing
That I should stop thinking the love-thoughts,
The charm-sticks fade and decay,
And yet,
The rumour of our love
Takes foot, and moves through the world.
We had no meeting.
But tears have, it seems, brought out a bright blossom
Upon the dyed tree of love.

SHITE

Tell me, could I have foreseen
Or known what a heap of my writings
Should lie at the end of her shaft-bench?

CHORUS

A hundred nights and more
Of twisting, encumbered sleep,
And now they make it a ballad,
Not for one year or for two only,
But until the days lie deep
As the sand's depth at Kefu.
Until the year's end is red with autumn,
Red like these love-wands,
A thousand nights are in vain.
I, too, stand at this gate-side:
You grant no admission, you do not show yourself
Until I and my sleeves are faded.
By the dew-like gemming of tears upon my sleeve,
Why will you grant no admission?

NISHIKIGI

And we all are doomed to pass
You, and my sleeves and my tears.
And you did not even know when three years had come to an
    end.
Cruel, ah, cruel!
The charm-sticks . . .

SHITE

    . . . were set up a thousand times;
Then, now, and for always.

CHORUS

Shall I ever at last see into that secret bride-room, which no other
    sight has traversed?

SHITE

Happy at last and well-starred,
Now comes the eve of betrothal;
We meet for the wine-cup.

CHORUS

How glorious the sleeves of the dance,
That are like snow-whirls!

SHITE

Tread out the dance.

CHORUS

Tread out the dance and bring music.
This dance is for Nishikigi.

SHITE

This dance is for the evening plays,
And for the weaving.

CHORUS

For the tokens between lover and lover:
It is a reflecting in the wine-cup.

CHORUS

Ari-aki,
The dawn!

Come, we are out of place;
Let us go ere the light comes,

[*To the* WAKI.

We ask you, do not awake,
We all will wither away.
The wands and this cloth of a dream.
Now you will come out of sleep,
You tread the border and nothing
Awaits you: no, all this will wither away.
There is nothing here but this cave in the field's midst.
To-day's wind moves in the pines;
A wild place, unlit, and unfilled.

KINUTA

CHARACTERS
WAKI, a country gentleman.
TSURE, the servant-maid YUGIRI.
SHITE, the wife.
Second Shite, ghost of the wife.

In Kinuta ('The Silk-board') the plot is as follows:
The Waki, a country gentleman, has tarried long in the capital.
He at last sends the Tsure, a maid-servant, home with a message
to his wife. The servant talks on the road. She reaches the Waki's
house and talks with the Shite (the wife). The chorus comments.
Finally, the wife dies. The chorus sing a death-song, after which
the husband returns. The second Shite, the ghost of the wife, then
appears, and continues speaking alternately with the chorus until
the close.

HUSBAND
I am of Ashiya of Kinshu, unknown and of no repute. I have
been loitering on in the capital entangled in many litigations. I
went for a casual visit, and there I have been tarrying for three full
years. Now I am anxious, over-anxious, about affairs in my home.
I shall send Yugiri homeward; she is a maid in my employ. Ho!
Yugiri! I am worried. I shall send you down to the country. You
will go home and tell them that I return at the end of this year.

MAID-SERVANT
I will go, Sir, and say that then you are surely coming. (*She
starts on her journey.*) The day is advancing, and I, in my travelling
clothes, travel with the day. I do not know the lodgings, I do not
know the dreams upon the road, I do not know the number of the
dreams that gather for one night's pillow. At length I am come
to the village—it is true that I was in haste—I am come at last to
Ashiya. I think I will call out gently. 'Is there any person or thing

299

in this house? Say that Yugiri is here in the street, she has just come back from the city.'

WIFE

Sorrow!—
Sorrow is in the twigs of the duck's nest
And in the pillow of the fishes,
At being held apart in the waves,
Sorrow between mandarin ducks,
Who have been in love
Since time out of mind.
Sorrow—
There is more sorrow between the united
Though they move in the one same world.
O low 'Remembering-grass',
I do not forget to weep
At the sound of the rain upon you,
My tears are a rain in the silence,
O heart of the seldom clearing.

MAID-SERVANT

Say to whomsoever it concerns that Yugiri has come.

WIFE

What! you say it is Yugiri? There is no need for a servant. Come to this side! in here! How is this, Yugiri, that you are so great a stranger? Yet welcome. I have cause of complaint. If you were utterly changed, why did you send me no word? Not even a message in the current of the wind?

MAID-SERVANT

Truly I wished to come, but his Honour gave me no leisure. For three years he kept me in that very ancient city.

WIFE

You say it was against your heart to stay in the city? While even in the time of delights I thought of its blossom, until sorrow had grown the cloak of my heart.

KINUTA

CHORUS

As the decline of autumn
In a country dwelling,
With the grasses failing and fading—
As men's eyes fail—
As men's eyes fail,
Love has utterly ceased.
Upon what shall she lean to-morrow?
A dream of the autumn, three years,
Until the sorrow of those dreams awakes
Autumnal echoes within her.
Now former days are changed,
They have left no shadow or trace;
And if there were no lies in all the world
Then there might come some pleasure
Upon the track of men's words.
Alas, for her foolish heart!
How foolish her trust has been.

WIFE

What strange thing is it beyond there that takes the forms of sound? Tell me. What is it?

MAID-SERVANT

A villager beating a silk-board.

WIFE

Is that all? And I am weary as an old saying. When the wandering Sobu[1] of China was in the Mongol country he also had left a wife and children, and she, aroused upon the clear cold nights, climbed her high tower and beat such a silk-board, and had perhaps some purpose of her heart. For that far-murmuring cloth could move his sleep—that is the tale—though he were leagues away. Yet I have stretched my board with patterned cloths, which curious birds brought through the twilit utter solitude, and hoped with such that I might ease my heart.

[1] So Wu.

MAID-SERVANT

Boards are rough work, hard even for the poor, and you of high rank have done this to ease your heart! Here, let me arrange them, I am better fit for such business.

WIFE

Beat then. Beat out our resentment.

MAID-SERVANT

It's a coarse mat; we can never be sure.

CHORUS

The voice of the pine-trees sinks ever into the web!
The voice of the pine-trees, now falling,
Shall make talk in the night.
It is cold.

WIFE

Autumn it is, and news rarely comes in your fickle wind, the frost comes bearing no message.

CHORUS

Weariness tells of the night.

WIFE

Even a man in a very far village might see. . . .

CHORUS

Perhaps the moon will not call upon her, saying: 'Whose night-world is this?'

WIFE

O beautiful season, say also this time is toward autumn, 'The evening moves to an end.'

CHORUS

The stag's voice has bent her heart toward sorrow,
Sending the evening winds which she does not see,
We cannot see the tip of the branch.
The last leaf falls without witness.
There is an awe in the shadow,

And even the moon is quiet,
With the love-grass under the eaves.

WIFE

My blind soul hangs like a curtain studded with dew.

CHORUS

What a night to unsheave her sorrows—
An hour for magic—
And that cloth-frame stands high on the palace;
The wind rakes it from the north.

WIFE

They beat now fast and now slow—are they silk-workers down in the village? The moon-river pours on the west.

CHORUS
(*strophe*)

The wandering Sobu is asleep in the North country,
And here in the East-sky the autumnal wind is working about from the West.
Wind, take up the sound she is beating upon her coarse-webbed cloth.

CHORUS
(*antistrophe*)

Beware of even the pines about the eaves,
Lest they confuse the sound.
Beware that you do not lose the sound of the travelling storm,
That travels after your travels.
Take up the sound of this beating of the cloths.

Go where her lord is, O Wind; my heart reaches out and can be seen by him; I pray that you keep him still dreaming.

WIFE

Aoi! if the web is broken, who, weary with time, will then come and seek me out? If at last he should come to seek me, let him call in the deep of time. Cloths are changed by recutting, hateful! love thin as a summer cloth! Let my lord's life be even so slight, for I have no sleep under the moon. O let me go on with my cloths!

Chorus

The love of a god with a goddess
Is but for the one night in passing,
So thin are the summer cloths!
The river-waves of the sky
Have cut through our time like shears,
They have kept us apart with dew.
There are tears on the Kaji leaf,
There is dew upon the helm-bar
Of the skiff in the twisting current.
Will it harm the two sleeves of the gods
If he pass?
As a floating shadow of the water grass,
That the ripples break on the shore?
O foam, let him be as brief.

Wife

The seventh month is come to its seventh day; we are hard on the time of long nights, and I would send him the sadness of these ten thousand voices—the colour of the moon, the breath-colour of the wind, even the points of frost that assemble in the shadow. A time that brings awe to the heart, a sound of beaten cloths, and storms in the night, a crying in the storm, a sad sound of the crickets, make one sound in the falling dew, a whispering lamentation, hera, hera, a sound in the cloth of beauty.

Maid-servant

What shall I say to all this? A man has just come from the city. The master will not come this year. It seems as if . . .

Chorus

The heart, that thinks that it will think no more, grows fainter; outside in the withered field the crickets' noise has gone faint. The flower lies open to the wind, the gazers pass on to madness, this flower-heart of the grass is blown on by a wind-life madness, until at last she is but emptiness.

[*The wife dies. Enter the husband, returning.*

HUSBAND

Pitiful hate, for my three years' delay, working within her has turned our long-drawn play of separation to separation indeed.

CHORUS

The time of regret comes not before the deed,
This we have heard from the eight thousand shadows.
This is their chorus—the shadowy blades of grass.
Sorrow! to be exchanging words
At the string-tip—
Sorrow! that we can but speak
With the bow-tip of the adzusa!
The way that a ghost returns
From the shadow of the grass—
We have heard the stories,
It is eight thousand times, they say,
Before regret runs in a smooth-worn groove,
Forestalls itself.

GHOST OF THE WIFE

Aoi! for fate, fading, alas, and unformed, all sunk into the river of three currents, gone from the light of the plum flowers that reveal spring in the world!

CHORUS

She has but kindling flame to light her track . . .

GHOST OF THE WIFE

. . . and show her autumns of a lasting moon.[1] And yet, who had not fallen into desire? It was easy, in the rising and falling of the smoke and the fire of thought, to sink so deep in desires. O heart, you were entangled in the threads. 'Suffering' and 'the Price' are their names. There is no end to the lashes of Aborasetsu, the jailor of this prison. O heart, in your utter extremity you beat the silks of remorse; to the end of all false desire Karma shows her hate.

[1] I.e. a moon that has no phases.

CHORUS

Ah false desire and fate!
Her tears are shed on the silk-board,
Tears fall and turn into flame,
The smoke has stifled her cries,
She cannot reach us at all,
Nor yet the beating of the silk-board
Nor even the voice of the pines,
But only the voice of that sorrowful punishment.

Aoi! Aoi!

Slow as the pace of sleep,
Swift as the steeds of time,
By the six roads of changing and passing
We do not escape from the wheel,
Nor from the flaming of Karma,
Though we wander through life and death;
This woman fled from his horses
To a world without taste or breath.

GHOST OF THE WIFE

Even the leaves of the katsu-grass show their hate of this under-world by the turning away of their leaves.

CHORUS

The leaves of the katsu show their hate by bending aside; and neither can they unbend nor can the face of o'ershadowed desire. O face of eagerness, though you had loved him truly through both worlds, and hope had clung a thousand generations, 'twere little avail. The cliffs of Matsuyama, with stiff pines, stand in the end of time; your useless speech is but false mocking, like the elfish waves. Aoi! Aoi! Is this the heart of man?

GHOST OF THE WIFE

It is the great, false bird called 'Taking-care.'

CHORUS

Who will call him a true man—the wandering husband—when even the plants know their season, the feathered and furred have their hearts? It seems that our story has set a fact beyond fable. Even Sobu, afar, gave to the flying wild-duck a message to be borne through the southern country, over a thousand leagues, so deep was his heart's current—not shallow the love in his heart. Kimi, you have no drowsy thought of me, and no dream of yours reaches toward me. Hateful, and why? O hateful!

Chorus

She recites the Flower of Law; and ghost is received into Butsu; the road has become enlightened. Her constant beating of silk has opened the flower, even so lightly she has entered the seed-pod of Butsu.

HAGOROMO

A Play in one Act

CHARACTERS
CHIEF FISHERMAN, HAKURYO.
A FISHERMAN.
A TENNIN.
CHORUS.

The plot of the play Hagoromo, the Feather-mantle, is as follows: The priest finds the Hagoromo, the magical feather-mantle of a Tennin, an aerial spirit or celestial dancer, hanging upon a bough. She demands its return. He argues with her, and finally promises to return it, if she will teach him her dance or part of it. She accepts the offer. The Chorus explains the dance as symbolical of the daily changes of the moon. The words about 'three, five, and fifteen' refer to the number of nights in the moon's changes. In the finale, the Tennin is supposed to disappear like a mountain slowly hidden in mist. The play shows the relation of the early Noh to the God-dance.

HAKURYO

Windy road of the waves by Miwo,
Swift with ships, loud over steersmen's voices.

Hakuryo, taker of fish, head of his house, dwells upon the barren pine-waste of Miwo.

A FISHERMAN

Upon a thousand heights had gathered the inexplicable cloud. Swept by the rain, the moon is just come to light the high house.

A clean and pleasant time surely. There comes the breath-colour of spring; the waves rise in a line below the early mist; the moon is still delaying above, though we've no skill to grasp it. Here is a beauty to set the mind above itself.

HAGOROMO

CHORUS

I shall not be out of memory
Of the mountain road by Kiyomi,
Nor of the parted grass by that bay,
Nor of the far seen pine-waste
Of Miwo of wheat stalks.

Let us go according to custom. Take hands against the wind here, for it presses the clouds and the sea. Those men who were going to fish are about to return without launching. Wait a little, is it not spring? will not the wind be quiet? This wind is only the voice of the lasting pine-trees, ready for stillness. See how the air is soundless, or would be, were it not for the waves. There now, the fishermen are putting out with even the smallest boats.

HAKURYO

I am come to shore at Miwo-no; I disembark in Matsubara; I see all that they speak of on the shore. An empty sky with music, a rain of flowers, strange fragrance on every side; all these are no common things, nor is this cloak that hangs upon the pine-tree. As I approach to inhale its colour, I am aware of mystery. Its colour-smell is mysterious. I see that it is surely no common dress. I will take it now and return and make it a treasure in my house, to show to the aged.

TENNIN

That cloak belongs to some one on this side. What are you proposing to do with it?

HAKURYO

This? this is a cloak picked up. I am taking it home, I tell you.

TENNIN

That is a feather-mantle not fit for a mortal to bear,
Not easily wrested from the sky-traversing spirit,
Not easily taken or given.
I ask you to leave it where you found it.

HAKURYO

How! Is the owner of this cloak a Tennin? So be it. In this downcast age I should keep it, a rare thing, and make it a treasure in the country, a thing respected. Then I should not return it.

TENNIN

Pitiful, there is no flying without the cloak of feathers, no return through the ether. I pray you return me the mantle.

HAKURYO

Just from hearing these high words, I, Hakuryo, have gathered more and yet more force. You think, because I was too stupid to recognize it, that I shall be unable to take and keep hid the feather-robe, that I shall give it back for merely being told to stand and withdraw?

TANNIN

A Tennin without her robe,
A bird without wings,
How shall she climb the air?

HAKURYO

And this world would be a sorry place for her to dwell in?

TENNIN

I am caught, I struggle, how shall I . . .?

HAKURYO

No, Hakuryo is not one to give back the robe.

TENNIN

Power does not attain . . .

HAKURYO

. . . to get back the robe. . . .

CHORUS

Her coronet,[1] jewelled as with the dew of tears, even the flowers that decorated her hair, drooping and fading, the whole

---

[1] Vide examples of state head-dress of kingfisher feathers in the South Kensington Museum.

chain of weaknesses[1] of the dying Tennin can be seen actually before the eyes. Sorrow!

TENNIN

I look into the flat of heaven, peering; the cloud-road is all hidden and uncertain; we are lost in the rising mist; I have lost the knowledge of the road. Strange, a strange sorrow?

CHORUS

Enviable colour of breath, wonder of clouds that fade along the sky that was our accustomed dwelling; hearing the sky-bird, accustomed, and well accustomed, hearing the voices grow fewer, the wild geese fewer and fewer, along the highways of air, how deep her longing to return! Plover and seagull are on the waves in the offing. Do they go or do they return? She reaches out for the very blowing of the spring wind against heaven.

HAKURYO
(*to the* TENNIN)

What do you say? Now that I can see you in your sorrow, gracious, of heaven, I bend and would return you your mantle.

TENNIN

It grows clearer. No, give it this side.

HAKURYO

First tell me your nature, who are you, Tennin? Give payment with the dance of the Tennin, and I will return you your mantle.

TENNIN

Readily and gladly, and then I return into heaven. You shall have what pleasure you will, and I will leave a dance here, a joy to be new among men and to be memorial dancing. Learn then this dance that can turn the palace of the moon. No, come here to learn it. For the sorrows of the world I will leave this new dancing with you for sorrowful people. But give me my mantle, I cannot do the dance rightly without it.

---

[1] The chain of weaknesses, or the five ills, diseases of the Tennin: namely, the Tamakadzura withers; the Hagoromo is stained; sweat comes from the body; both eyes wink frequently; she feels very weary of her palace in heaven.

HAKURYO

Not yet, for if you should get it, how do I know you'll not be off to your palace without even beginning your dance, not even a measure?

TENNIN

Doubt is of mortals; with us there is no deceit.

HAKURYO

I am again ashamed. I give you your mantle.

CHORUS

The young sprite now is arrayed, she assumes the curious mantle; watch how she moves in the dance of the rainbow-feathered garment.

HAKURYO

The heavenly feather-robe moves in accord with the wind.

TENNIN

The sleeves of flowers are being wet with the rain.

HAKURYO

All three are doing one step.

CHORUS

It seems that she dances.
Thus was the dance of pleasure,
Suruga dancing, brought to the sacred east.
Thus was it when the lords of the everlasting
Trod the world,
They being of old our friends.
Upon ten sides their sky is without limit,
They have named it, on this account, the enduring.

TENNIN

The jewelled axe takes up the eternal renewing, the palace of the moon-god is being renewed with the jewelled axe, and this is always recurring.

Chorus

(commenting on the dance)

The white kiromo, the black kiromo,
Three, five into fifteen,
The figure that the Tennin is dividing.
There are heavenly nymphs, Amaotome,[1]
One for each night of the month,
And each with her deed assigned.

Tennin

I also am heaven-born and a maid, Amaotome. Of them there
are many. This is the dividing of my body, that is fruit of the
moon's tree, Katsura.[2] This is one part of our dance that I leave
to you here in your world.

Chorus

The spring mist is widespread abroad; so perhaps the wild
olive's flower will blossom in the infinitely unreachable moon.
Her flowery head-ornament is putting on colour; this truly is sign
of the spring. Not sky is here, but the beauty; and even here comes
the heavenly, wonderful wind. O blow shut the accustomed path
of the clouds. O, you in the form of a maid, grant us the favour of
your delaying. The pine-waste of Miwo puts on the colour of
spring. The bay of Kiyomi lies clear before the snow upon Fuji.
Are not all these presages of the spring? There are but few ripples
beneath the piny wind. It is quiet along the shore. There is naught
but a fence of jewels between the earth and the sky, and the gods
within and without,[3] beyond and beneath the stars, and the moon
unclouded by her lord, and we who are born of the sun. This
alone intervenes, here where the moon is unshadowed, here in
Nippon, the sun's field.

Tennin

The plumage of heaven drops neither feather nor flame to its own
diminution.

[1] Cf. 'Paradiso', xxiii. 25:
    'Quale nei plenilunii sereni
    Trivia ride tra le ninfe eterne.'
[2] A tree something like the laurel.
[3] 'Within and without', gei, gu, two parts of the temple.

Chorus

Nor is this rock of earth overmuch worn by the brushing of that feather-mantle, the feathery skirt of the stars: rarely, how rarely. There is a magic song from the east, the voices of many and many: and flute and sho, filling the space beyond the cloud's edge, seven-stringed; dance filling and filling. The red sun blots on the sky the line of the colour-drenched mountains. The flowers rain in a gust; it is no racking storm that comes over this green moor, which is afloat, as it would seem, in these waves.

Wonderful is the sleeve of the white cloud, whirling such snow here.

Tennin

Plain of life, field of the sun, true foundation, great power!

Chorus

Hence and for ever this dancing shall be called 'a revel in the East.' Many are the robes thou hast, now of the sky's colour itself, and now a green garment.

Semi-Chorus

And now the robe of mist, presaging spring, a colour-smell as this wonderful maiden's skirt—left, right, left! The rustling of flowers, the putting on of the feathery sleeve; they bend in air with the dancing.

Semi-Chorus

Many are the joys in the east. She who is the colour-person of the moon takes her middle-night in the sky. She marks her three fives with this dancing, as a shadow of all fulfilments. The circled vows are at full. Give the seven jewels of rain and all of the treasure, you who go from us. After a little time, only a little time, can the mantle be upon the wind that was spread over Matsubara or over Ashitaka the mountain, though the clouds lie in its heaven like a plain awash with sea. Fuji is gone; the great peak of Fuji is blotted out little by little. It melts into the upper mist. In this way she (the Tennin) is lost to sight.

KAGEKIYO

A Play in one Act, by Motokiyo

CHARACTERS

SHITE, KAGEKIYO old and blind.
TSURE, a girl, his daughter, called HITOMARU.
TOMO, her attendant.
WAKI, a villager.
THE scene is in HIUGA.

GIRL AND ATTENDANT
(chanting)

What should it be; the body of dew, wholly at the mercy of wind?

GIRL

I am a girl named Hitomaru from the river valley Kamegaye-ga-
    Yatsu,
My father, Akushichi-bioye Kagekiyo,
Fought by the side of Heike,
And is therefore hated by Genji.
He was banished to Miyazaki in Hiuga,
To waste out the end of his life.
Though I am unaccustomed to travel,
I will try to go to my father.

GIRL AND ATTENDANT
(describing the journey as they walk across the bridge and the stage)

Sleeping with the grass for our pillow,
The dew has covered our sleeves.

[*Singing*.

Of whom shall I ask my way
As I go out from Sagami province?
Of whom in Totomi?

315

I crossed the bay in a small hired boat
And came to Yatsuhashi in Mikawa;
Ah, when shall I see the City-on-the-cloud?

ATTENDANT

As we have come so fast, we are now in Miyazaki of Hiuga.
It is here you should ask for your father.

KAGEKIYO

(in another corner of the stage)

Sitting at the gate of the pine wood I wear out the end of my years. I cannot see the clear light, I do not know how the time passes. I sit here in this dark hovel, with one coat for the warm and the cold, and my body is but a framework of bones.

CHORUS

May as well be a priest with black sleeves. Now having left the world in sorrow, I look on my withered shape. There is no one to pity me now.

GIRL

Surely no one can live in that ruin, and yet a voice sounds from it. A beggar, perhaps. Let us take a few steps and see.

KAGEKIYO

My eyes will not show it me, yet the autumn wind is upon us.

GIRL

The wind blows from an unknown past, and spreads our doubts through the world. The wind blows, and I have no rest, nor any place to find quiet.

KAGEKIYO

Neither in the world of passion, nor in the world of colour, nor in the world of non-colour, is there any such place of rest; beneath the one sky are they all. Whom shall I ask, and how answer?

GIRL

Shall I ask the old man by the thatch?

KAGEKIYO

Who are you?

KAGEKIYO

GIRL
Where does the exile live?

KAGEKIYO
What exile?

GIRL
One who is called Akushichi-bioye Kagekiyo, a noble who fought with Heike.

KAGEKIYO
Indeed? I have heard of him, but I am blind, I have not looked in his face. I have heard of his wretched condition and pity him. You had better ask for him at the next place.

ATTENDANT
(to girl)
It seems that he is not here, shall we ask further?

[*They pass on.*

KAGEKIYO
Strange, I feel that woman who has just passed is the child of that blind man. Long ago I loved a courtesan in Atsuta, one time when I was in that place. But I thought our girl-child would be no use to us, and I left her with the head man in the valley of Kamegaye-ga-yatsu; and now she has gone by me and spoken, although she does not know who I am.

CHORUS
Although I have heard her voice,
The pity is, that I cannot see her.
And I have let her go by
Without divulging my name.
This is the true love of a father.

ATTENDANT
(at further side of the stage)
Is there any native about?

VILLAGER
What do you want with me?

317

ATTENDANT

Do you know where the exile lives?

VILLAGER

What exile is it you want?

ATTENDANT

Akushichi-bioye Kagekiyo, a noble of Heike's party.

VILLAGER

Did not you pass an old man under the edge of the mountain as you were coming that way?

ATTENDANT

A blind beggar in a thatched cottage.

VILLAGER

That fellow was Kagekiyo. What ails the lady, she shivers?

ATTENDANT

A question you might well ask, she is the exile's daughter. She wanted to see her father once more, and so came hither to seek him. Will you take us to Kagekiyo?

VILLAGER

Bless my soul! Kagekiyo's daughter. Come, come, never mind, young miss. Now I will tell you, Kagekiyo went blind in both eyes, and so he shaved his crown and called himself 'The blind man of Hiuga.' He begs a bit from the passers, and the likes of us keep him; he'd be ashamed to tell you his name. However, I'll come along with you, and then I'll call out, 'Kagekiyo!' and if he comes, you can see him and have a word with him. Let us along. (*They cross the stage, and the villager calls*) Kagekiyo! Oh, there, Kagekiyo!

KAGEKIYO

Noise, noise! Some one came from my home to call me, but I sent them on. I couldn't be seen like this. Tears like the thousand lines in a rain storm, bitter tears soften my sleeve. Ten thousand things rise in a dream, and I wake in this hovel, wretched, just a

nothing in the wide world. How can I answer when they call me
by my right name?

CHORUS

Do not call out the name he had in his glory. You will move
the bad blood in his heart. (*Then, taking up* KAGEKIYO'S *thought*)
I am angry.

KAGEKIYO

Living here . . .

CHORUS

(*going on with* KAGEKIYO'S *thought*)

I go on living here, hated by the people in power. A blind man
without his staff. I am deformed, and therefore speak evil; excuse
me.

KAGEKIYO

My eyes are darkened.

CHORUS

Though my eyes are dark I understand the thoughts of another.
I understand at a word. The wind comes down from the pine trees
on the mountain, and snow comes down after the wind. The
dream tells of my glory. I am loath to wake from the dream. I hear
the waves running in the evening tide, as when I was with Heike.
Shall I act out the old ballad?

KAGEKIYO

(*to the villager*)

I had a weight on my mind, I spoke to you very harshly; excuse
me.

VILLAGER

You're always like that, never mind it. Has any one been here
to see you?

KAGEKIYO

No one but you.

VILLAGER

Go on! That is not true. Your daughter was here. Why couldn't you tell her the truth, she being so sad and so eager? I have brought her back now. Come now, speak with your father. Come along.

GIRL

Oh, Oh, I came such a long journey, under rain, under wind, wet with dew, over the frost; you do not see into my heart. It seems that a father's love goes when the child is not worth it.

KAGEKIYO

I meant to keep it concealed, but now they have found it all out. I shall drench you with the dew of my shame, you who are young as a flower. I tell you my name, and that we are father and child, yet I thought this would put dishonour upon you, and therefore I let you pass. Do not hold it against me.

CHORUS

At first I was angry that my friends would no longer come near me. But now I have come to a time when I could not believe that even a child of my own would seek me out.

[*Singing.*

Upon all the boats of the men of Heike's faction
Kagekiyo was the fighter most in call,
Brave were his men, cunning sailors,
And now even the leader
Is worn out and dull as a horse.

VILLAGER

(*to* KAGEKIYO)

Many a fine thing is gone, sir; your daughter would like to ask you. . . .

KAGEKIYO

What is it?

VILLAGER

She has heard of your fame from the old days. Would you tell her the ballad?

KAGEKIYO

KAGEKIYO

Towards the end of the third month, it was in the third year of Juei. We men of Heike were in ships, the men of Genji were on land. Their war-tents stretched on the shore. We awaited decision. And Noto-no-Kami Noritsune said: 'Last year in the hills of Harima, and in Midzushima, and in Hiyodorigoye of Bitchiu, we were defeated time and again, for Yoshitsune is tactful and cunning. Is there any way we can beat them?' Kagekiyo thought in his mind: 'This Hangan Yoshitsune is neither god nor a devil, at the risk of my life I might do it.' So he took leave of Noritsune and led a party against the shore, and all the men of Genji rushed on them.

CHORUS

Kagekiyo cried, 'You are haughty'. His armour caught every turn of the sun. He drove them four ways before him.

KAGEKIYO
(*excited and crying out*)

Samoshiya! Run, cowards!

CHORUS

He thought, how easy this killing. He rushed with his spear-haft gripped under his arm. He cried out, 'I am Kagekiyo of the Heike.' He rushed on to take them. He pierced through the helmet vizards of Miyonoya. Miyonoya fled twice, and again; and Kagekiyo cried: 'You shall not escape me!' He leaped and wrenched off his helmet. 'Eya!' The vizard broke and remained in his hand and Miyonoya still fled afar, and afar, and he looked back crying in terror, 'How terrible, how heavy your arm!' And Kagekiyo called at him. 'How tough the shaft of your neck is!' And they both laughed out over the battle, and went off each his own way.

CHORUS

These were the deeds of old, but oh, to tell them! to be telling them over now in his wretched condition. His life in the world is weary, he is near the end of his course. 'Go back,' he would say to his daughter. 'Pray for me when I am gone from the world, for

321

I shall then count upon you as we count on a lamp in the darkness . . . we who are blind.' 'I will stay,' she said. Then she obeyed him, and only one voice is left.

We tell this for the remembrance. Thus were the parent and child.

NOTE

Fenollosa has left this memorandum on the stoicism of the last play: I asked Mr. Hirata how it could be considered natural or dutiful for the daughter to leave her father in such a condition. He said, 'that the Japanese would not be in sympathy with such sternness now, but that it was the old Bushido spirit. The personality of the old man is worn out, no more good in this life. It would be sentimentality for her to remain with him. No good could be done. He could well restrain his love for her, better that she should pray for him and go on with the work of her normal life.'

PART IV

I give the next two plays, Awoi no Uye and Kakitsubata, with very considerable diffidence. I am not sure that they are clear; Japanese with whom I have discussed them do not seem able to give me much help. Several passages which are, however, quite lucid in themselves, seem to me as beautiful as anything I have found in Fenollosa's Japanese notes, and these passages must be my justification. In each case I give an explanation of the story so far as I understand it. In one place in Kakitsubata I have transferred a refrain or doubled it. For the rest the plays are as literal as the notes before me permit.

AWOI NO UYE

A Play by Ujinobu

INTRODUCTION

The story, as I understand it, is that the 'Court Lady Awoi' (Flower of the East) is jealous of the other and later co-wives of Genji. This jealousy reaches its climax, and she goes off her head with it, when her carriage is overturned and broken at the Kami festival. The play opens with the death-bed of Awoi, and in Mrs. Fenollosa's diary I find the statement that 'Awoi, her struggles, sickness, and death are represented by a red, flowered kimono, folded once length-wise, and laid at the front edge of the stage.'

The objective action is confined to the apparitions and exorcists. The demon of jealousy, tormenting Awoi, first appears in the form of the Princess Rakujo, then with the progress and success of the exorcism the jealous quintessence is driven out of this personal ghost, and appears in its own truly demonic ('hannya')

323

form—'That awful face with its golden eyes and horns revealed.' The exorcist Miko is powerless against this demon, but the yamabushi exorcists, 'advancing against it, making a grinding noise with the beads of their rosaries and striking against it,' finally drive it away.

The ambiguities of certain early parts of the play seem mainly due to the fact that the 'Princess Rokujo', the concrete figure on the stage, is a phantom or image of Awoi no Uye's own jealousy. That is to say, Awoi is tormented by her own passion, and this passion obsesses her first in the form of a personal apparition of Rokujo, then in demonic form.

This play was written before Ibsen declared that life is a 'contest with the phantoms of the mind.' The difficulties of the translator have lain in separating what belongs to Awoi herself from the things belonging to the ghost of Rokujo, very much as modern psychologists might have difficulty in detaching the personality or memories of an obsessed person from the personal memories of the obsession. Baldly: an obsessed person thinks he is Napoleon; an image of his own thought would be confused with scraps relating perhaps to St. Helena, Corsica, and Waterloo.

The second confusion is the relation of the two apparitions. It seems difficult to make it clear that the 'hannya' has been cast out of the ghostly personality, and that it had been, in a way, the motive force in the ghost's actions. And again we cannot make it too clear that the ghost is not actually a separate soul, but only a manifestation made possible through Awoi and her passion of jealousy. At least with this interpretation the play seems moderately coherent and lucid.

Rokujo or Awoi, whichever we choose to consider her, comes out of hell-gate in a chariot, 'because people of her rank are always accustomed to go about in chariots. When they, or their ghosts, think of motion, they think of going in a chariot, therefore they take that form.' There would be a model chariot shown somewhere at the back of the stage.

The ambiguity of the apparition's opening line is, possibly, to arouse the curiosity of the audience. There will be an air of mystery, and they will not know whether it is to be the chariot associated with Genji's liaison with Yugawo, the beautiful heroine of the play Hajitomi, or whether it is the symbolic chariot drawn by a sheep, a deer, and an ox. But I think we are nearer the mark if we take Rokujo's enigmatic line, 'I am come in three chariots,' to mean that the formed idea of a chariot is derived from these events and from the mishap to Awoi's own chariot, all of which have combined and helped the spirit world to manifest itself concretely. Western students of ghostly folk-lore would tell you that the world of spirits is fluid and drifts about seeking shape. I do not wish to dogmatize on these points.

The Fenollosa-Hirata draft calls the manifest spirit 'The Princess Rokujo', and she attacks Awoi, who is represented by the folded kimono. Other texts seem to call this manifestation 'Awoi no Uye', i.e. her mind or troubled spirit, and this spirit attacks her body. It will be perhaps simpler for the reader if I mark her speeches simply 'Apparition', and those of the second form 'Hannya'.

I do not know whether I can make the matter more plain or summarize it otherwise than by saying that the whole play is a dramatization, or externalization, of Awoi's jealousy. The passion makes her subject to the demon-possession. The demon first comes in a disguised and beautiful form. The prayer of the exorcist forces him first to appear in his true shape, and then to retreat.

But the 'disguised and beautiful form' is not a mere abstract sheet of matter. It is a sort of personal or living mask, having a ghost-life of its own; it is at once a shell of the princess, and a form, which is strengthened or made more palpable by the passion of Awoi.

Scene in Kioto

DAIJIN

I am a subject in the service of the Blessed Emperor Shujakuin. They have called in the priests and the high priests for the sickness of Awoi no Uye of the house of Sadaijin. They prayed, but the gods give no sign. I am sent to Miko, the wise, to bid her pray to the spirits. Miko, will you pray to the earth?

MIKO

Tenshojo, chishojo,
Naigeshojo, Rakkonshojo.

Earth, pure earth,
Wither, by the sixteen roots
(Wither this evil)!

APPARITION

It may be, it may be, I come from the gate of hell in three coaches. I am sorry for Yugawo and the carriage with broken wheels. And the world is ploughed with sorrow as a field is furrowed with oxen. Man's life is a wheel on the axle, there is no turn whereby to escape. His hold is light as dew on the Basho leaf. It seems that the last spring's blossoms are only a dream in the mind. And we fools take it all, take it all as a matter of course. Oh, I am grown envious from sorrow. I come to seek consolation. (*Singing.*) Though I lie all night hid for shame in the secret carriage, looking at the moon for sorrow, yet I would not be seen by the moon.

Where Miko draws the magical bow,
I would go to set my sorrow aloud.

(*Speaking.*) Where does that sound of playing come from? It is the sound of the bow of Adzusa!

MIKO

Though I went to the door of the square building, Adzumaya——

APPARITION

—you thought no one came to knock.

MIKO

How strange! It is a lady of high rank whom I do not know. She comes in a broken carriage, a green wife clings to the shaft. She weeps. Is it——

DAIJIN

Yes, I think I know who it is. (*To the Apparition.*) I ask you to tell me your name.

APPARITION

In the world of the swift-moving lightning I have no servant or envoi, neither am I consumed with self-pity. I came aimlessly hither, drawn only by the sound of the bow. Who do you think I am? I am the spirit of the Princess Rokujo,[1] and when I was still in the world, spring was there with me. I feasted upon the cloud with the Sennin,[2] they shared in my feast of flowers. And on the Evening of Maple Leaves I had the moon for a mirror. I was drunk with colour and perfume. And for all my gay flare at that time I am now like a shut Morning-glory, awaiting the sunshine. And now I am come for a whim, I am come uncounting the hour, seizing upon no set moment. I would set my sorrow aside. Let some one else bear it awhile.

CHORUS

Love turns back toward the lover, unkindness brings evil return. It is for no good deed or good purpose that you bring back a sorrow among us, our sorrows mount up without end.

APPARITION

The woman is hateful! I cannot keep back my blows.

[*She strikes.*

MIKO

No. You are a princess of Rokujo! How can you do such things? Give over. Give over.

APPARITION

I cannot. However much you might pray. (*Reflectively, as if detached from her action, and describing it.*) So she went toward the pillow, and struck. Struck.

MIKO

Then standing up——

[1] As in Western folk-lore, demons often appear first in some splendid disguise.
[2] Spirits not unlike the Irish 'Sidhe'.

APPARITION

This hate is only repayment

MIKO

The flame of jealousy——

APPARITION

——will turn on one's own hand and burn.

MIKO

Do you not know?

APPARITION

Know! This is a just revenge.

CHORUS

Hateful, heart full of hate,
Though you are full of tears
Because of others' dark hatred,
Your love for Genji
Will not be struck out
Like a fire-fly's flash in the dark.

APPARITION

I, like a bush——

CHORUS

——am a body that has no root.
I fade as dew from the leaf,
Partly for that cause I hate her,
My love cannot be restored . . .
Not even in a dream.

It is a gleam cast up from the past. I am full of longing. I
would be off in the secret coach, and crush her shade with me.

DAIJIN

Help. Awoi no Uye is sinking. Can you find Kohijiri of
Tokokawa?

KIOGEN

I will call him. I call him.

WAKI (KOHIJIRI)

Do you call me to a fit place for prayer? To the window of the nine wisdoms, to the cushion of the ten ranks, to a place full of holy waters, and where there is a clear moon?

KIOGEN

Yes, yes.

WAKI

How should I know? I do not go about in the world. You come from the Daijin. Wait. I am ready. I will come.

[He crosses the stage or bridge.

DAIJIN

I thank you for coming.

WAKI

Where is the patient?

DAIJIN

She is there on that bed.

WAKI

I will begin the exorcism at once.

DAIJIN

I thank you. Please do so.

WAKI
(beginning the ritual)

Then Gioja called upon En no Gioja, and he hung about his shoulders a cloak that had swept the dew of the seven jewels in climbing the peaks of Tai Kou and of Kori in Riobu. He wore the cassock of forbearance to keep out unholy things. He took the beads of red wood, the square beads with hard corners, and whirling and striking said prayer. But one prayer.

Namaku, Samanda, Basarada.

[During this speech the APPARITION *has disappeared. That is, the first* SHITE, *the* PRINCESS OF ROKUJO. *Her costume was 'The under kimono black satin, tight from the knees down, embroidered*

*with small, irregular, infrequent circles of flowers; the upper part,
stiff gold brocade, just shot through with purples, greens, and reds.']*
[*The* HANNYA *has come on. Clothed in a scarlet hakama, white upper
dress, and 'The terrible mask with golden eyes.' She has held a white
scarf over her head. She looks up. Here follows the great dance
climax of the play*].

HANNYA
(*threatening*)

Oh, Gioja, turn back! Turn back, or you rue it.

WAKI

Let whatever evil spirit is here bow before Gioja, and know
that Gioja will drive it out.

[*He continues whirling the rosary*

CHORUS
(*invoking the powerful good spirits*)

On the east stand Gosanze Miowo.

HANNYA
(*opposing other great spirits*)

On the south stand Gundari Yasha.

CHORUS

On the west stand Dai Itoku Miowo.

HANNYA

On the north stand Kongo——

CHORUS
——Yasha Miowa.

HANNYA

In the middle Dai Sei——

CHORUS
Fudo Miowo

Namaku Samanda Basarada!
Senda Makaroshana Sowataya

330

Wun tarata Kamman,
Choga Sessha Tokudai Chiye
Chiga Shinja Sokushin Jobutsu.

HANNYA
(overcome by the exorcism)

O terrible names of the spirits. This is my last time. I cannot return here again.

CHORUS

By hearing the scripture the evil spirit is melted. Bosatsu came hither, his face was full of forbearance and pity. Pity has melted her heart, and she has gone into Buddha. Thanksgiving.

KAKITSUBATA

By Motokiyo

Either Motokiyo or Fenollosa seems to have thought that the sage Narihira was in his day the incarnation of a certain Bosatsu or high spirit. Secondly, that the music of this spirit was known and was called 'Kohi' or 'Gobusaki's' music. Narihira seems, after favour, to have been exiled from the court, and to have written poems of regret.

In the play a certain priest, given to melancholy, and with a kindliness for the people of old stories, meets with the spirit of one of Narihira's ladies who had identified herself with the Iris, that is to say, the flowers are the thoughts or the body of her spirit.

She tells him of her past and of Narihira's, and how the music of Gobusaki will lift a man's soul into paradise. She then returns to her heaven.

The rest is, I hope, apparent in the play as I have set it.

CHARACTERS

The Scene is in Mikawa

SPIRIT OF THE IRIS, KAKITSUBATA.
A PRIEST.
CHORUS.

PRIEST

I am a priest who travels to see the sights in many provinces; I have been to Miyako city and seen all the ward shrines and places of interest; I will now push on to the east country. Every night it is a new bed and the old urge of sorrow within me. I have gone by Mino and Owari without stopping, and I am come to Mikawa province to see the flowers of Kakitsubata in the height of their full season. Now the low land is before me, I must go down and peer closely upon them.

Time does not stop and spring passes,

The lightfoot summer comes nigh us,
The branching trees and the bright unmindful grass
Do not forget their time,
They take no thought, yet remember
To show forth their colour in season.

SPIRIT
What are you doing here in this swamp?

PRIEST
I am a priest on my travels. I think these very fine iris. What place is this I am come to?

SPIRIT
Eight Bridges, Yatsubashi of Mikawa, an iris plantation. You have the best flowers before you, those of the deepest colour, as you would see if you had any power of feeling.

PRIEST
I can see it quite well; they are, I think, the Kakitsubata iris that are set in an ancient legend. Can you tell me who wrote down the words?

SPIRIT
In the Ise Monogatari you read, 'By the eight bridges, by the web of the crossing waters in Kumode, the iris come to the full, they flaunt there and scatter their petals.' And when some one laid a wager with Narihira he made an acrostic which says, 'These flowers brought their court dress from China.'

PRIEST
Then Narihira came hither? From the far end of Adzuma?

SPIRIT
Here? Yes. And every other place in the north, the deep north.

PRIEST
Though he went through many a province, what place was nearest his heart?

SPIRIT
This place, Yatsubashi.

PRIEST

Here with the wide-petalled iris
On the lowlands of Mikawa.

SPIRIT

Throughout the length and width of his journeys——

PRIEST

Their colour was alive in his thought.

SPIRIT

He was Narihira of old, the man of the stories.

PRIEST

Yet this iris. . . .

SPIRIT

(*still standing by the pillar and bending sideways*)
These very flowers before you——

CHORUS

—are not the thing of importance. She would say:
'The water by the shore is not shallow.
The man who bound himself to me
Returned times out of mind in his thought
To me and this cobweb of waters.'
It was in this fashion he knew her, when he was strange in this
place.

SPIRIT

I should speak.

PRIEST

What is it?

SPIRIT

Though this is a very poor place, will you pass the night in my
cottage?

PRIEST

Most gladly. I will come after a little.

[*Up to this point the spirit has appeared as a simple young girl of the
locality. She now leaves her pillar and goes off to the other side of the*

KAKITSUBATA

stage to be dressed. She returns in her true appearance, that is, as the great lady beloved of old by Narihira. She wears a black hoshiben crest or hat, an overdress of gauze, purple with golden flowers, an underdress of glaring orange with green and gold pattern. This shows only a little beneath the great enveloping gauze.]

SPIRIT

(to tire-women)

No, no. This hat, this ceremonial gown, the Chinese silk, Karaginu, . . . Look!

PRIEST

How strange. In that tumble-down cottage; in the bower, a lady clad in bright robes! In the pierced hat of Sukibitai's time. She seems to speak, saying, 'Behold me!'

What can all this mean?

KAKITSUBATA

This is the very dress brought from China,
Whereof they sing in the ballad,
'Tis the gown of the Empress Takago,
Queen of old to Seiwa Tenno,[1]
She is Narihira's beloved,
Who danced the Gosetsu music.
At eighteen she won him,
She was his light in her youth.

This hat is for Gosetsu dancing,
For the Dance of Toyo no Akari.
Narihira went covered in like.
A hat and a robe of remembrance!
I am come clothed in a memory.

PRIEST

You had better put them aside. But who are you?

THE LADY

I am indeed the sprit, Kakitsubata, the colours of remembrance.
And Narihira was the incarnation of the Bosatsu of Gokusaki's

[1] Emperor of Japan, A.D. 859-876.

music. Holy magic is run through his words and through the notes of his singing, till even the grass and the flowers pray to him for the blessings of dew.

PRIEST

A fine thing in a world run waste,
To the plants that are without mind,
I preach the law of Bosatsu.

LADY

This was our service to Buddha,
This dance, in the old days.

PRIEST
(hearing the music)

This is indeed spirit music.

LADY

He took the form of a man.

PRIEST

Journeying out afar
From his bright city.

LADY

Saving all——

PRIEST
——by his favour.

CHORUS

Going out afar and afar
I put on robes for the dance.

LADY

A robe for the sorrow of parting.

CHORUS

I send the sleeves back to the city.

LADY

This story has no beginning and no end,
No man has known the doer and no man has seen the deed.

KAKITSUBATA

In the old days a man
Wearing his first hat-of-manhood
Went out hunting
Toward the town of Kasuga in Nara.

We think it was in the time
Of the reign of Nimmio Tenno.

He was granted by Imperial Decree
Reading: 'About the beginning of March,
When the mists are still banked upon Ouchiyama the moun-
    tain. . . .'
He was granted the hat-insignia, sukibitai,
As chief messenger to the festival of Kasuga.

LADY

An unusual favour.

CHORUS

It was a rare thing to hold the plays and Genbuku ceremony in
the palace itself. This was the first time it had happened.
The world's glory is only for once,
Comes once, blows once, and soon fades,
So also to him: he went out
To seek his luck in Adzuma,
Wandering like a piece of cloud, at last
After years he came
And looking upon the waves at Ise and Owari,
He longed for his brief year of glory:
        The waves, the breakers return,
        But my glory comes not again,
            Narihira, Narihira,
        My glory comes not again.
    He stood at the foot of Asama of Shinano, and saw the smoke
curling upwards.

337

LADY

The smoke is now curling up
From the peak of Asama.

> Narihira, Narihira,
> My glory comes not again.

CHORUS

Strangers from afar and afar,
Will they not wonder at this?
He went on afar and afar
And came to Mikawa, the province,
To the flowers Kakitsubata
That flare and flaunt in their marsh
By the many-bridged cobweb of waters.

'She whom I left in the city?' thought Narihira. But in the long tale, Monogatari, there is many a page full of travels . . . and yet at the place of eight bridges the stream-bed is never dry.
He was pledged with many a lady.
The fire-flies drift away
From the jewelled blind,
Scattering their little lights
And then flying and flying:

Souls of fine ladies
Going up into heaven.

And here in the under-world
The autumn winds come blowing and blowing,
And the wild ducks cry: 'Kari! . . . Kari!'
I who speak, an unsteady wraith,
A form impermanent, drifting after this fashion,
Am come to enlighten these people.
Whether they know me I know not.

SPIRIT

A light that does not lead on to darkness.

CHORUS
(singing the poem of Narihira's)
No moon!

338

The spring
Is not the spring of the old days,
My body
Is not my body,
But only a body grown old.

Narihira, Narihira,
My glory comes not again.

CHORUS

Know then that Narihira of old made these verses for the Queen
of Seiwa Tenno. The body unravels its shred, the true image
divides into shade and light. Narihira knew me in the old days.
Doubt it not, stranger. And now I begin my dance, wearing the
ancient bright mantle.

[*Dance and its descriptions.*

SPIRIT

The flitting snow before the flowers:
The butterfly flying.

CHORUS

The nightingales fly in the willow tree:
The pieces of gold flying.

SPIRIT

The iris Kakitsubata of the old days
Is planted anew.

CHORUS

With the old bright colour renewed.

SPIRIT

Thus runs each tale from its beginning,
We wear the bright iris crest of Azame.

CHORUS

What are the colours of the iris?
Are they like one another, the flower,
Kakitsubata, Ayame.

[*The grey and olive robed chorus obscure the bright dancer.*
What is that that cries from the tree?

[*The spirit is going away, leaving its apparition, which fades as it returns to the aether.*

SPIRIT

It is only the cracked husk of the locust.

CHORUS

(closing the play)

The sleeves are white like the snow of the Uno Flower
Dropping their petals in April.
Day comes, the purple flower
  Opens its heart of wisdom,
It fades out of sight by its thought.
The flower soul melts into Buddha.

NOTE

I have left one or two points of this play unexplained in the opening notice. I do not think any one will understand the beauty of it until he has read it twice. The emotional tone is perhaps apparent. The spirit manifests itself in that particular iris marsh because Narihira in passing that place centuries before had thought of her. Our own art is so much an art of emphasis, and even of over-emphasis, that it is difficult to consider the possibilities of an absolutely unemphasized art, an art where the author trusts so implicitly that his auditor will know what things are profound and important.

The Muses were 'the Daughters of Memory'. It is by memory that this spirit appears, she is able or 'bound' because of the passing thought of these iris. That is to say, they, as well as the first shadowy and then bright apparition, are the outer veils of her being. Beauty is the road to salvation, and her apparition 'to win people to the Lord ' or 'to enlighten these people' is part of the ritual, that is to say, she demonstrates the 'immortality of the soul' or the 'permanence or endurance of the individual personality' by her apparition—first, as a simple girl of the locality; secondly, in the ancient splendours. At least that is the general meaning of the play so far as I understand it.   E. P.

CHORIO

By Nobumsitu (who died in the 13th year of Yeisho, A.D. 1516)

CHARACTERS

The Scene is in China

FIRST SHITE, an old man.
SECOND SHITE, KOSEKKO.
WAKI, CHORIO.

PART I

WAKI

I am Chorio,[1] a subject of Koso of Kan, though I am busy in service I had a strange dream that there was in Kahi an earthen bridge, and that as I leaned on the bridge-rail there came an old man on horseback. And he dropped one of his shoes and bade me pick up the shoe. I thought this uncivil, yet he seemed so uncommon a figure and so gone on in old age that I went and picked up the shoe. 'You've a true heart,' he said, 'come back here in five days' time, and I will teach you all there is to know about fighting.'

He said that, and then I woke up, and now it's five days since the dream, and I am on my way to Kahi.

Dawn begins to show in the sky. I am afraid I may be too late. The mountain is already lit, and I am just reaching the bridge.

SHITE

Chorio, you are late, you have not kept your promise. I came quite early, and now it is much too late. Hear the bell there.

CHORUS

Too late now. Come again. Come in five days' time if you carry a true heart within you. And I shall be here, and will teach

---

[1] Chinese. Chang Liang died 187 B.C. Koso of Kan = Kao Tsu, first Emperor of the Han dynasty. Kahi = Hsia-p'ei, in the north of Kiangsu. Kosekko = Huang Shih Kung, Yellow Stone Duke.

you the true craft of fighting. Keep the hour, and keep true to your promise. How angry the old man seemed. How suddenly he is gone. Chorio, see that you come here in time.

CHORIO

He is angry. I am sorry. Why do I follow a man wholly a stranger? Foolish. Yet, if he would teach me his secrets of strategy. . . .

CHORUS

I think that he will come back. He does not like wasting his time. Still, he will come back again. See, he has gone away happy.

PART II

CHORIO

'Frost tinges the jasper terrace,
A fine stork, a black stork sings in the heaven,
Autumn is deep in the valley of Hako,
The sad monkeys cry out in the midnight,
The mountain pathway is lonely.'

CHORUS

The morning moonlight lies over the world
And flows through the gap of these mountains,
White frost is on Kahi bridge, the crisp water wrinkles beneath it,
There is no print in the frost on the bridge,
No one has been by this morning.
Chorio, that is your luck. That shadow shows a man urging his
    horse.

OLD MAN

I am the old man, Kosekko. Since Chorio is loyal in service, no fool, ready at learning . . .

CHORUS

Since he cares so much for the people . . .

CHORIO

KOSEKKO
His heart has been seen in high heaven.

CHORUS
The Boddisatwa are ready to bless him.

KOSEKKO
I will teach him the secrets of battle.

CHORUS
He says he will teach Chorio to conquer the enemy, and to rule well over the people. He urges his horse and seeing this from far off, seeing the old man so changed in aspect, with eye gleaming out and with such dignity in his bearing, Chorio has knelt down on the bridge awaiting Kosekko.

KOSEKKO
Chorio, you are come in good time. Come nearer and listen.

CHORIO
Chorio then stood up and smoothed out his hat and his robe.

KOSEKKO
I know quite well he is wise, but still I will try him.

CHORUS
Kosekko kicked off his shoe so it fell in the river. Then Chorio leapt in for the shoe, but the river flowed between rocks; it was full of currents and arrow-like rapids. He went diving and floating and still not reaching the shoe.[1]

See how the waves draw back. A thick mist covers the place, a dragon moves in darkness, ramping among the waves, lolling its fiery tongue. It is fighting with Chorio; see, it has seized on the shoe.

CHORIO
Chorio drew his sword calmly.

CHORUS
He struck a great blow at the dragon; there was terrible light on his sword. See, the dragon draws back and leaves Chorio with the

[1] One must consider this as dance motif.

shoe. Then Chorio sheathed his sword and brought up the shoe to Kosekko, and buckled it fast to his foot.

Kosekko

And Kosekko got down from his horse.

Chorus

He alighted, saying, 'Well done. Well done.' And he gave a scroll of writing to Chorio, containing all the secret traditions of warfare. And Kosekko said, 'That dragon was Kwannon. She came here to try your heart, and she must be your goddess hereafter.'

Then the dragon went up to the clouds, and Kosekko drew back to the highest peak, and set his light in the sky; was changed to the yellow stone.

GENJO

By Kongo

Story from Utai Kimmō Zuye

In China, under the Tō dynasty (A.D. 604-927), there was a biwa player named Renjōbu, and he had a biwa called Genjō. In the reign of Nimmyō Tennō (A.D. 834-850) Kamon no Kami Sadatoshi met Renjōbu in China, and learnt from him three tunes, Ryūsen (The Flowing Fountain), Takuboku[1] (The Woodpecker), and the tune Yōshin. He also brought back to our court the biwa named Genjō.

Murakami Tenno (947-967) was a great biwa player. One moonlight night, when he was sitting alone in the Southern Palace, he took the biwa Genjo and sang the old song:

> Slowly the night draws on
> And the dew on the grasses deepens.
> Long after man's heart is at rest
> Clouds trouble the moon's face—
> Through the long night till dawn.

Suddenly the spirit of Renjōbu appeared to him and taught him two new tunes, Jōgen and Sekishō (the Stone Image). These two, with the three that Sadatoshi had brought before, became the Five Biwa Tunes.

[1] The words of 'Takuboku' are—

> In the South Hill there's a bird
> That calls itself the woodpecker.
> When it's hungry, it eats its tree;
> When it's tired, it rests in the boughs.

> Don't mind about other people;
> Just make up your mind what you want.
> If you're pure, you'll get honour;
> If you're foul, you'll get shame.
>
> By Lady Tso, A.D. 4th cent.

These five tunes were transmitted to Daijo Daijin Moronaga, who was the most skilful player in the Empire.

Moronaga purposed to take the biwa Genjō and go with it to China in order to perfect his knowledge. But on the way the spirit of Murakami Tennō appeared to him at Suma under the guise of an old salt-burner.[1]

PART I

The Scene is in Settsu

CHARACTERS

FIRST SHITE, an old man.
TSURE, an old woman.
TSURE, Fujiwara no Moronaga.
SECOND SHITE, the Emperor Murakami.
TSURE, Riujin, the Dragon God.
WAKI, an attendant of Moronaga.

WAKI

What road will get us to Mirokoshi,[2] far in the eight-folded waves?

MORONAGA

I am the Daijo Daijin Moronaga.

WAKI

He is my master, and the famous master of the biwa, and he wishes to go to China to study more about music, but now he is turning aside from the straight road to see the moonlight in Suma and Tsu-no-Kuni.[3]

MORONAGA

When shall I see the sky-line of Miyako, the capital? We started at midnight. Yamazaki is already behind us.

[1] Note supplied by A. D. W.
[2] China
[3] Tsu-no-Kuni is the poetical name for Settsu province.

GENJO

WAKI

Here is Minato river and the wood of Ikuta; the moon shows between the black trees, a lonely track. But I am glad to be going to Mirokoshi. The forest of Koma is already behind us. Now we are coming to Suma.

Now we have come to the sea-board, Suma in Tsu-no-Kuni. Let us rest here a while and ask questions.

OLD MAN AND OLD WOMAN

It's a shabby life, lugging great salt tubs, and yet the shore is so lovely that one puts off one's sorrow, forgets it.

OLD MAN

The setting sun floats on the water.

OLD MAN AND OLD WOMAN

Even the fishermen know something grown out of the place, and speak well of their sea-coast.

OLD WOMAN

The isles of Kii show through the cloud to the southward.

OLD MAN

You can see the ships there, coming through the gateway of Yura.

OLD WOMAN

And the pine-trees, as far off as Sumiyoshi.

OLD MAN

And the cottages at Tojima, Koya, and Naniwa.

OLD WOMAN

They call it the island of pictures.

OLD MAN

Yet no one is able to paint it.

OLD MAN AND OLD WOMAN

Truly a place full of charms.

CHORUS

The air of this place sets one thinking. Awaji, the sea, a place of fishermen, see now their boats will come in. The rain crouches

347

low in the cloud. Lift up your salt tubs, Aie! It's a long tramp, heavy working. Carry along, from Ise Island to the shore of Akogi. There is no end to this business. The salt at Tango is worse. Now we go down to Suma. A dreary time at this labour. No one knows aught about us. Will any one ask our trouble?

OLD MAN

I will go back to the cottage and rest.

WAKI

(at the cottage door)

Is any one home here? We are looking for lodging.

OLD MAN

I am the man of the place.

WAKI

This is the great Daijin Moronaga, the master of biwa, on his way to far Mirokoshi. May we rest here?

OLD MAN

Please take him somewhere else.

WAKI

What! you won't give us lodging. Please let us stay here.

OLD MAN

The place isn't good enough, but you may come in if you like.

OLD WOMAN

When they were praying for rain in the garden of Shin-sen (Divine Fountain), he drew secret music from the strings of his biwa——

OLD MAN

——and the dragon-god seemed to like it. The clouds grew out of the hard sky of a sudden, and the rain fell and continued to fall. And they have called him Lord of the Rain.

OLD WOMAN

If you lodge such a noble person——

GENJO

OLD MAN
—I might hear his excellent playing.

BOTH
It will be a night worth remembering.

CHORUS
The bard Semimaru played upon his biwa at the small house in Osaka, now a prince will play in the fisherman's cottage. A rare night. Let us wait here in Suma. The pine-wood shuts out the wind and the bamboo helps to make stillness. Only the little ripple of waves sounds from a distance. They will not let you sleep for a while. Play your biwa. We listen.

WAKI
I will ask him to play all night.

MORONAGA
Maybe it was spring when Genji was exiled and came here into Suma, and had his first draught of sorrow, of all the sorrows that come to us. And yet his travelling clothes were not dyed in tears. Weeping, he took out his small lute, and thought that the shore wind had in it a cry like his longing, and came to him from far cities.

CHORUS
That was the sound of the small lute and the shore wind sounding together, but this biwa that we will hear is the rain walking in showers. It beats on the roof of the cottage. We cannot sleep for the rain. It is interrupting the music.

OLD MAN
Why do you stop your music?

WAKI
He stopped because of the rain.

OLD MAN
Yes, it is raining. We will put our straw mats on the roof.

OLD WOMAN
Why?

349

OLD MAN

They will stop the noise of the rain, and we can go on hearing his music.

BOTH

So they covered the wooden roof.

CHORUS

And they came back and sat close to hear him.

WAKI

Why have you put the mats on the roof.

OLD MAN

The rain sounded out of the key. The biwa sounds 'yellow bell', and the rain gives a 'plate' note. Now we hear only the 'bell'.

CHORUS

We knew you were no ordinary person. Come, play the biwa yourself.

OLD MAN AND OLD WOMAN

The waves at this side of the beach can play their own biwa; we did not expect to be asked.

CHORUS

Still they were given the biwa.

OLD MAN

The old man pulled at the strings.

OLD WOMAN

The old woman steadied the biwa.

CHORUS

A sound of pulling and plucking, 'Barari, karari, karari, barari,' a beauty filled full of tears, a singing bound in with the music, unending, returning.

MORONAGA

Moronaga thought——

GENJO

CHORUS

—I learned in Hi-no-Moto all that men knew of the biwa, and now I am ashamed to have thought of going to China. I need not go out of this country. So he secretly went out of the cottage. And the old man, not knowing, went on playing the biwa, and singing 'Etenraku', the upper cloud music, this song:

'The nightingale nests in the plum tree, but what will she do with the wind?

Let the nightingale keep to her flowers.'

The old man is playing, not knowing the guest has gone out.

OLD WOMAN

The stranger has gone.

OLD MAN

What! he is gone. Why didn't you stop him?

BOTH

So they both ran after the stranger.

CHORUS

And taking him by the sleeve, they said, 'The night is still only half over. Stay here.'

MORONAGA

Why do you stop me? I am going back to the capital now, but later I will return. Who are you? What are your names?

BOTH

Emperor Murakami, and the lady is Nashitsubo.

CHORUS

To stop you from going to China we looked on you in a dream, by the sea-coasts at Suma. So saying, they vanished.

PART II

THE EMPEROR MURAKAMI

I came up to the throne in the sacred era of Gengi,[1] when the fine music came from Mirokoshi, the secret and sacred music, and

[1] A.D. 901-923.

the lutes Genjo, Seizan,[1] and Shishimaru. The last brought from the dragon world. And now I will play on it.

And he looked out at the sea and called on the dragon god, and played on 'Shishimaru'.

The lion-dragon floated out of the waves, and the eight goddesses of the dragon stood with him, and he then gave Moronaga the biwa. And Moronaga took it, beginning to play. And the dragon king moved with the music, and the waves beat with drum rhythm. And Murakami took up one part. That was music. Then Murakami stepped into the cloudy chariot, drawn by the eight goddesses of the dragon, and was lifted up beyond sight. And Moronaga took a swift horse back to his city, bearing that biwa with him.

[1] The lute Seizan. See first speech of 'Tsunemasa'.

APPENDIX I

SHUNKWAN, by Motokiyo (b. 1374, d. 1455).

Plot.—When Kiyomori[1] was at the height of his power three men plotted against him. They were detected and exiled to Devil's Island; 'for many years they knew the spring only by the green new grass, and autumn by the turning of the leaves.'

Then when Kiyomori's daughter was about to give birth to a child, many prisoners and exiles were pardoned in order to propitiate the gods, and among them Shunkwan's companions, but not the chief conspirator Shunkwan.

On the ninth day of the ninth month, which day is called 'Chöyo' and is considered very lucky, because Hosö of China drank ceremonial wine on that day and lived 7000 years, the two exiled companions of Shunkwan are performing service to their god Kumano Gongen. They have no white prayer cord, and must use the white cord of their exile's dress; they have no white rice to scatter, and so they scatter white sand. With this scene the Noh opens. Shunkwan, who alone is a priest, enters, and should offer a cup of saké, as in the proper service for receiving pilgrims, but he has only a cup of water.

While this ceremony is in progress, the imperial messengers arrive with the emperor's writ; they pronounce the names of Yasu-yori and Naritsune, but not Shunkwan's. He thinks there must be some error. He seizes the paper and reads, and is frenzied with grief. He tries to detain his companions, but the messengers hurry them off. Shunkwan seizes the boat's cable. The messenger cuts it. Shunkwan falls to earth, and the others go off, leaving him alone.

This is, of course, not a 'play' in our sense. It is a programme for a tremendous dance.

Modus of Presentation (Asakusa, October 30, 1898).—The companions wear dull blue and brown. Shunkwan's mask is of a

[1] Kiyomori, 1118-81.

dead colour, full of wrinkles, with sunken cheeks and eyes. His costume is also of blue and brown. The finest singing and dancing are after the others have entered the boat. Everything is concentrated on the impression of a feeling.

The scene is in 'an island of Stasuma'.

KOI NO OMONI ('THE BURDEN OF LOVE'), said to be by the Emperor Gohanazono (1429-65).

Plot.—Yamashina Shoshi was the emperor's gardener, and as the court ladies were always walking about in the garden, he fell in love with one of them. He wished to keep this secret, but in some way it became known. Then a court officer said to him, 'If you can carry this light and richly brocaded burden on your back, and carry it many thousand times round the garden, you will win the lady you love.' But for all its seeming so light and being so finely ornamented, it was a very heavy load, and whenever he tried to lift it he fell to the ground, and he sang and complained of it, and at last he died trying to lift it.

And the court officer told the lady, and she was filled with pity and sang a short and beautiful song, and the ghost of Shoshi came and sang to her of the pain he had in this life, reproaching her for her coldness.

Modus.—From the very first the burden of love lay in the centre front of the stage, thus 'becoming actually one of the characters'. It was a cube done up in red and gold brocade and tied with green cords. The hero wore a mask, which seemed unnecessarily old, ugly, and wrinkled. His costume subdued, but rich. The court lady gorgeously dressed, with smiling young girl's mask and glittering pendant, East-Indian sort of head-dress.

The lady sat at the right corner, immobile, rather the lover's image of his mistress than a living being. He sings, complains, and tries several times to lift the burden, but cannot. The court officer sits a little toward the right-back. Shoshi dies and passes out.

The officer addresses the lady, who suddenly seems to come to life. She listens, then leaves her seat, half-kneels near the burden, her face set silently and immovably toward it. This is more graphic and impressive than can well be imagined. All leave the stage save this silent figure contemplating the burden.

The Shoshi's ghost comes in, covered with glittering superb brocades, he uses a crutch, has a mane of flying grey hair, and a face that looks like an 'elemental'.

KANAWA, THE IRON RING, by Motokiyo.

Story.—In the reign of Saga Tenno there was a princess who loved unavailingly, and she became so enraged with jealousy that she went to the shrine of Kibune and prayed for seven days that she might become a hannya. On the seventh day the god had pity, and appeared to her and said, 'If you wish to become a hannya go to the Uji river and stay twenty-five days in the water.' And she returned rejoicing to Kioto, and parted her hair into five strands and painted her face and her body red, and put an iron ring on her head with three candles in it. And she took in her mouth a double fire-stick, burning at both ends. And when she walked out in the streets at night people thought her a devil.

From this it happens that when Japanese women are jealous they sometimes go to a temple at night wearing an iron ring (Kanawa) with candles in it. Sometimes they use also a straw doll in the incantation.

Modus.—First comes Kiogen, the farce character, and says he has had a god-dream, and that he will tell it to the woman who is coming to pray.

Then comes the woman. Kiogen asks if she comes every night. He tells her his dream, and how she is to become a hannya by the use of Kanawa. She goes. Her face changes en route. Enter the faithless husband, who says he lives in Shimokio, the Lower City, and has been having very bad dreams. He goes to the priest Abē, who tells him that a woman's jealousy is at the root of it, and that his life is in danger that very night. The husband confesses his infidelity. The priest starts a counter exorcism, using a life-sized straw doll with the names of both husband and wife put inside it. He uses the triple takadana[1] and five coloured 'gohei', red, blue, yellow, black, white. Storm comes with thunder and lightning.

[1] Generally called mitegura.

The woman appears. She and the chorus sing, interrupting each other—she complaining, the chorus interpreting her thoughts. She approaches her husband's pillow with the intention of killing him. But the power of the exorcism prevails, and she vanishes into the air.

MATSUKAZE, by Kiyotsugu.

A wandering priest sees the ghost of the two fisher girls, Matsukaze and Murasame, still gathering salt on the seashore at Suma. They still seem to feel the waves washing over them, and say, 'Even the shadows of the moon are wet', 'The autumn wind is full, full of thoughts, thoughts of the sea'. They seem to wish to be back in their old hard life, and say the moon is 'envious' of the ghost life, and will only shine on the living; that the dews are gathered up by the sun, but that they lie like old grass left to rot on the sea-beach. 'How beautiful is the evening at Suma for all the many times we have seen it and might be tired with seeing it. How faint are the fishermen's voices. We see the fisher boats in the offing. The faint moon is the only friend. Children sing under the field-sweeping wind; the wind is salt with the autumn. O how sublime is this night. I will go back to shore, for the tide is now at its full. We hang our wet sleeves over our shoulders, salt dripping from them. The waves rush to the shore, a stork sings in the reeds. The storm gathers in from all sides; how shall we pass through this night. Cold night, clear moon, and we two in deep shadow.'

APPENDIX II

FENOLLOSA's notes go into considerable detail as to how one must place large jars under the proper Noh stage for resonance: concerning the officials in the ministry of music in the reign of some emperor or other; concerning musical instruments, etc.; concerning special ceremonies, etc. A part of this material can, I think, be of interest only to scholars; at least I am not prepared to edit it until I know how much or how little general interest there is in the Japanese drama and its methods of presentation. Many facts might be extremely interesting if one had enough knowledge of Noh, and could tell where to fit them in. Many names might be rich in association, which are, at the present stage of our knowledge, a rather dry catalogue.

Still, I may be permitted a very brief summary of a section of notes based, I think, on a long work by Professor Ko-haka-mura.

Certain instruments are very old (unless we have pictures of all these instruments, a list of Japanese names with the approximate dates of their invention will convey little to us). Music is divided roughly into what comes from China, from Korea, and what is native. 'Long and short songs, which sang out the heart of the people, were naturally rhythmic.' Foreign music . . . various schools and revolutions . . . priests singing in harmony (?) with the biwa. Puppet plays (about 1596, I think, unless the date 1184 higher on the page is supposed to be connected with 'the great genius Chikamatsu'). Chikamatsu, author of 97 jōruri plays, lived 1653-1724. Various forms of dancing, female dancing, 'turning piece', some forms of female dancing forbidden. Music for funerals and ceremonies.

'The thoughts of men, when they are only uttered as they are, are called "tada goto", plain word. But when they are too deep for "plain word" we make "pattern decoration" (aya), and have fushi (tones) for it.'

An emperor makes the first koto from 'decayed' wood; the sound of it was very clear and was heard from afar.

Field dances, shield dances, etc. 'In the ninth month of the fourteenth year of Temmu (A.D. 686), the imperial order said: "The male singers and female flute blowers must make it their own profession, and hand it down to their descendants and make them learn." Hence these hereditary professions.'

'In the festival of Toka, court ladies performed female dancing, ceremony of archery, wrestling (so the note seems to read). In the Buddhist service only foreign music was used.'

More regulations for court ceremonies, not unlike the general meticulousness of 'Leviticus'.

Buddhism, growing popularity of Chinese music. 'In Daijosai, the coronation festival, it was not the custom to use Chinese music. But in this ceremony at Nimmio Tenno's coronation, on the day of the dinner-party, they collected pebbles before the temple, planted new trees, spread sheets on the ground, scattered grain to represent the seashore, and took out boats upon it, and a dance was performed imitating fishermen picking up seaweed.

In the festival of the ninth month, literary men offered Chinese poems, so it may be that the music was also in Chinese style.

In the time of Genkio (1321-23), mention of a troupe of 140 dancers.

Udzumusa Masena (?) gives a list of pieces of music brought over from China. 'Sansai Zuye', an old Japanese encyclopedia, certainly gives this list. Some of these names may be interesting as our knowledge of Noh increases. At any rate, I find already a few known names, notably the seawave dance mentioned in the Genji play already translated. I therefore give a partial list, which the reader may skip at his pleasure:

Brandish dancing, breaking camp music, virtue of war, whirling circle music, spring nightingale singing, heaven head jewel life, long life, jewel tree, back-garden flower (composed by a princess of China), King of Rakio (who always wore a mask on his face when he went into battle), congratulation temple, 10,000 years (Banzi), black-head music, Kan province, five customs, courtesy and justice music, five saints' music, pleasant spring, pleasant heart, playing temple, red-white peach pear flower, autumn wind, Rindai (a place in the out-of-the-way country of To), green sea-waves (sei kai ha), plucking mulberry old man, King of Jin breaking camp, divine merit, great settling great peace, returning castle music, turning cup, congratulation king benevolence. Three pieces for sword-dancing: great peace, general music, the palace of Komon; beating ball, music of (?) Ringin Koku. 'A wild duck curving her foot is the dancing of Bosatsu mai.' Kariobinga bird,[1] barbaric drinking wine, dinner drinking, 'Inyang'[2] castle peace. Music of Tenjiku,[3] in which the dancers

---

[1] The Kariobinga bird belongs to the Gyokuraku Jōdo or Paradise of Extreme Felicity. The name is Sanskrit, the thing Indian.

[2] The name Inyang is wrong, but I cannot find the correct name.

[3] Tenjiku = India.

are masked to look like sparrows, scattering hands, pluck off head, Princess of So, perfumed leaves, 10,000 autumns' music.

APPENDIX III

CARE AND SELECTION OF COSTUMES
(From another talk with Umewaka Minoru)

THE clothes are put away in tanso (?), the costly ones on sliding boards, only a few at a time. Ordinary ones are draped in nag-mochi (oblong chests). The best ones are easily injured, threads break, holes come, etc.

Costumes are not classified by the names of the rôles, but by the kind of cloth or by cut or their historic period, and if there are too many of each sort, by colour, or the various shape of the orna-mental patterns. The best are only used for royal performances. The costume for Kakitsubata is the most expensive, one of these recently (i.e. 1901) cost over 500 yen. (*Note.*—I think they are now more expensive.—E. P.)

One does not always use the same combination of costumes; various combinations of quiet costumes are permitted. His sons lay out a lot of costumes on the floor, and Umewaka makes a selection or a new colour scheme as he pleases. This does not take very long.

All his costumes were made before Isshin, and he will not have new ones. When the daimios sold their costumes after the revolu-tion, he might have bought the most splendid, but he was poor. He saved a few in his own house. He collected what he could afford from second-hand shops. Many went abroad. He sold his own clothes and furniture to buy masks. Only Mayeda of Kashu kept his masks and costumes.

Varia.—The notations for singing are very difficult. Takasago is the most correct piece. If a student sings with another who sings badly, his own style is ruined.

Umewaka's struggles to start Noh again after the downfall of the old regime seem to have been long and complicated. Fenollosa has recorded them with considerable detail, but without very great clarity. This much seems to be certain, that without Umewaka's persistence through successive struggles and harassing disappointments, the whole or a great part of the art might have been lost.

THE END

DUST FOR SPARROWS[1]

From the French of
Rémy de Gourmont

[1] i.e.: small size bird-shot, note also the idiom Tirer sa poudre aux moineaux. Sprecare le proprie risorse.

TRANSLATOR'S NOTE

In June, 1915, Rémy de Gourmont wrote to me that because of ill health he could send me, for a proposed literary venture, only 'indications of ideas' not *pages accomplies*. The section of his unpublished work headed Dust for Sparrows (Poudre aux Moineaux) is presumably of that period, physical fatigue, war fatigue combining against the author. I do not offer an excuse for these detached and semi-detached paragraphs; I simply wish to indicate that they must be considered in their relation to the rest of his work.

The following pages are not intended as epigrams; they are indications and transitions of thought; in them is the lucidity which had characterized Rémy de Gourmont's best work; they are not so highly energized as a selection of passages from thirty of his critical books would be, but they are nearly all concerned with some problem of contemporary philosophy—directly, not as vague general speculation. They are given especially for those to whom de Gourmont's work is familiar; those to whom it is not, will possibly find a finer aroma after consideration of that work as a whole, remembering Les Chevaux de Diomèdes and the critical work beginning in Le Livre des Masques, which practically established a whole new generation in French literature.

Naturally, the thoughts in such a note-book as the present are of varying degrees of importance; some would have been amplified, others erased; the translator, at any rate, begs to be excused the responsibility of erasure and believes that the giving of a complete text will be the only satisfactory procedure.

Things Thought, Felt, Seen, Heard, and Dreamed

I

When we believe it needful to say something which we, at any rate, judge useful for the progression of ideas, or the knowledge of verity, we must not hesitate: Better exposure to another's censure than to our own self-contempt.

2

A two line peremptory assertion is not always presumptuous; it is a way of forcing meditation.

3

We have more difficulty in ascribing consciousness to an inert body than to a living thing. Yet, even among those who deny the existence of the soul, the general idea of the *self* is of something unmoveable and of one piece.

4

Even when we arrive at the conviction that free will (*liber arbitrio*) is nothing but an illusion, we still find repugnant a conclusion, thence, that the *self* is a complexity; so greatly do we feel it a unity—so great is the *impression* of unity which we get from it. What prevents us from supposing that the instants of the sensation of being succeed each other, in us, as rapidly as the fragmentary images of the cinema, which in their succession produce the illusion of life?

5

The brook-water seems to stop, lazily to reflect the bank's beauties as its mirror: Error: water never the same, running, ever renewed.

6

The water again, the agitation of its transparency, now deforming its reflections in confusion, now a veridic mirror, might give us, perhaps, a figure for passing vagrancy of the mind?

7

The mechanism of whistling, which instinctively reproduces all the musical modulation, seems to indicate that intelligence is, in origin, purely imitative. Everything is, of necessity, reflected in it; an instability or an uncompellable vibratability obliges the child to reproduce all the sounds he hears, all the movements he sees.

8

There is at times a mental activity whereof the mechanism seems inconceivably complicated: as in the faithful execution of a portrait: arduous labour for the brush, it is realized instantly and to perfection in a mirror.

9

And, in times past, the civilized exemplified the intellectual torpor of the Pampas Indians by pointing out that when the latter were taken from their huts to a city, they showed no surprise at seeing their faces in mirrors. . . . The mentally torpid being those who had not taken count of the fact that the earliest men must have been struck by the phenomenon of reflection upon first regarding their features in placid water.

10

The idea of God is like a limitless mirror in which the physical and moral image of man passes from the relative to the absolute.

11

In the near-arctic, the pale oblique sun and the whitish unanimity of the landscape either suppress shadows almost altogether, or give them excessive value. The gods of Scandinavian mythology may have for origins these colossal figures, fantastic, disproportioned, which the early Norsemen saw before them in the indefinite perspective of the snowscape.

12

In the eternal activity of wanting to understand the structure of this thing which thinks, feels, and wills inside itself; there is a something of the infant who turns the mirror about to see if there isn't another *him* hidden behind it.

13

If in the new creations of man's wit—however original they appear—we could clearly distinguish all the elements, immediate or distant, from which they derive, as we can with new varieties of plants, their originality would be found reduced to a labour of joining, and one would see that their novelty consists only in the style, that seal of paternity.

14

When one analyses the language, seeking the origin and evolution of words, one discovers that there are among the most venerated (*prestigeuses*) phrases, some like Spanish statues covered with gold and velvet, celebrated for their miracles, and having wooden insides.

15

Every thought is a stem, potentially flower and fruit; some suggest, question the unknown, interview truth; some affirm.

[All this little series of paragraphs should be taken in relation to Gourmont's essay on style. E. P.]

16

If we cannot think without words, without articulating them mutely to ourselves, as is shown by the movements of our throats and tongues; how can we admit telepathy, lacking a wireless alphabet for its purpose?

17

And if this thought transmission were possible, one would have so perfected the process that the Telepathic Company would have already ruined Marconi.

18

Wasting my time imagining the mechanism of memory, I have represented it to myself as a noisily crowded department store. The inspectors tell you where a given line is to be found, the clerks are behind their counters, others look up things in the catalogue, and all with order and simplicity in the midst of a terrible apparent confusion.

19

When we are persecuted and obsessed by the search for a forgotten word, we unconsciously take note that it has been invoiced, and that it ought to appear. The search is made in the phantom department store without our knowledge, and some one suddenly brings it to us.

20

The ages of faith have heaped upon our minds such amassments of rhetoric and mystery, that now, when we seek natural explanations for lofty and beautiful things, we seem to commit a coarse triviality.

21

The difference between popular and savant music is very likely the same as that between lace and packing cloth. Distance enormous, but not perhaps, a matter of substance.

22

To judge how high a child's talent will reach, do not attend so much to his greater and smaller facility for assimilating technical notions, but watch to see whether his eyes are occasionally clouded with tears of enthusiasm in the work.

23

Melodic and rhythmic music really *says* [Italics mine. E. P.] nothing; but it gives us the impression of hearing marvelous verse the sense of which we think we divine, by means of emotive association. Symphonic music, as it evolves nothing, is merely a prose absolutely denuded of sense, and it gives many people at the opera the impression of facing a Chinese play accompanied on a tom-tom.

24

At thirty the spring of curiosity is broken, the mind becomes sedentary; at fifty and after the body can enjoy only table and bed.

25

Never have literary works seemed so beautiful to me as when at a theatre, or in reading, because of lack of habit or lacking a complete knowledge of the language, I lost the meaning of many phrases. This threw about them a light veil of somewhat silvery shadow, making the poetry more purely musical, more ethereal. [This is the most dangerous of confessions; it offers a basis for an attack on all the Gourmontian criticism; and yet it is probably true autobiography. The enjoyable, silvery, and ethereal incomprehension may, however, be safer for some minds than for others. E. P.]

26

The need which intelligent men have for hearing good music is only a pretext for lifting themselves above prosaic reality into the world of agreeable sensations, of beautiful ideas and chimeras.

27

There are memories like old mirrors with part of their quick-silver gone. Recollections take, in them, an admirable clarity, but they are full of wholly empty lacunae.

28

Man is no longer the centre of creation. Yet subjectively he has not yet abandoned that centrality, seeing that the universe still exists solely for him, in so far as he is the sole being who transforms sensation into consciousness.

29

But for the nervous system we might consider all our body as an exterior world.

30

Since perfect psychic health is as impossible as absolute physical health our best course is to seek out the defects of our intelligence, and if incurable, to circumscribe or neutralize them by will or by any appropriate moral system.

31

The source of what good there is in confession may come from the fact that many mental defects, being sins, are curable by the shame of avowal and the punishment of the penance.

32

Certain monomanias are presumably, in the mental mechanism, about what hernias are in the intestines; they do not disturb the general functioning, but they are an annoyance and may cause serious accidents.

33

At times, and even very often, we are set upon by unthought about memories of days, of particular places; memories to which we attach no significance. By what association of ideas are these reminiscences brought us? We can not make out, for what is produced is an association of sensations. A grey cold bit of weather without wind, or some other bit equally characteristic brings us the recollection of an analogous day which had given us a special impression. What happens for times happens also for places, and for all impressions which travel in pairs.

34

In ageing, at the memory of the innumerable days when we have been caught by the sight of trees naked with autumn, or spring bourgeoning, it seems that we are millenarians. Each revolution of the earth is, as the ancients thought it, a poem complete: each day of spring or winter which remains out in the memory is recalled as a season, as a year.

35

Images are not decisive arguments, but, as engravings for a complicated text, they may well serve as a prop or as a guide to intelligence.

36 and 37

The superstitions of incurable gamblers clearly indicate the mental defect from which they suffer, for, utterly incredulous, they attribute providential virtues to hazard, and prove that phobias and tics are very closely akin. Among their prejudices there is however one which is, at bottom, justifiable, and there does seem to be some truth in the idea of the run of luck (*veine*), of the favourable moment: chance, which rules the world according to mysterious laws, has caprices. If we throw a thousand black and a thousand white balls into a glass globe and whirl it around vigorously, we see that the colours do not arrange themselves in ysmmetry, but form, on the contrary, groups of each colour on an asymmetrical background. In life as in the game of chance, things do not arbitrarily follow each other; but neither, on the other hand, do they show the logic of an architecture.

38

The wisdom of antiquity tries to inform us that there is no great intelligence without its grain of folly. There would probably be more exactitude in saying that for an intelligence to give its full measure it needs the spur-point of some taint from which it must deliver and redeem itself.

39

A solid and well-balanced intelligence in a healthy body will always be content with doing no more than is necessary to preserve its happy vegetative condition.

40

In great characters the explosive interior force proceeds not from a natural equilibrium, but on the contrary, from an active energy which keeps continual watch lest it escape save at the opportune moment and in the required degree.

41

The best psychological method for a writer who wants veridically to describe the deeds and actions of criminals or to linger over any other point contrary to morality, is to feign having dreamed the matter. In this way one may, temporarily and without fear of law, lay hold on the conduct, and reconstruct the sensibility of a bandit.

42

It is annoying, but true, that nearly all the superior men who are pleasing by their own fireside, are so not because one likes them, but because one admires them, flatters them, and accepts their dictatorship.

43

At times we are set upon by a profound and unjustifiable sense of shame. This ought to be because of some evil action, or some crime we have dreamt we committed.

44

We have two affective sensibilities: one of the first go, apropos of prosaic and quotidien things; and the other deeper, almost invariable. Old men shrug their shoulders at love and recall their youthful extravagances with contempt only. Yet when they reflect, they are not only capable of sighing at the memory of an unhappy passion, but one sees them weep in reading, or in seeing on the stage, some tender story, as for example Romeo and Juliet.

45

There is, it is unfortunate, no deeper abyss than that which separates abstract will from reality.

46

If mute curses cause death, those who desire the death of an husband are the least rare among criminals.

47

Abnegation can not exist without naïveté: exaggeratedly modest opinion of oneself and exaggeratedly favourable opinion of those whom one admires.

48

Who, miser or poor man, is most wretched? Doubtless the miser, for the poor man knows that his unhappiness is not in himself; he retains the hope of riches; while the miser knows that he will never be cured of his mania, which should make him hateful even to himself.

49

It is observed that the doctors most in public esteem are those in whom the minimum of talent is joined to the greatest astuteness.

50

It is a fact, established by science, that idiots understand animals better than any one else.

51

Any one can verify the dementia of a raving lunatic; but is it not strange that there are learned men to decide upon the feebleness or surety of the intelligence of slightly unbalanced persons? Is the plenitude of mental faculties conceivable? Have people not, on the contrary, concluded that genius and madness are equal?

52

What is most admirable in music is the hearing and soul of men.

53

Hearing being the instrument by which all the loftiest ideas and sensations reach our consciousness; the art related to this sense is that which most exalts the mind and goes deepest down into the heart.

54

Is it not curious that for the coldest and most skeptical temperaments, for those most given to buffoonery or calculation, a day comes, the Bonaparte appears, and they find themselves embarked upon most extraordinary adventures?

55

There are souls whom one can bless like the sun, which sheds prodigal his warmth and pleasure upon all he lightens.

56

There are people born debtors by temperament. Between them and the creditor there is an unclimbable wall, a wall over which nothing passes.

57

Heroes have not the tendency to complaint. They are not snivellers albeit having acquaintance with tears. Were this not so they would be monsters, inadmirable. There would be nothing in them but pride.

58

Love of children is the greatest of loves, for though it is egoistic in its essence, it has no equal in abnegation.

59

Games which excite one because, like cards, they bank on one's *amour-propre,* are doubtless an excellent school for character. They call for invaluable faculties, and furnish arms for the struggle for life, especially for politicians and parliamentarians. One might designate them as sedentary fencing.

60

Pious works unmask the Pharisee. But it would be a grave error to misjudge noble souls who have suffered human weakness. To make literary and historical psychology from this, would be like showing a room with tapestries turned face to the wall.

61

There is a woman with whom we never attain complete sincerity, even though we know that she knows us inside out and that we, ourselves, may count on her benevolence.

63

In their normal state the English overdo their respect and attentions to women in order that, thus, acquired habit may preserve them from indecency when they lose control of themselves.

64

It is nearly evident that those who advocate the death penalty are in closer affinity to the assassins than those who oppose it.

65

There are people deeply convinced that there exists between them and the proletariat a veritable difference of quality, which makes these latter bear without suffering the miseries of life to which they are accustomed.

66

There is nothing more perverted by convention than the sense of smell. Analogous odours produce different impressions according as they have one source or another.

67

The origin of certain repulsions which we feel from things which animals find excellent, lies probably in certain confusions in the child mind and even in the man's mind, between shame and disgust; between virtue and dirtiness; vice and bodily cleanliness.

68

Physical disgust begins as instinctive repulsion; it becomes insuperable in becoming a moral prejudice.

69

[Manuscript undecipherable. E. P.]

70

Milan, the moral capital of Italy, its most active centre of thought, art, and industry, was, in the old days, pregnant of the modern, the monastic, and conventual city par excellence.

71

The head of one lunatic genius may contain more wisdom than those of one hundred thousand idiots.

72

There are words so ordinary, and which have assumed in our minds an aspect so characteristic and precise, that on hearing, they almost give us the sensation of the things which they designate.

73

I have known very religious men in all the professions, as I have known also convinced deists and spiritualists, who were *nevertheless* quite intelligent, very enlightened, very well-balanced in all manifestations of practical activity. Which may, all of it, serve to demonstrate that when one passes out of the realm of the knowable the knowledge of atheist and believer are of perfectly equal equivalence.

74

I have observed that when we Latins have an altercation with Anglo-Saxons we look at the position of their hands before attending to their speech.

75

It is evident that religion does not ameliorate people's characters. I have known many almost devout persons who were none the less, in ordinary life, very nasty, especially to their inferiors.

76

It has been, perhaps, profound wisdom on the part of the Church not to make herself the paladin of all the great human causes, and even to sanction certain crimes, such as slavery, but it is certain that this conduct has alienated from her all generous hearts, all those who thirst for justice.

77

It is evident that for the English, the most important part of their religion is that it is Anglican. Most young Englishmen would without much difficulty renounce their part in paradise if they knew that one does not speak English in heaven, that one does not play tennis, that bull-dogs are not admitted, and that one does not have tea with little cakes daily at 5 p.m.

79

Modesty is the essential characteristic of mankind. The history of religions proves it, for man adores everything, positively everything before adoring himself.

80

The progress realized by the physical sciences permits us to conceive mechanical contrivances far superior to Vaucasson's famous duck; mechanisms endowed with the rudimentary sensibility which is found in the lower organisms, lacking a brain, but provided with will and a memory.

To what point will this unlimited scientific progress attain? Will it discover the automaton of greater and still greater sensibility, and get more intelligent? And if so, what *rôle* will this machine play in politics?

81

If love did not contain the secret of life, it would be but the most egoist of the passions, or an agreeable pastime in perhaps debatable taste.

82

There are insects whose life is more logically proportioned than ours; one act for eating, one for sleep, one for *l'amour*. For the first act they have a sort of repugnance; for the second they fold up, seem oldish, become dry as one's boot soles, but for the third they put on their finest raiment, and having suppressed the horrors of digestion, they can hardly be persuaded to suck the honey from flowers to keep from dying of thirst.

83

Women who call in all the sciences to correct the troubles of their exterior life, rarely attempt to appease within themselves the tragedies of nutrition.

84

Ignorance is the name generally given to non-knowledge of the names of things. Anent which: A patient arrives. The doctor examines him and prescribes. The patient starts to leave discontented, turns at the door with, 'But, Doctor, what is the trouble with my ear?' The Doctor reflects a moment and then pronounces the generic technical term for all ear troubles: '*Otitis*'. The patient goes out calm and satisfied. 'Ah, it is an "otitis"!'

85

The great majority of people who travel by electric tram-way are totally ignorant of the mechanism, yet one must not on this account call them ignorant. There is no middle in such a case between the ignorant and the savant, one either understands or does not understand the technique. As for the phenomenon in itself, it is a mystery in one case as in the other.

86

There are quite honourable people who go in terror of judges; as others in terror of bandits.

87

A confessor with whom I enjoy conversation upon dubious topics, told me that the aversion from soap, displayed by the pious, is justified; and that he had observed that the tendency to sin had increased in proportion to the popularization of bathtubs and such like utensils.

88

As scoundrels are everywhere more numerous than honest people, it is but natural that the 'decrees of justice' are more often legal swindles than acts enforcing the right.

89

Nothing seems to me more touching or more ludicrous than a poor devil mourning for a millionaire's death. It is a bullock weeping for the death of Gargantua.

90

Young and pretty women detest old women who try not to appear old, not because they fear traitorous competition, but because no one likes to see himself grotesquely caricatured.

90-a

Humanity is composed not only of two sexes. It is formed of three, which do not love one another: the child, the adult, and the aged.

91

There are men who dye their hair not from coquetry, but for the same reason they have their boots polished: that is, the bureaucratic sense of the fitness of things.

92

It is completely false to say that cosmetics and dyeing fool no one. The first gives an illusion of beauty, prolongs youth, and seduces by revealing, be they feigned or real, the secret anxieties of a temperament. As for dyes, they at least lead toward an error. When we see a woman whose age we do not know, if she is carefully dyed we give her, in any case, fewer years than are hers.

93

If abnegation is the basis of friendship, it is not exaggerated to say that friendship constitutes the basis of all great human affections.

94

Kindness redeems the greatest defects, almost as the purity of its lines and the immaculate whiteness of its material preserve a statue against time's ravages.

95

The man whom I have heard discourse most abundantly about women and love was one of my servants, and neither I nor any one else was able to learn that he had ever had more than one love affair, and that with a German woman who made eyes for mechanical dolls.

96

Everything is miraculous except the things labelled miracles. Most miraculous the transmission of thought through air; if the invention had been cleverly and secretly worked the pretences of supernatural agency would have taken in fools; on the other hand the real miracle once known and stripped of novelty, becomes only habitual fact, and lacks all miraculous prestige.

97

The governing classes have exploited every hoax for the domination of the masses. This has not prevented these very classes from falling into their own trap with the course of years; and the shadow of centuries, joined to the initial mystery, has apotheosized all the charlatans and mountebanks.

98

Neither science nor metaphysic has carried us a hair's breadth beyond the boundary of the knowable. This absolute ignorance of the beyond, this impenetrability of the shadow which on all sides circumscribes us is the last hope which sustains man's boundless anxiety. If no one knows anything, why not take this anxiety into account (that is, as a factor in the problem)?

99

Behind almost every egoistic high living old bachelor there hides a weeping sentimentalist.

100

There are people who by force of mediocrity, by absence of temperament, lack of natural taste for anything whatsoever, give the impression of austerity. They have the air of following automatically and without any effort the strict line of a discipline.

101

We frequently hear said of someone who is chasing fortune precipitate, 'I like him, he's a fighter'; in reality Mr So-and-So is an unscrupulous person who dares risk being gaoled for his manner of doing business.

102

The greater number of skeptics whom I have known were of the type in fashion in the eighteenth century, who if it thundered while they were eating ham-omelette on Good Friday would hurl the plate through the window, saying: 'What a fuss about a mere omelette!'

103

If in the midst of nihilism the most complete of ideas needs only a feminine smile or the squalling of an infant to drive everything out of our heads, why pledge ourselves to reject the arguments of feeling? Is life a problem of mathematics? In our ignorance of all finality is not a pleasant sensation more important to our happiness than an exact piece of reasoning?

104

Borrowers at the end of their tether usually tap people who have helped them before, not only because they count on their kindness or weakness, but because they feel that precedent makes for a servitude.

105

To-day when one presents certain young folk with 'the case of the mandarin' one has to go into detailed explanations, for they think they are being made fun of; one ends by posing the question in this form: would you strangle your millionaire bachelor uncle, whose heir you are, if you were sure of not being found out?

106

The most terrible tyrants have been those who had the horror of action, those who would not shed blood themselves; who never laid eyes on their victims, but had them coldly eliminated; as if making mental operations which dealt with abstractions only.

107

The theatricality common among vain, mediocre persons has produced the opposite type which always looks gloomy in public, though it smiles and enjoys itself privately. There are, likewise, others almost professionally happy and pleasant in society, who suddenly turn lugubrious as soon as one stops gushing over them, as soon as they stop trying to please those about them.

108

The men grossest and most tyrannic in intimacy are those who are, from baseness or pusillanimity, most honeyed to strangers.

109

When in certain celebrated novels we observe the intimate relations of mother and daughter, for example, in high European society, we find in their attitudes and words a deal of manner. Is this not simply because we are vexed at seeing them endowed with a culture more finely developed than ours?

110

A life of great emotional satisfactions, even if crossed by fracas and difficulties, is worth more than an existence sacrificed in the chase of a fortune which comes too late, when the vital spring is broken; the solitary man is nothing but an expensive watch, marking inutile hours.

111

It is fortunate for women coldly correct and incapable of generous impulse, that they very rarely take count of the intimate contempt included in the homages offered to their respectability.

112

There are people with souls so desiccated, so lacking in sap that to talk with them is like chewing a blotter. [Vide Catullus on dryness. E. P.]

113

Strange return to casuistry!

It is odd that in a period whose characteristic is unscrupulous egoism, the favourite subject of many novels is an act contrary to the social pact, for which the committer is tortured by remorse despite the fact that he believed it permissible; despite the fact that he had so judged it in accordance with nature's morality.

114

We need believe in nothing which passes the domain of natural intelligence; nevertheless we may suppose the affirmers of a supreme cause nearer verity than the deniers, for the first lot approach more nearly to natural logic and the aspirations of the human soul; at the same time their belief helps to make life less bitter and harsh. There is neither fortune nor moral compensation in life comparable to the tranquillity of the dying of a just man who has confidence in resurrection and in the supreme rewards.

115

Generally, men happiest in youth have a gloomy age, for they do not see that with the slide of time the qualities which drew to them the sympathy of others must needs be replenished by new acquisitions.

116

The greatest collective suicide was Egypt's, a people which preferred to endure as mummy, rather than to prolong an empire. To spend sums and enormous labour in honouring death is to go pigheadedly contrary to the future, that is, to life.

117

People who really, or pretendedly, pay no attention to what they eat are either not elevated, or obstinately refuse to elevate themselves above humanity. The race is voracious in proportion to its savagery and bestiality; as it is tamed it shows tastes and predilections proportional to the level it has reached. The parrot is fussy about its food, the dog has very marked tastes, the monkey is a gourmet, the ass likes thistles, and the pig all he is given or finds.

118

In the Genius, the contrary of Cervantes' immortal pair, it is Sancho Panza, not the knight, who commits follies.

119

In the case of genius, as with all intelligences, there is a duality resulting from the tensions, minima or maxima, with which he works. Hence comes it that men of extraordinary gifts may seem equal or even inferior to the ordinary, when from disdain or weariness they give way to laziness of mind.

120

Great men have a habit, when they arrive at celebrity, of no longer changing their silhouette. Thus they get the satisfaction of contemplating themselves in the very lines of the future statue.

121

Poverty, condition propitious to sanctity, is by even that, a school for character, and, for the great spirit, a spur to audacious action. Without it humanity would drowse in contented mediocrity, and we should have no more heroes either of thought or of action.

122

Those who establish laws establish also prejudice and the *droits du seigneur*.

123

As the beautiful has no sex and as the female body is the object of eternal and passionate male praise, it is not extraordinary that for certain feminine eyes there is nothing more beautiful than the holy body of Venus.

124

One conceives the intimate friendship of a young man and young woman, but they need only exposure, as the two elements of an explosive; they go off at the slightest disturbance.

125

The romantics, nearing thirty, were full of despair, they died young, they committed hari-kari. Why? Probably because they had false ideas about everything, especially about love which they conceived only as a cult or an orgy. A state of perpetual physical and moral instability could lead only to the cemetery or to madness.

126

As the truths have traversed many centuries in the mask of paradox, it is good to affirm that there is a profound difference between commerce and theft. The first spoils the client with his consent, the second consults only its own desires.

127

Man's will is a conscious application of the fatalities which rule the universe: a balance which knows what it does when we forbid it to act automatically.

128

One may have friends whom one does not value; but it is impossible to be friends with certain people whom one respects.

129

When fathers really attend to the education of their sons they will insist on an ethical teaching which implies a virile contempt of life and a strict respect for one's own convictions; seeing that man is by nature a rapacious being, endowed with all the instincts of animality, and that an artificial civilization makes him every day more cunning and dangerous.

130

Earthly justice can't be much good among people who have accepted as divine justice a system wherein the sins of the fathers are visited upon the children, and for whom a scoundrel respecting their dogmas and following their rites is of more worth than a saint who hasn't the luck to be a believer.

131

The church has had this profound idea, namely that crime does not exclude redemption nor even sanctity.

132

Upon the day of aridity, shadow, and sadness, perhaps an ember of love conserved beneath so many ashes, will set the world on fire, and cause life, purified by grief, to be reborn warmer and more agreeable than ever.

133

One of the most decided partisans of the death penalty I have ever met confessed to me one day that he had insisted on his mistress having three abortions, and that she had died of the complications ensuing upon the third intervention. He sighed, adding, 'Poor little thing, I was very fond of her.'

134

The only cheap and quick justice is that one can do oneself, without, of course, lèse-society.

135

At the marriage of a French prince and a Spanish infanta, one of the items of the celebration was to have been a grilling of Jews and of people who had fallen back into heresy. It was only omitted at the request of the French ambassador; they had to be content with a bull-fight.

136

The ferocity which marks the Spanish fanatic is not European; it is Asiatic and African and must have been brought in by the Moors and converted Jews.

137

There is no doubt that there should be a difference between the spirit of justice and its legal application; as for example when this serves to open public life to a family reduced to misery.

138

Superstition is rather more human than religion, because it has no morality.

139

There is a science; there is especially an art which cannot read.

140

Torquemada is the best demonstration of the affinity between the temperaments of fanatic and assassin.

141

It is easy to understand that those who have had a childhood unhappy and full of mortifications and injustices have even to an advanced age a soul melancholy and yet avid of pleasures.

142

The social life in superior civilizations is too harsh, too arid, too sad to be bearable without the aid of excitements. Wine is the best of these stimulants, being agreeable, noble, and having the sanction of antiquity.

143

All vices are of interior origin. Cards do not make the gambler nor a bottle the drunkard.

144

If one deprived humanity of the pleasures of good wine, life would be rather like catholicism without *fiestas* and without art.

145

If gambling to amuse oneself or drinking a few glasses of wine were enough to turn a normal man into a drunkard or a gambler who in this world would be without these two vices?

146

To-day as in Horace's time good wine continues to be the consolation of life, and the sole means of evoking, for an instant, happy hours, or the fevers of love, when youth is no more but a memory.

147

Bernard Palissy said that all birth pangs are painful, especially those of intelligence. Nevertheless, the creative fever gives transports of enthusiasm and divine inebriations.

148

The art which cannot, in a verse, a phrase, a melody, a brushstroke evoke all of an instant of life may be a goldsmith's product; it is not, at any rate, art.

149

The Napoleonic épopée was really a resurrection of Julius Caesar; transferred from Rome to Paris and having Gauls to carry his triumphant eagles . . . to the borders of Europe. The war of 1870 was the return of the barbarians. Will we see Caesar resuscitated or will the Latin eagles remain for ever vanquished by the other proud eagles?

150

Various of the books ridiculed by Cervantes in Don Quixote were used by Wagner in writing his musical poems. This shows that one may have plastic genius and the highest sense of the comic without possessing an atom of poetry.

151

The Italians are the cleverest interpreters of the grand passions. They are perhaps the only people who can play Shakespeare. But he who can do the greater cannot do the less, although Novelli has almost proved the contrary. One must not put a race horse in carriage shafts or demand pirouettes of an elephant.

152

The sanguinary vehemence of the southerner is not in most cases the outburst of a brutal temperament. May it not be a great love of justice, a great cult of friendship which makes him drive a knife into the heart of a companion who is dishonest in business, cheater at cards, or disloyal in affections?

153

A sacred orator has told us that one of the greatest proofs of the infinitude of God's kindness is that he has put poison in the serpent's mouth and not on the lips of woman.

154

If women suspected the amenities mental and even spoken which men address to them in the impatience of the delay?

155

One sole thing distinguishes mankind from the animals, making man the most ferocious of all, especially against his own species: it is fanaticism.

156

Many people, moreover intelligent ones, care far more for what men say than for what they do.

157

Charity as practised in Christian countries is good in itself and even indispensible, but rests in final analysis on the charity of a master who, having over-driven his slaves all their lives, sends them to hospital when they are ill or to an asylum when old age has made them impotent.

158

Hearts corrodible by human tears are condemned to all the defeats, for true tears are abundant and false tears are a deluge. Beware of imitations.

159

At passing into adolescence, brought up as they have been in accordance to a strict moral code which exalts purity of sentiments, children generally suffer and are indignant at seeing not the inconsequence of strangers but of their own parents. It must be a fairly bad world where the fathers find themselves obliged to teach their children a moral code which they despise; inculcating conditions which, after their entry into life, the children will respect no more than they themselves do.

THINGS THOUGHT, FELT, SEEN, ETC.

160

The right to revolution, legitimate though it may be, like that of legitimate defence, has been greatly discredited by having been so much abused.

161

Evidently the English suffragettes are in a bad way. Love is really the goal of all human struggles; if women had penetrated this verity they might easily have had all the world's government in their hands.

. . . .

165

Bismarck in repudiating the paternity of the aphorism: might makes right, committed an act of inconsequence, or more probably of diplomatic hypocrisy.

166

Revolutions are necessary incidents in progressive evolution. It would be preferable to avoid them; but history shows, unfortunately, that humanity has never made a step forward . . . or let us say, rather, that the demands of the majority have never forced a concession from the egoism of the minority . . . save across blood and fire. St Paul said, it is some time ago: *Sine sanguinis effusione nulla fuit remissio.* (No remission of sins without blood.)

167

The privileges of the aristocracy before the (French) revolution were not less grounded than those of the present bourgeoisie, yet how indignant are the great-grand-nephews of those who had Louis XVI guillotined, when some other stratum of future bourgeois wants to make effective this motto of Liberty-Equality-Fraternity, which has up to now been used only as a decoration.

168

Without the sentimental cult of the fatherland, nations are to-day only great commercial houses, united or separated by interest, and carrying the egoism of alliances to such a pitch that it is permissible to hate one's ally of last evening, and to arm against him, since for reasons of supremacy or to frustrate cupidity, he will be your enemy on the morrow. Italy and Austria, for example.

169

The divorce law is useless and hypocrite, first because it has no effect upon custom; secondly because free love, if honest, should not hide behind legal formulas.

170

Because of the fatality of relation of government over the governed, there is often nothing so like a tyrant as his implacable enemy when the latter has come into power.

171

What is most to be feared from the participation of women in government is that they will adopt a morality and sensibility as precarious as those of the male; which will cause an appreciable decline in the forces which maintain the cohesion and equilibrium of society.

172

The wishes of public opinion are always accomplished in the long run, despite the biased speeches of politicians and the vicious practices of governments; as life triumphs over 'Dulcamara's Mixture' and the impostures of apothecaries.

173

It is quite probable that the gravity of social demands as well as the anarchist madness comes from the enormous and ill-distributed funds spent on public instruction, which forms a pernicious intellectual proletariat, while leaving thousands of unfortunates in absolute intellectual indigence.

174

If there is no social problem, but only a working-man's problem, in the Argentine, we must despair of the ideality of a country in which the masses are stirred only for the sake of bettering an immediate situation and without any plan or higher aspiration whatsoever for the future.

175

There are only two differences between the constitutional and parliamentary monarchies of Europe and the South American republics: first, in the monarchies the head of the state is more or less hereditarily legitimate, who doesn't much matter; and in the republics he is apocryphally elective; second, in the monarchies there is a true democracy and in the republics there is a false aristocracy of plebeians.

176

A monarchy where a socialist minister comes into power is plausible, but as sincere as a papacy with an academy of atheists serving for sacred college.

177

A religion, moral code, civilization, politics which have not the fundamental intention of aiding the well-being and happiness of mankind are necessarily false and pernicious.

178

A politics which would sacrifice the happiness of present generations for that of future generations would be suicidal, for being incapable of its own perfection humanity would live in a perpetual and useless sacrifice.

179

There is no indignation more sincere or more comic than that of a capitalist fighting with workmen who demand successive increases in pay.

'But where will they stop, the lunatics?'

Yes, they will stop when they are as cracked as you are yourself, sir.

180

The best thing in republics is the loyalty and almost religious affection of the people for the great men who incarnate the national tradition. That is to say, it is precisely the same force which has preserved monarchies through the ages.

181

What sincerity can we find in public indignation against functionaries who profit by their public place to transact private business—in countries where the politicians cheat the State, where the business men smuggle, where no one has the slightest scruple about making declarations contrary to the fiscal interest.

182

Political and social constitutions founded on bourgeois criteria can go on without pains of opposition if the favoured do not abuse their privileged position. The people, as ages experience and the realities of the moment demonstrate, if it attains small but secure situations, if it escapes, from above, the excitements of those who would exploit it without pity; from beneath, the excitements of those who would do so with some moderation, the *people* is anti-revolutionary.

183

Everyone pities orphans. But children set between a base father and a brutal mother!

184

Civil wars are by far harsher and more cruel than international wars, because blows are more painful from friends than from strangers; because one fights with more rage against people one knows and whom one knows to be conscious and voluntary enemies than against those who attack us only in obedience to a will exterior to themselves. Two soldiers of different nations embrace without bitterness when peace arrives, two protagonists in civil war separate huffily because they hated each other before, because they have fought with hate, and because after to-morrow they will start 'getting ready for the next'.

185

I have often observed that men most attached to their political leaders complain in private that these latter shower rewards and honours more freely upon far less devoted co-religionists. They do not understand, firstly, that private intercourse has in it a touch of servitude, and, secondly, that one must always give more to those whose defection one fears than to those whose fidelity is assured.

186

The day when the riches of this world are divided, not absurdly into equal parts, but equitably divided, one will no longer see houses fit for birds of paradise next to hovels fit only for rats, cities will be clean, and full of honest people; crime and contagious disease will be almost unknown; vice will no longer gnaw the viscera of the rich, nor of the poor; suburbs will no longer be nests of *apaches*, and streets where the wild conditions are eternally dominant, where it rains, snows, and where one receives the wind as in a forest, will become galleries sheltered from disagreeable extremes, when the state of the weather demands it.

187

The brutal militarism of William First, the thief of giants; joined to the idealism of the old universities; beer swillings plus the music of Beethoven; *schlager* duels, contempt for ladies of indeterminate reputation plus the adoration of inaccessible Marguerites, have given birth to the most savant, the strongest, the most idealistic, the most law-respecting, and the most barbarous people in Europe.

188

Journalism, in normal epochs, when it is not an impartial censor of public life, nor a truthful vehicle of daily information, is changed, as one has often seen it, into a violent apostle of morality plus the art of blackmail. Which is, after all, to end as it began in the person of its creator, Pietro Aretino. (Whose apocryphal writings are published plus the soubriquets *il veritabile, il divino*. E. P.)

189

Why should one, of necessity, consider the criminal as an unbalanced person utterly lacking in sensibility? Are not the accidents of the *milieu* in which he is born enough to account for the conjunction of the savage's rudimentary sensitization with the sharpened wit of civilized man?

190

The next paragraph will pass as a joke, yet I am convinced that when feminism triumphs, yes on that day and without further procrastination, the origin of humanity's profound evils will be discovered to rest in the mute war between thin women and fat women.

191

An intelligence examining the earth from above without knowing civilization, nor formulating an idea of countries and frontiers, would end by saying in face of the various activities of agglomerations of humans, that they lived according to their density and its relation to the land which feeds them, sometimes resisting, sometimes penetrating them peacefully—and that this latter condition tended to predominate.

192

When socialists become owners and find themselves at the head of a business in difficulties, instead of convoking their employees and forming a cooperative affair, they behave like other bourgeois, and lower the wages. They then excuse themselves and blame it on *force majeure* and when the danger is over, those who have helped them surmount it find themselves where they were before.

193

Perhaps the English are the greatest people on earth, for their acts in general bear the stamp of frankness and are always modeled on life's realities.

194

To speak evil of the French would be a useless, ridiculous task, for one would never attain the severity of mind which they themselves employ in self-criticism.

195

In Paris, the centre of a very ancient civilization, the *apache* is the product of certain districts only; in South America, in the midst of new heterogeneous civilization, the *indian* appears in all classes of society. The phenomenon is the same: Rudimentary sensibility plus intelligence over-sharpened by necessity and the 'hot house' (*serre chaude*) of the milieu.

196

The Church, marvellous weapon of the social order, has had the profound wisdom to permit mystic monomanias to perfect themselves and at the same time to limit propagation; establishing celibacy for priests, cloistration for ecstatics, and the active exercise of charity for souls given to abnegation and incurably wounded by the world.

197

It is the duty of superior men definitely to take the first place and to make people who base their social eminence on wealth alone feel their inferiority. One should notice the intimate petulance with which these little gentlemen obey the request when one states it clearly.

198

Under the race's total drive, the return blow (*la revanche*) has taken during half a century's effort the form of submarine, auto, and aeroplane. The Frenchman, seeing himself smaller and less numerous than the German, has sought to make up the difference by a reckless bravery which gives him the deciding advantages in time and in space.

199

Men born in contradiction to the social pact make a breach in the conventions which close unjustly before them. A life consciously and uniquely martyrized is worth just that much more.

200

Only the political ballet-dancers (*coryphées*) can understand all the sorts of bitterness; all the concealed hatreds which are concentrated in the soul of a servant.

201

Public opinion brands governments as thieves when their depredations injure the general welfare; when the times are prosperous, when the official purses are not filled *too* full, opinion grumbles a little, but in the main shrugs its shoulders.

[*Here end the numbered paragraphs of the manuscript.*]

202

Art is the means of giving plastic, perceivable (*sensible*) life to things, ideas, sensations, feelings, and passions. By use of forms, precarious and poetically magnified, it eternalizes all the interior and exterior manifestations of *l'attimo fugente*. It gives to all sensations, and to the prolongations of them, the seal of its generalizing synthesis. In indefinitely enlarging the field of thought and the dimensions of life, it manages to give us the best of all consolations: the illusion of immortality.

203

Let one attribute what importance one will to the fact, it is nevertheless certain that all men of genius and all those who have had the most extraordinary influence over the destinies of humanity or of their country, have had blue eyes. Christ was a blue-eyed Jew.

204

Men with black eyes are too violent and too nervous to command well. The chief ought to be a man calm, reflective, energetic, equitable, capable of pardoning a negligence, but never a breach of discipline. These qualities are most often found in blue-eyed men. This is the secret, or at any rate the symptom of the secret, which enabled the Barbarians to dominate and regenerate the Latin world.

205

The right sort, the man who judges himself with sincerity and takes count of that fragile and shadowy thing, the human soul, is the only sort of man who has the right to kill another man in self-defence.

206

Two great and apparently paradoxical merits: to exaggerate without exaggeration in a story; and to declaim without declamation in the tribune.

207

The greater part of the 'enlightened public' admires parliamentary speeches and political editorials as if they were fine works of art. This shows that the artistic criteria of the crowds is superior to that of cultivated people, even though they do not confuse Trefoil and masonry.

208

Musical interpretations, copies of works of plastic art, need only in order to be good, stick closely to the text, as is also the case with translations; but neither one nor the other is worth anything unless the copyist or translator possesses something more than technical competence and mechanical cleverness.

209

The fundamental condition of good prose is that it should be natural and rhythmic as the movements of breathing. (*Vide* also the Essay on Style.)

210

I confess that when I first looked at Leonardo's Mona Lisa, I was astonished. I had never seen any woman with such a silly expression.

211

The chief obstacle against which *débutants* in letters have to struggle is that they do not know that it is the essential that one must put into a story and that the accessory should be put aside. For this reason their first pages, even when they denote a great talent, are puerile and heavy.

212

The deficiency in lay instruction is that it does not teach men how to die.

213

Art and science are *at bottom* the same, since without geometry there is no architecture, and since geometry has been engendered by experience, man creating the space which geometry studies. What we call art is the scientifically ruled translation of the agreeable sensations which we get from the appearances and qualities of things; and science is the perception of the harmonious beauty of the universe and a practical means of economizing thought in the practical applications of this.

214

The less talent and competence a man has in the science he practises, the more downright and imperative he is.

Thank God that in order to free the human mind from this tyranny, Henri Poincaré has demonstrated with mathematic evidence that without chance there would have been no science, and that it is chance alone which corrects the inevitable errors which defective senses and defective instruments cause in all scientific work.

215

The first time one sees a realist play in a theatre, the care for the staging and the interpretation makes all the details effective with meticulous patience; one has the sensation of watching a painting which moves and speaks. Then the eye gets promptly used to the trick and it becomes boring because one notices that it isn't life but a simple copy of its superficial elements.

216

Renaissance princes received great artists in their palaces and loaded them with favours. Among us, people in high society, when there appears a man of extraordinary intellectual gifts but in modest circumstances, treat him as a poor relation whom they receive in *négligé*, and do not invite to their parties. Talent ill-dressed is become something ridiculous. Better an imbecile with cash.

217

One is a Jew when one lends two or three thousand pesos at ten per cent per month; one is an Hebrew when one hypothecates at fourteen per cent per annum; one is an Israelite when, in partnership with a Christian, one carries on business with the government yielding one hundred and fifty per cent in utilities. [Apropos of which one can still see in Verona a mediaeval lion's mouth for the denunciation of usurers and unjust, usurious contracts. E. P.]

218

Given two husbands with similar temperaments, which will feel most outraged, the one whose wife confesses that she loves another man chastely; or the one whose wife says that in a moment of enthusiasm she has given herself to a man whom she did not love and whom she now detests?

219

There are psychologists who mock at Shakespeare because in several of his plays he gives a decisive *rôle* to sorcerers. They do not know that to-day among the people most dramas of passion are managed and exploited by *somnambules* (fortune tellers, trance mediums, et ceteri) according to their fancy.

220

A very curious investigation (family papers hitherto kept secret) has revealed that Ernest Renan was descended from a son whom Abelard had by Heloise—after the famous surgical intervention of Canon Fulbert.

221

Verlaine, Villiers de l'Isle Adam, and Wagner . . . The first and second lived amid the tables of night cafés and ended in hospital. Wagner realized his prodigious dream because a lunatic was king of Bavaria.

Oh! marvelous influence of criticism?

222

The day when the irremediable instability of every scientific verity is proclaimed we shall see the fall of the last Bastile.

223

The sensations of love, like the vibrations of music, move all the nervous system at once; because of this the voice of the beloved has, during youth, such prestige, the most chaste and fugitive contact electrifies us and leaves a prolonged sensation of gentleness upon the brushed nerve tip; it is as if we felt the musical waves of a 'cello divinely stroking the skin, having reached us through the air and through objects in contact with us.

224

It is as absurd to nourish and to exercise one's soul with the aim of attaining possession of Truth as to nourish and exercise one's body with the aim of making it immortal.

225

The dream is a cupful of death which gives us—without the ennui of disenchantment, without the ravages of alcohol, and without the chagrin of leaving the world before having solved its enigma—the most entire of pleasures, the unmixed sweetness of not existing.

The End

MISCELLANEOUS POEMS

CONVERSATIONS IN COURTSHIP

*From Boris de Rachewiltz's Italian versions of
Egyptian hieroglyphic texts*

HE SAYS:
Darling, you only, there is no duplicate,
More lovely than all other womanhood,
    luminous, perfect,
A star coming over the sky-line at new year,
    a good year,
Splendid in colors,
    with allure in the eye's turn.
Her lips are enchantment,
    her neck the right length
        and her breasts a marvel;
Her hair lapislazuli in its glitter,
    her arms more splendid than gold.
Her fingers make me see petals,
    the lotus' are like that.
Her flancs are modeled as should be,
    her legs beyond all other beauty.
Noble her walking
        (vera incessu)
My heart would be a slave should she enfold me.
Every neck turns—that is her fault—
    to look at her.
Fortune's who can utterly embrace her;
    he would stand first among all young lovers.
Deo mi par esse
    Every eye keeps following her
        even after she has stepped out of range,
A single goddess,
    uniquely.

SHE SAYS:
His voice unquiets my heart,
 It's the voice's fault if I suffer.
My mother's neighbor!
     But I can't go see him,
 Ought she to enrage me?

MOTHER:
Oh, stop talking about that fellow,
 the mere thought of him is revolting.

SHE:
I am made prisoner 'cause I love him.

MOTHER:
But he's a mere kid with no brains.

SHE:
So am I, I am just like him
and he don't know I want to put my arms round him.
   THAT would make mama talk . . .
May the golden goddess make fate,
 and make him my destiny.

Come to where I can see you.
 My father and mother will then be happy
 Because everyone likes to throw parties for you
  And they would get to doing it too.

SHE SAYS:
I wanted to come out here where it's lovely
 and get some rest,
Now I meet Mehy in his carriage
 with a gang of other young fellows,
  How can I turn back?

Can I walk in front of him
    as if it did not matter?
Oh, the river is the only way to get by
    and I can't walk on the water.

    My soul you are all in a muddle.
If I walk in front of him my secret will show,
    I'll blurt out my secrets; say:
                Yours!

And he will mention my name and
    hand me over to just any one of them
        who merely wants a good time.

SHE SAYS:
My heart runs out if I think how I love him,
    I can't just act like anyone else.
It, my heart, is all out of place
    It won't let me choose a dress
        or hide back of my fan.
I can't put on my eye make-up
                or pick a perfume.

"Don't stop, come into the house."
    That's what my heart said, one time,
And does, every time I think of my beloved.
    Don't play the fool with me, oh heart.
        Why *are* you such an idiot?
Sit quiet! keep calm
        and he'll come to you.
And my alertness won't let people say:
    This girl is unhinged with love.
When you remember him
    stand firm and solid,
        don't escape me.

HE SAYS:

I adore the gold-gleaming Goddess,
                Hathor the dominant,
                        and I praise her.

I exalt the Lady of Heaven,
    I give thanks to the Patron.
She hears my invocation
    and has fated me to my lady,
Who has come here, herself, to find me.
    What felicity came in with her!
I rise exultant
    in hilarity
           and triumph when I have said:
                Now,
And behold her.
    Look at it!
           The young fellows fall at her feet.
Love is breathed into them.

I make vows to my Goddess,
    because she has given me this girl for my own.
I have been praying three days,
    calling her name.
For five days she has abandoned me.

SHE SAYS:

I went to his house, and the door was open.
    My beloved was at his ma's side
        with brothers and sisters about him.
Everybody who passes has sympathy for him,
    an excellent boy, none like him,
        a friend of rare quality.
He looked at me when I passed
    and my heart was in jubilee.
If my mother knew what I am thinking
    she would go to him at once.

O Goddess of Golden Light,
   put that thought into her,
    Then I could visit him
And put my arms round him while people were looking
And not weep because of the crowd,
    But would be glad that they knew it
     and that you know me.
What a feast I would make to my Goddess,
    My heart revolts at the thought of exit,
If I could see my darling tonight,
     Dreaming is loveliness.

HE SAYS:
Yesterday. Seven days and I have not seen her.
    My malady increases;
      limbs heavy!
        I know not myself any more.
High priest is no medicine, exorcism is useless:
    a disease beyond recognition.

I said: She will make me live,
  her name will rouse me,
Her messages are the life of my heart
  coming and going.
My beloved is the best of medicine,
  more than all pharmacopoeia.
My health is in her coming,
  I shall be cured at the sight of her.
Let her open my eyes
  and my limbs are alive again;
Let her speak and my strength returns.
Embracing her will drive out my malady.
  Seven days and
      she has abandoned me.

"ASK NOT UNGAINLY"

from Horace

Ask not ungainly askings of the end
Gods send us, me and thee, Leucothoë;
Nor juggle with the risks of Babylon,
     Better to take whatever,
Several, or last, Jove sends us. Winter is winter,
Gnawing the Tyrrhene cliffs with the sea's tooth.

Take note of flavors, and clarity's in the wine's manifest.
Cut loose long hope for a time.
We talk. Time runs in envy of us,
Holding our day more firm in unbelief.

(*Odes,* Book I, 11)

"BY THE FLAT CUP"

from Horace

By the flat cup and the splash of new vintage
What, specifically, does the diviner ask of Apollo? Not
Thick Sardinian corn-yield nor pleasant
Ox-herds under the summer sun in Calabria, nor
Ivory nor gold out of India, nor
Land where Liris crumbles her bank in silence
Though the water seems not to move.

Let him to whom Fortune's book
Gives vines in Oporto, ply pruning hook, to the
Profit of some seller that he, the seller,

May drain Syra from gold out-size basins, a
Drink even the Gods must pay for, since he found
It is merchandise, looking back three times,
Four times a year, unwrecked from Atlantic trade-routes.

Olives feed me, and endives and mallow roots.
Delight had I healthily in what lay handy provided.
Grant me now, Latoe:

> Full wit in my cleanly age,
Nor lyre lack me, to tune the page.

(*Odes*, Book I, 31)

"THIS MONUMENT WILL OUTLAST"

from Horace

This monument will outlast metal and I made it
More durable than the king's seat, higher than pyramids.
Gnaw of the wind and rain?

> Impotent
The flow of the years to break it, however many.

Bits of me, many bits, will dodge all funeral,
O Libitina-Persephone and, after that,
Sprout new praise. As long as
Pontifex and the quiet girl pace the Capitol
I shall be spoken where the wild flood Aufidus
Lashes, and Daunus ruled the parched farmland:

Power from lowliness: "First brought Aeolic song to Italian
fashion"—
Wear pride, work's gain! O Muse Melpomene,
By your will bind the laurel.

> My hair, Delphic laurel.

(*Odes*, Book III, 30)

TO FORMIANUS' YOUNG LADY FRIEND

AFTER VALERIUS CATULLUS

All Hail; young lady with a nose
        by no means too small,
With a foot unbeautiful,
        and with eyes that are not black,
With fingers that are not long, and with a mouth undry,
And with a tongue by no means too elegant,
You are the friend of Formianus, the vendor of cosmetics,
And they call you beautiful in the province,
And you are even compared to Lesbia.

O most unfortunate age!

CATULLUS: XXVI

This villa is raked of winds from fore and aft,
All Boreas' sons in bluster and yet more
Against it is this TWO HUNDRED THOUSAND sesterces,
All out against it, oh my God:
                some draft.

CATULLUS: LXXXV

I hate and love. Why? You may ask but
It beats me. I feel it done to me, and ache.

ROMA

Rutilius Claudius Namantianus
(flourished 416 A.D.)

Again and again I kiss thy gates at departing
And against our will leave thy holy door-stone,
Praying in tears and with praises
   such words as can pierce our tears.

Hear us, Queen, fairest in all the earth, ROMA,
Taking post twixt the sky's poles,
Nurse of men! Mother of gods,
     do thou hear us.
Ever we hymn thee and will, while the Fates can have power.
No guest can forget thee.
   It were worse crime than forgetting the sun
If we ceased holding thy honor in heart,
Thou impartial as sunlight to the splash of all outer sea-bords.
All that Apollo over-rides in his quadriga
Hast thou combined into equity:
Many strange folk in one fatherland,
To their good, not seeking to dominate;
Gavest law to the conquered as consorts;
Made city what had been world.

They say that Venus was thy mother, that is by Aeneas,
Mars for father hadst'ou through Romulus,
Making mild armed strength, she in conquest:
One god in two natures;
     Joy out of strife by sparing
O'ercamest the sources of terror
  In love with all that remains.

INSCRIPTIO FONTIS

From the Latin of Andrea Navagero

(16th Century)

Lo! the fountain is cool and
    none more hale of waters.
Green is the land about it,
    soft with the grasses.
And twigged boughs of elm
    stave off[1] the sun.

There is no place more charmed
    with light-blown airs,
Though Titan in utmost flame
    holdeth the middle sky,
And the parched fields burn with
    the oppressing star.

Stay here thy way, O voyager,
    for terrible is now the heat;
Thy tired feet can go no further now.
Balm here for weariness is
    sweet reclining,
Balm 'gainst the heat, the winds,
    and greeny shade!
And for thy thirst the lucid fount's assuaging.

[1]Arceo.

CERTAIN POEMS OF KABIR

(Hindi: 1440-1518)

From the English versions of Kali Mohan Ghose

I

The spring season is approaching,
Who will help me meeting with my dearest?
How shall I describe the beauty of the dearest,
Who is immersed in all beauties?
That color colors all the pictures of this universe,
Body and mind alike
Forget all things else in that beauty.
He who has these ideas,
The play of the spring is his.
This is the word which is unutterable.
Saith Kabir: There are very few who know this mystery.

II

My beloved is awakened, how can I sleep?
Day and night he is calling me,
And instead of responding to his call
I am like an unchaste girl, living with another.
Saith Kabir: O clever confidant,
The meeting with the dearest is not possible without love.

III

The scar aches day and night.
Sleep is not come.
Anxious for meeting with the dearest,
The father's house is not attractive at all.
The sky-gate opens,
The temple is manifested,
There now is the meeting with the husband.

I make oblation of my mind and body:
To the dearest the cup of the dearest!
Let flow the quick shower of rain from your eyes.
Cover your heart
With the intense deep blue
Assembling of the cloud.
Come near to the ear of the dearest,
Whisper to him your pain.
Saith Kabir: Here bring the meditation of the dearest,
Today's treasure of the heart.

IV

It is true, I am mad with love. And what to me
Is carefulness or uncarefulness?
Who, dying, wandering in the wilderness,
Who is separated from the dearest?
My dearest is within me, what do I care?
The beloved is not asundered from me,
No, not for the veriest moment.
And I also am not asundered from him.
My love clings to him only,
Where is restlessness in me?
Oh my mind dances with joy,
Dances like a mad fool.
The rāginis of love are being played day and night,
All are listening to that measure.
Rāhu, the eclipse, Ketu, the Head of the Dragon,
And the nine planets are dancing,
And Birth and Death are dancing, mad with Ananda.
The mountain, the sea and the earth are dancing,
The Great Adornment is dancing with laughter and tears
    and smiles.
Why are you leaving "the world,"
You, with the *tilak*-mark on your forehead?
While my mind is a-dancing through the thousand stages of
    its moon,
And the Lord of all his creation has found it acceptable dancing.

V

O deserted bride,
How will you live in the absence of your beloved,
Without hunger in the day,
Sleepless in the night-watches,
And every watch felt as if
It were the aeon of Kaliyuga?
The beautiful has deserted you in the full passion of his April.
Alas the fair is departed!
O thou deserted,
Now begin to give up your house and your having.
Go forth to the lodge of the forest,
Begin to consider his name.
And if there he shall come upon you,
Then alone will you be come to your joy.
Eager as the caught fish for its water,
Be thou so eager to return!
Shapeless, formless and without line,
Who will be come to meet you,
O beautiful lady?
Take recognisance of your own wed Lord,
Behold him out of the center of your meditations,
Strip off the last of your errors,
And know that Love is your lord.
Saith Kabir: There is no second. Aeon
After aeon
Thou and I are the same.

VI

Very difficult is the meeting with him,
How shall I be made one with my beloved?
After long consideration and after caution
I put my feet on the way, but every time
They have trembled and slipped aside.
The slippery path leads upward and the feet can not hold to it.
The mind is taken in shyness,

For fear of the crowd
And out of respect to the family.
Oh where is my far beloved?
And I in the family dwelling!
And I can not escape my shyness!

VII

How shall it be severed,
This love between thee and me?
Thou art lord, and I servant,
As the lotus is servant of water.
Thou art lord, and I servant,
As the Chakora is servant of moonlight
And watches it all the night long.
The love between thee and me is from beginning to ending,
How can it end in time?
Saith Kabir: As the river is immersed in the ocean,
My mind is immersed in thee.

VIII

Rishi Nārad, that hast walked upon the winding path of the air,
That hast walked there playing the Vinā and singing thy song
    to Hari,
Rishi Nārad, the beloved is not afar off,
I wake not, save in his waking,
I sleep not, save in his slumber.

IX

O receiver of my heart,
Do thou come into my house.
My mind and body
Are but a pain, in thy absence.
When they say that I am your mistress
The shame of it is upon me.
If heart lie not upon heart,
How is the heart of love there?
The rice has no savor, the night is passed and is sleepless.

In the house and in the way of the forest my mind and thought
    have no rest.
Love-cup to the maid: water-cup to famished of thirst.
Is there one, bearer of fortune, to make clear my heart to my
    beloved?
Kabir is at the end of his patience
And dies without sight of his beloved.

X

O bearer of love, give voice to the well-omened song.
The great lord is come to my house,
After employing my body in his love
I shall employ my mind.
The five mysteries will be enlightened with love.
The receiver of my heart, today is the guest in my house,
I am grown mad with my youth.
The pool of my body will be the place of pilgrimage.
Near by will Brahmā chant Vedas,
The mind will be fused with my lover.

O opportune, and well-omened,
The three and thirty tunes of curious sound here with the sound
    of Ananda.
The paired lovers of the universe are assembled.
Saith Kabir: This day I set out for my marriage
With a bridegroom who is deathless.
In the quarter of my body there is music in process,
Thirty and six rāginis are bound up into the burthen.
The bridegroom hath April play with me.
As Krishna with Rādhā, playing at the spring festival of
    Harililā,
I play at the spraying of colors, I and my beloved.
The whole universe is curious today.
Love and the rain of love are come hither with their showers.

CHANSSON DOIL

From the Provençal of Arnaut Daniel

(12th Century)

I

I'll make a song   with exquisite
Clear words, for buds are blowing sweet
Where the sprays meet,
And flowers don
Their bold blazon
Where leafage springeth greenly
O'ershadowing
The birds that sing
And cry in coppice seemly.

II

The bosques among   they're singing fleet.
In shame's avoid my staves compete,
Fine-filed and neat,
With love's glaives on
His ways they run;
From him no whim can turn me,
Although he bring
Great sorrowing,
Although he proudly spurn me.

III

For lovers strong   pride is ill won,
And throweth him who mounts thereon.
His lots are spun
So that they fling

Him staggering,
His gaudy joys move leanly,
He hath grief's meat
And tears to eat
Who useth Love unseemly.

IV

Though tongues speak wrong   of wrangles none
Can turn me from thee. For but one
Fear I have gone
Dissembling;
Traitors can sting,
From their lies I would screen thee,
And as they'd treat
Us, with deceit,
Let fate use them uncleanly.

V

Though my swath long   's run wavering
My thoughts go forth to thee and cling,
Wherefore I sing
Of joys replete
Once, where our feet
Parted, and mine eyes plainly
Show mists begun
And sweetly undone,
For joy's the pain doth burn me.

VI

Save 'neath Love's thong I move no thing,
And my way brooks no measuring,
For right hath spring
In that Love's heat
Was ne'er complete
As mine, since Adam.   'Tween me

And sly treason
No net is spun,
Wherefore my joy grows greenly.

CODA

Lady, whoe'er demean thee
My benison
Is set upon
Thy grace where it moves queenly.

RICA CONQUESTA

THE SONG "OF HIGH ALL-ATTAINING"

From Arnaut Daniel

I

Did Lord Love lay upon me his wide largess
As I bear mine to her, with open heart,
He'd set no bar between me and the great,
For I'm borne up and fall as this love surges;
Yet, reckoning how she is the peak of worth,
I mount in mine own eyes by daring her
'Till heart and mind cry out that I'll attain
This rich conquest that's set for my attaining.

II

I care not though delay delay enlarges,
For I sweep toward, and pool me in such part
That the mere words she speaks hold me elate.
I'd follow her until they sing my dirges.
Sure as I can tell gold from brassy earth
She is without alloy; without demur
My faith and I are steadfast in her train
Until her lips invest me, past all feigning.

III

The good respite recalls me and then discharges
A sweet desire wherewith my flanks so smart,
Yet quietly I bear my beggared state
For o'er all other peaks her grace emerges;
Whoe'er is noblest seemeth of base birth
Compared to her; let him play justicer
Who 'th seen how charm, worth, wit and sense all reign,
Increase and dwell and stay where she dwells reigning.

IV

Don't think my will will waste it o'er its marges
(She is so fair!), divide it or depart;
Nay, by the dove, God's ghost, the consecrate,
My mind's not mine, nor hers if it diverges!
No man desires, in all the wide world's girth,
Fortune, with such desires as are astir
In me herward, and they reap my disdain
Who deem love's pain a thing for light sustaining.

V

Ah "All-Supreme," leave me no room for charges
That you are miserly. My love's sans art,
Candid, my heart cannot shake off its weight;
It's not the sort that bottle-madness urges,
But, as night endeth day, doth day my mirth.
I bow me toward you where my vows concur,
Nor think my heart will ever be less fain,
The flame is in my head and burns unwaning.

VI

A cursed flame eat through your tongues and targes,
Sick slanderers until your sick eyes start
And go blind; 'till your vile jests abate
We loose our steeds and mancs.   And loss submerges
Almost love's self. God damn you that your dearth

Of sense brings down the shame that we incur.
Sad fools! What blighting-star grows you this bane
To kill in you th' effect of all our training?

VII

Lady, I've borne delay and will again
Bear long delay in trust of high attaining.

FOR RIGHT OF AUDIENCE

From Arnaut Daniel

I

In a new cause my song again
Moves in my throat, with altered mien,
No, don't think any hope springs green
Of making fair song of my pain;
    But 'till she who hath blamed me wrongly 'll cry
"Mercy!" I'll sing it out before the crowd,
For she'll not let me speak with her alone.

II

'Tis grace and pardon I would gain
Did not her action come between
Me and my right of asking e'en,
Though mercy could the thief sustain,
    When all of his own deeds had passed him by,
Unto my life no respite is allowed
Unless, where my rights fail, mercy be shown.

III

Hath a man rights at love? No grain,
Yet fools think they've some legal lien;
And she'll blame you, with heart serene,

That ships for Bar* sink in mid-main
Or 'cause the French don't come from Gascony.
And for such faults I am nigh in my shroud,
Since, by my God! I've shown such faults or none.

IV

That place where his desire hath lain
A man leaves loath, this I well ween,
Yet there be some with breasts so mean
That they to take back gifts are fain.
    As for myself, my love can not run dry,
Not though she robs my all, where she's most proud.
My love, in lack of joy, is stronger grown.

Envoi

Please ye, Lords fellows, now maintain
Me, whom she would in all demean.
Pray to her thus (until she lean
Toward me and make her mercy plain):
    "Fair for our sake let Arnaut's song draw nigh!"
I may not name her, cry ye all aloud
That Arnaut came to court, his heart is known.

CANZON: OF THE TRADES
AND LOVE

From Arnaut Daniel

I

Though this measure quaint confine me,
And I chip out words and plane them,
    They shall yet be true and clear
When I finally have filed them.

---

* Literally: "That ships wreck ere they get to Bar (*i.e.*, the port of Bari), and 'cause the French are not Gascons."

Love glosses and gilds them knowing
  That my song has for its start
One who is worth's hold and warrant.

II

  Each day finer I refine me
  And my cult and service strain them
    Toward the world's best, as ye hear,
    "Hers" my root and tip have styled them.
And though bitter winds come blowing,
  The love that rains down in my heart
Warmeth me when frost's abhorrent.

III

  To long masses I resign me,
    Give wax-lights and lamps, maintain them
    That God win me issue here.
    Tricks of fence? Her charm's beguiled them.
Rather see her, brown hair glowing;
  And her body fine, frail art,
Than to gain Lucerna for rent!

IV

  Round her my desires twine me
  'Till I fear lest she disdain them.
    Nay, need firm love ever fear?
    Craft and wine, I have exiled them.
Yet her high heart's overflowing
  Leaves my heart no parched part;
Lo, new verse sprouts in the current.

V

  If they'd th' empire assign me
  Or the Pope's chair, I'd not deign them
    If I could not have her near.

My heart's flames have so high piled them,
If she'll not, ere th' old year's going
   Kiss away their deadly smart,
Dead am I and damned, I warrant.

VI

Though these great pains so malign me
I'd not have love's powers restrain them
   —Though she turn my whole life drear—
See, my songs have beamed and tiled them.
Yes, love's work is worse than mowing,
   And ne'er pains like mine did dart
Through Moncli for Audierent.

VII

I, Arnaut, love the wind, doing
   My hare-hunts on an ox-cart,
And I swim against the torrent.

NOTE

Manning, in his "Scenes and Portraits," compares Dante's
similes—similes like those of the arsenal at Venice, or of the hoar
frost—to the illuminated capital letters in mediaeval manuscript.
Daniel in this canzon has produced the same effect, and solely by
suggestion, by metaphor that is scarce metaphor, by suggestive
verbs; thus in stanza I he makes his vignette in the shop of the
joiner and finisher, in II the metal-worker's shop with a glimpse
through the open window; in III the church, and in the last
lines of it: "I love her more than one who should give me
Lucerne," he puts in perhaps a woman, with the light of the altar
candles about her, paying dues to the ecclesiastical suzerain; in IV
the low-lying fields, where the grain is fostered by the river-flush;
in V Rome, of the church and empire; in VI the suggestion is
fainter, though it may be of a farm hand working in a grey, barren
stretch of field. I have translated it badly even if my idiom does

mean about the same as the Provençal.

The last line of stanza VI on "Moncli n'Audierna" has given rise to a good deal of fruitless conjecture. Obviously Arnaut cites them as a pair of famous lovers, just as he cites Paris and Helen in his third canzon, but no such lovers are to be found either in classical myth or in romance tradition.

Turning, however, to Virgil's ninth eclogue I find the following in lines 10-11 and 44:

Omnia carminibus vestrum servasse Menalcan.
M. Audieras, et fama fuit; sed carmina tantum, etc.

. . .

Quid, quae te pura solum sub nocte canentem Audieram?

Given these lines in modern print, one would advance scarce further; Arnaut had been, however, to a monastic school: he knew some Latin; he knew not only of Paris and Helen but of Atalanta and Meleager, though only one of their names is given in Ovid's account of the hunting through Caledon. His Latin was, let us say, no better than mine—learning for learning's sake had not appealed to him. His Latin text was not only in miniscule manuscript but it was full of all manner of abbreviations, and in the matter of unusual proper names—like Menalcas—the scribe would have been more than usually prone to go wrong.

This eclogue is not over easy to read. "Menalcas" appears in three different case forms—"-an," "-as," "-a." The content of the eclogue is very like that of a Provençal canzon; parts of it are almost pure Provençal in the matter of vocabulary. It would have charmed by being not too unfamiliar. One more detail: the "M" in line 11, which stands for the speaker, Moeris, is not unlike the "N" which is Provençal for "donna," or "lady." The parts of the verb *audio,* in lines 11 and 45, both begin with capital letters; in both places the final consonant, "s" or "m," would or might have been written above the "a," with nothing to indicate whether it fell before or after. Translating on this hypothesis without too much regard to the Latin syntax, with which Arnaut would have been much less familiar than he was with the Latin vocabulary, we get, in the first case, something like this: "Monalca, or Menacla (or some such person), served with songs (all, yours, his, in all things), the lady Audierna or Audieras"; and in the second: "What, thou alone 'neath the clear night singing, Audierna." "Audiart" is, of course, perfectly good Provençal; de Born and others mention a lady of that name, so that if Arnaut had seen the first part of the name he might easily have mistaken it for a Latin form or variation; in any case, even supposing he had read it correctly and forgotten the spelling in the book, the transition was not beyond the bounds of the possible. At least, it is no worse a mistake than that by which "Sir Sagramore the unbridled" becomes "Sir Sagramour the desirous." I make the suggestion for what it is worth.

LO FERM VOLER

From Arnaut Daniel

Firm desire that doth enter
My heart will not be hid by bolts nor nailing
Nor slanderers who loose their arms by lying
And dare not fight with even twigs and switches.
Yea, by some jest, there where no uncle enters
I'll have my joy in garden or in chamber.

I remember oft that chamber
Where, to my loss, I know that no man enters
But leaves me free as would a brother or uncle.
I shake in ev'ry part except my nails
As doth a child, for fear, before the switch
For fear I shall not come unto her arms.

A WAR SONG

From the Provençal of Bertrand de Born
(c. 1140-1214)

Well pleaseth me the sweet time of Easter
That maketh the leaf and the flower come out.
And it pleaseth me when I hear the clamor
Of the birds, their song through the wood;
And it pleaseth me when I see through the meadows
The tents and pavilions set up, and great joy have I
When I see o'er the campagna knights armed and horses arrayed.

And it pleaseth me when the scouts set in flight the folk with their
    goods;
And it pleaseth me when I see coming together after
    them an host of armed men.
And it pleaseth me to the heart when I see strong
    castles besieged,
And barriers broken and riven, and I see the host on
    the shore all about shut in with ditches,
And closed in with lisses of strong piles.

"QUANT L'HERBA FRESQ
EL FUELL APAR"

From the Provençal of Bernart de Ventadorn
(1148-1195)

When grass starts green and flowers rise
Aleaf in garden and in close
And philomel in dulcet cries
And lifted notes his heart bestows,

426

Joy I've in him and in the flowers joy,
E'en joy in me have I yet more employ,
Hath joy in her in whom my joy is cast,
She is such joy as hath all joys o'erpast.

I love her so and so her prize,
I fear her and such thoughts oppose
That my poor words dare not arise,
Nor speech nor deeds my heart disclose.

And yet she knows the depth of my annoy
And, when she will, she will her grace employ;
For God's love, Love, put now our love to test
For time goes by and we here waste his best.

THE LARK

From Bernart de Ventadorn

When I see the lark a-moving
For joy his wings against the sunlight,
Who forgets himself and lets himself fall
For the sweetness which goes into his heart;
Ai! what great envy comes unto me for him whom I see so
    rejoicing!

I marvel that my heart melts not for desiring.
Alas! I thought I knew so much
Of Love, and I know so little of it, for I cannot
Hold myself from loving
Her from whom I shall never have anything toward.
She hath all my heart from me, and she hath from me all my wit
And myself and all that is mine.
And when she took it from me she left me naught
Save desiring and a yearning heart.

LAS GRANS BEAUTATZ

From the Provençal of Folquet de Romans

Her beauty and the fineness of her thought,
And her true heart and all the food of praise,
And her high speech and the newfangled ways
That color hath when to her cheek 'tis brought
Give me the will for song and knowledge of it.
Such were my song but such fears crowd above it
I dare not say 'tis you of whom I'm fain,
And know not what shall count me loss or gain.

My love of her so secretly is wrought
That none save I and Love know love's assay,
And on my heart the flame in secret preys;
Yet knowing this, you are not much distraught.
And yet I have such fear lest you reprove it,
That my heart scarce dares show you that you move it.
Yet if, when we're alone I daren't speak out,
At least my songs shall say what I'm about.

DESCANT ON A THEME BY CERCALMON

When the sweet air goes bitter,
And the cold birds twitter
Where the leaf falls from the twig,
I sough and sing

      that Love goes out
    Leaving me no power to hold him.

Of love I have naught
Save trouble and sad thought,

And nothing is grievous
    as I desirous,
Wanting only what
No man can get or has got.

With the noblest that stands in men's sight,
If all the world be in despite
    I care not a glove.
Where my love is, there is a glitter of sun;
God give me life, and let my course run

      'Till I have her I love
      To lie with and prove.

I do not live, nor cure me,
Nor feel my ache—great as it is,
For love will give
    me no respite,
Nor do I know when I turn left or right
  nor when I go out.

      For in her is all my delight
      And all that can save me.

I shake and burn and quiver
From love, awake and in swevyn,
Such fear I have she deliver
          me not from pain,
    Who know not how to ask her;
    Who can not.
Two years, three years I seek
And though I fear to speak out,
          Still she must know it.

If she won't have me now, Death is my portion,
    Would I had died that day

I came into her sway.
God! How softly this kills!
When her love look steals on me.

Killed me she has, I know not how it was,
 For I would not look on a woman.

Joy I have none, if she make me not mad
 Or set me quiet, or bid me chatter.
Good is it to me if she flout
 Or turn me inside out, and about.
 My ill doth she turn sweet.

How swift it is.
 For I am traist and loose,
 I am true, or a liar,
 All vile, or all gentle,
 Or shaking between,
      as she desire,
I, Cercalmon, sorry and glad,
 The man whom love had
      and has ever;
 Alas! whoe'er it please or pain,
 She can me retain.

I am gone from one joy,
From one I loved never so much,
 She by one touch
 Reft me away;
 So doth bewilder me
 I can not say my say
     nor my desire,
And when she looks on me
 It seems to me
    I lose all wit and sense.

The noblest girls men love
'Gainst her I prize not as a glove
Worn and old.
Though the whole world run rack
And go dark with cloud,
Light is
Where she stands,
And a clamor loud
                    in my ears.

MERE AU SAUVEOUR

From the Provençal of Williaume Li Viniers

Maiden and Virgin loyal
In whom here Christ's Godhead.
As child glorious royal
Was conceived, born, nourished
Sweet maid be thy heart full fed
May his love and his grace allay
Thee this day,
When the Holy Ghost
By God's son honored Thee most.

Lady imperious
O marvelous fleur-de-lys,
The holy fruit for us
Thou hast born specially
Ah, rose branch and sovran tree
Thou hast the flower, and fleet
Odor sweet
Whereby paradise
Shall be brought before our eyes.

"DIEU! QU'IL LA FAIT"

From the French of Charles D'Orléans (1391-1465)

God! that mad'st her well regard her,
How she is so fair and bonny;
For the great charms that are upon her
Ready are all folks to reward her.
Who could part him from her borders
When spells are always renewed on her?
God! that mad'st her well regard her,
How she is so fair and bonny.
From here to there to the sea's border,
Dame nor damsel there's not any
Hath of perfect charms so many.
Thoughts of her are of dream's order:
God! that mad'st her well regard her.

ROME

From the French of Joachim du Bellay (1524-1560)

'Troica Roma resurges.'—PROPERTIUS

O thou new comer who seek'st Rome in Rome
And find'st in Rome no thing thou canst call Roman;
Arches worn old and palaces made common,
Rome's name alone within these walls keeps home.

Behold how pride and ruin can befall
One who hath set the whole world 'neath her laws,
All conquering, now conquered, because
She is Time's prey and Time consumeth all.

Rome that art Rome's one sole last monument,
Rome that alone has conquered Rome the town,
Tiber alone, transient and seaward bent,
Remains of Rome. O world, thou unconstant mime!
That which stands firm in thee Time batters down,
And that which fleeteth doth outrun swift time.

AIR: SENTIR AVEC ARDEUR

La Marquise de Boufflers
(1711–1786)

Say what you will in two
Words and get thru.
Long, frilly
Palaver is silly.

Know how to read? you MUST
Before you can write. An idiot
Will always
Talk a lot.

You need not always narrate;
    cite; date,
But listen a while and not say: "I! I!"
Want to know why?

The ME is tyrannical;
    academical.
Early, late
Boredome's cognate mate
    in step at his side
And I with a ME, I fear,
                yet again!

433

Say what you will in two
Words and get thru!
Long, frilly
Palaver is silly.

CABARET VERT

From the French of Jean Arthur Rimbaud (1854-1891)

Wearing out my shoes, 8th day
On the bad roads, I got into Charleroi.
Bread, butter, at the Green Cabaret
And the ham half cold.

Got my legs stretched out
And was looking at the simple tapestries,
Very nice when the gal with the big bubs
And lively eyes,

Not one to be scared of a kiss and more,
Brought the butter and bread with a grin
And the luke-warm ham on a colored plate,

Pink ham, white fat and a sprig
Of garlic, and a great chope of foamy beer
Gilt by the sun in that atmosphere.

COMEDY IN THREE CARESSES

From Rimbaud

She hadn't much left on, and the big trees,
With no discretion, swished
Their leaves over the window-pane
Teasingly, so near, so near.

Half naked in my big chair,
She put her hands together
And her little toes tickled the floor,
Quivering comfortably, and so small.

I watched a little sprouting flush,
The color of wax, flutter
Like a smile over her neat breasts:
Fly on a rose bush.

I kissed her traced ankles
And she smiled a longish smile, bad **sign**
That shattered out into clear trills,
Crystalline.

Her little feet scampered under her shift:
"Will you *stop* now!!"
After the first permitted boldness,
The smile pretending coldness?

Her poor eyelids fluttered under my lips
As I kissed her eyes
And she threw back her weakling head:
"That's better now," she said.

"But I have something still to . . ."
I chucked the rest between her breasts
In a caress that brought a kindly smile,
Benevolence, all of it.

She hadn't much left on, and the big trees
Swished their leaves over the window-pane
At ease, teasingly, and so near.

ANADYOMENE

From Rimbaud

As it might have been from under a green tin coffin-lid,
A woman's head with brown over-oiled hair
Rises out of a theatre box, slow and stupid
With ravages in rather poor repair.

Then ups the fat grey neck and bulgy shoulder-blades,
The shortish back going out and in
And the fat, in clumsy slabs under the skin,
Seems ready to emerge without further aids.

LICE-HUNTERS

From Rimbaud

When the kid's forehead is full of red torments
Imploring swarms of dreams with vague contents,
Two large and charming sisters come
With wafty fingers and silvery nails, to his bedroom.

They set the kid by a wide-open window where
A tangle of flowers bathes in the blue air
And run fine, alluring, terrible
Fingers through his thick dew-matted hair.

He hears the rustling of their timid breath
Flowered with the long pinkish vegetable honies underneath
Or broken anon, sibilant, the saliva's hiss
Drawn from a lip, or a desire to kiss.

He hears their black eyelashes beat in that quietude
and "Crack!" to break his inebriated indolences
Neath their electric and so soft fingers death assails
The little lice beneath their regal nails.

And Lo! there mounts within him Wine of Laziness—a squiffer's
    sigh
Might bring delirium—and the kid feels
Neath the slowness of their caresses, constantly
Wane and fade a desire to cry.

RUS

From the French of Laurent Tailhade
(1854-1919)

What lures the antient truss-maker from his shoppe whose luxury
Sucked in the passers-by,
Is his garden at Auteuil where zinnias void of all odor or stink
Look like varnished zinc.

That's where he, of an evening, comes to taste the aromatic air
In his flannel coat and rocking-chair
As factories of suet and animal
Black spread out the whiff and flavor from Grenelle.

Although free-thinking and a quite free mason,
He thinks a favoring god in propitious hour
Gave him such refuge—a goldfish dying in the fountain basin—

While, with Chinese lanterns in a moorish tower
His "young lady" hums to and fro
Spicing his raspberry syrup with a couplet by Nadaud.

PIERROTS

From the French of Jules Laforgue
(1860-1887)
(Scène courte mais typique)

Your eyes! Since I lost their incandescence
Flat calm engulphs my jibs,
The shudder of *Vae soli* gurgles beneath my ribs.

You should have seen me after the affray,
I rushed about in the most agitated way
Crying: My God, my God, what will she say?!

My soul's antennae are prey to such perturbations,
Wounded by your indirectness in these situations
And your bundle of mundane complications.

Your eyes put me up to it.
I thought: Yes, divine, these eyes, but what exists
Behind them? What's there? Her soul's an affair
    for oculists.

And I am sliced with loyal aesthetics.
Hate tremolos and national frenetics.
In brief, violet is the ground tone of my phonetics.[1]

I am not 'that chap there' nor yet 'The Superb'
But my soul, the sort which harsh sounds disturb,
Is, at bottom, distinguished and fresh as a March herb.

My nerves still register the sounds of 'contra-bass',
I can walk about without fidgeting when people pass,
Without smirking into a pocket-looking-glass.

[1] N.B. To emend it sometime to "... and yet my local color is violet." E.P.

Yes, I have rubbed shoulders and knocked off my chips
Outside your set but, having kept faith in your eyes,
You might pardon such slips.

Eh, make it up?
                              Soothings, confessions;
These new concessions
Hurl me into such a mass of divergent impressions.

STROPHES

*From the French ("Symphonie de Novembre")
of Oscar Wenceslas de Lubicz-Milosz*
(1877-1939)

It will be as it is in this life, the same room,
Yes, the same! and at daybreak, the bird of time in the leafage,
Pale as a dead woman's face; and the servants
Moving; and the icy, hollow noise of the fountain-taps,

Terrible, terrible youth; and the heart empty.
Oh! it will be as it is in this life; the poor voices,
The winter voices in the worn-out suburbs;
And the window-mender's cracked street-cry;

The dirty bonnet, with an old woman under it
Howling a catalogue of stale fish, and the blue-apron'd fellow
Spitting on his chapped hands
And bellowing like an angel of judgement,

It will be exactly as here and in this life, and the table,
The bible, Goethe, the ink with the same temporal odor,
Paper, pale; woman, white thought-reader!
Pen, the portrait,

It will be the same,
My child, as in this life, the same garden,
Long, long, tufted, darkish, and, at lunch-time,
Pleasure of being together; that is—
People unacquainted, having only in common
A knowledge of their unacquaintance—
And that one must put on one's best clothes
To go into the night—at the end of things,
Loveless and lampless;
It will be the same as in this life,
The same lane in the forest; and at mid-day, in mid-autumn
When the clean road turns like a weeping woman
To gather the valley flowers,
We will cross in our walks,
    As in the yesterday you have forgotten,
    In the gown whose color you have forgotten.

"VEDUT' HO LA LUCENTE STELLA DIANA"

From the Italian of Guido Guinicelli (died 1274)

I have seen the shining star of the dawn
Appearing ere the day yieldeth its whiteness.
It has taken upon itself the form of a human face,
Above all else meseems it gives splendor.
A face of snow, color of the ivy-berry,
The eyes are brilliant, gay, and full of love,
And I do not believe that there is a Christian maid in the world
So full of fairness or so valorous.
Yea, I am so assailed of her worth,
With such cruel battling of sighs,
That I am not hardy to return before her;
Thus may she have cognizance of my desires:
That without speaking, I would be her servitor
For naught save the pity that she might have of my anguish.

SONNET TO GUIDO CAVALCANTI

From Guido Orlandi (13th Century)

Say what is Love, whence doth he start,
Through what be his courses bent,
Memory, substance, accident?
A chance of eye or will of heart?

Whence he state or madness leadeth?
Burns he with consuming pain?

Tell me, friend, on what he feedeth,
How, where, and o'er whom doth he reign?

Say what is Love, hath he a face?
True form or vain similitude?
Is the Love life, or is he death?

Thou shouldst know for rumor saith:
Servant should know his master's mood—
Oft art thou ta'en in his dwelling-place.

CANTICO DEL SOLE

From the Italian of St. Francis of Assisi
(1182-1226)

Most high Lord,
Yours are the praises,
The glory and the honors,
And to you alone must be accorded
All graciousness; and no man there is
Who is worthy to name you.
Be praisèd, O God, and be exalted,
My Lord, of all creatures,
And in especial of the most high Sun
Which is your creature, O Lord, that makes clear
The day and illumines it,
Whence by its fairness and its splendor
It is become thy face;
And of the white moon (be praised, O Lord)
And of the wandering stars,
Created by you in the heaven
So brilliant and so fair.
Praisèd be my Lord, by the flame

Whereby night groweth illumined
In the midst of its darkness,
For it is resplendent,
Is joyous, fair, eager; is mighty.
Praisèd be my Lord, of the air,
Of the winds, of the clear sky,
And of the cloudy, praisèd
Of all seasons whereby
Live all these creatures
Of lower order.
Praisèd be my Lord
By our sister the water,
Element meetest for man,
Humble and chaste in its clearness.
Praised be the Lord by our mother
The Earth that sustaineth,
That feeds, that produceth
Multitudinous grasses
And flowers and fruitage.
Praisèd be my Lord, by those
Who grant pardons through his love,
Enduring their travail in patience
And their infirmity with joy of the spirit.
Praisèd be my Lord by death corporal
Whence escapes no one living.
Woe to those that die in mutual transgression
And blessed are they who shall
Find in death's hour thy grace that comes
From obedience to thy holy will,
Wherethrough they shall never see
The pain of the death eternal.
Praisè and give grace to my Lord,
Be grateful and serve him
In humbleness e'en as ye owe.
Praisè him all creatures!

HER MONUMENT, THE IMAGE CUT THEREON

From the Italian of Giacomo Leopardi

(1798-1837)

Such wast thou,
Who art now
But buried dust and rusted skeleton.
Above the bones and mire,
Motionless, placed in vain,
Mute mirror of the flight of speeding years,
Sole guard of grief
Sole guard of memory
Standeth this image of the beauty sped.

O glance, when thou wast still as thou art now,
How hast thou set the fire
A-tremble in men's veins; O lip curved high
To mind me of some urn of full delight,
O throat girt round of old with swift desire,
O palms of Love, that in your wonted ways
Not once but many a day
Felt hands turn ice a-sudden, touching ye,
That ye were once! of all the grace ye had
That which remaineth now
Shameful, most sad
Finds 'neath this rock fit mould, fit resting place!

And still when fate recalleth,
Even that semblance that appears amongst us
Is like to heaven's most 'live imagining.
All, all our life's eternal mystery!

To-day, on high
Mounts, from our mighty thoughts and from the fount
Of sense untellable, Beauty
That seems to be some quivering splendor cast
By the immortal nature on this quicksand,
And by surhuman fates
Given to mortal state
To be a sign and an hope made secure
Of blissful kingdoms and the aureate spheres;
And on the morrow, by some lightsome twist,
Shameful in sight, abject, abominable
All this angelic aspect can return
And be but what it was
With all the admirable concepts that moved from it
Swept from the mind with it in its departure.

Infinite things desired, lofty visions
'Got on desirous thought by natural virtue,
And the wise concord, whence through delicious seas
The arcane spirit of the whole Mankind
Turns hardy pilot . . . and if one wrong note
Strike the tympanum,
Instantly
That paradise is hurled to nothingness.

O mortal nature,
If thou art
Frail and so vile in all,
How canst thou reach so high with thy poor sense;
Yet if thou art
Noble in any part
How is the noblest of thy speech and thought
So lightly wrought
Or to such base occasion lit and quenched?

AUTUNNO

From the Italian of Saturno Montanari
(1918-1941)

Autumn, so many leaves
pass with the wind, I see
the worn-out rain
gather aloft again.

Aimless or vagabond,
a walking sadness, beyond
the deep-cut road:
horses weary of load.

A whirring noise, new night there
empty in monotone:
the Ave Maria
no prayer.

STAGIONE DI FIORI

From Montanari

Time of almonds in flower
and songs half spoken;
walnut's bough now
keeps sun off threshed oats.

Time comes again
from the shepherd's pens:
shy flowers in wind
each year, thus, with no pain;

Renews the rillets, and dews.
White thorn, darkens in pine
with new spikes, a heaven of birds
sing to line.

Comes joy's season, that does no ill
for our brother the sun, aloft,
keeps it too languid and still
for any evil.

POMERIGGIO DI LUGLIO

From Montanari

Road in the open there,
all sun and grain-dust
      and sour air
from the canal bank,

Ditch-water higher now
with the tide,
      turns violet and red.

A swallow for shuttle, back,
forth, forth, back
      from shack to
marsh track;
      to the far
sky-line that's fading now.
A thin song of a girl plucking grain,
a child cries from the threshing floor.

NOTTE DIETRO LE PERSIANE

From Montanari

When the light
goes, men shut behind blinds
their life, to die for a night.

And yet
through glass and bars
some dream a wild sunset,
waiting the stars.

Call these few, at least
the singers, in whom
hope's voice is yeast.

L'ULTIMA ORA

From Montanari

When the will to singing fails
and there be left him no choice
but to rest without singing voice,
forever, unending, arms crossed,

Let it be by the roadside
where the ditch is wide and deep
and the smell of his fields, in sleep
can come to him, and the note of the robin,

And the elms can be there companionable
to him, as evening draws to its close
in the savor of spring time,
melancholy a little, ending together.